D1368726

2 6

$3⁰⁰

THE RISE AND FALL
OF THE
AIRCRAFT CARRIER

THE RISE AND FALL OF THE AIRCRAFT CARRIER

Bernard Ireland

Marshall Cavendish

Prepared for Marshall Cavendish Books Limited
by Colourviews Limited, Birmingham

Editor: E. L. (Bill) Cornwell
Designers: Chris Lower and Eddie Pitcher
Picture research: E. L. Cornwell

Published by Marshall Cavendish Books Limited
58 Old Compton Street
London W1V 5PA

© Marshall Cavendish Limited 1979, 1983

First printing 1979
Second printing 1983

Printed and bound by L.E.G.O., Vicenza, Italy

ISBN 0 85685 711 4

Front endpaper: A view of HMS 'Furious' after final conversion but before the small island superstructure was added, showing the retractable compass platform and aerial masts.

Opposite title page: A Blackburn Baffin torpedo bomber, successor to the Ripon and initially named Ripon V, approaching to land on HMS 'Courageous', with a destroyer as rescue attendant.

This page: A Grumman F14A Tomcat swing-wing two-seat 'air superiority' fighter, capable of Mach 2.3 plus, taxying to a catapult for launching from nuclear-powered carrier USS 'Enterprise'.

Overleaf: HMS 'Bulwark' during her commando carrier role, recovering some of her Wessex helicopters, of which she carried about 20 as well as providing accommodation for 750 troops and their equipment.

Back endpaper: Last of the four Forrestal-class fleet carriers, the first US postwar design, USS 'Independence', pictured at Guantanamo Naval Base, Cuba, in 1969.

INTRODUCTION

From the Middle Ages to the dawn of the twentieth century the warship was dependent almost entirely upon the gun; a ship's effectiveness was reckoned by the number and calibre of the guns it carried. Then, seemingly fortuitously, just as it appeared that something of a plateau had been reached – that the gun's size and range were likely to be improved only marginally in the future – aircraft arrived on the scene.

Development of the aeroplane was swift and the potential of its usage at sea was rapidly appreciated. When the aircraft carrier became a reality, exercises soon confirmed an ability to observe and strike an enemy at ranges hitherto impossible. Between the Wars rival maritime powers forged the carrier into a weapon so flexible and so effective that the 'era of the big gun' became merely another chapter in the age-old history of the sea.

During World War II the carrier was seldom out of the news and its absolute dominance in the Pacific theatre justifies the prominence the great carrier actions are given in this book. But its reign as mistress of the seas promised to be short-lived as postwar missile technology first took over its role of bearer of the 'ultimate weapon' and then, at least in theory, transformed the carrier into a hopelessly vulnerable target.

The powerful anti-carrier lobby's case was further strengthened by massively spiralling costs and, until recently, few could be found bold enough to predict any future for the big multi-role battle carrier. Until, that is, the Soviet challenger to the Western Alliance's sea dominance added the aircraft carrier to its own armoury with every appearance of intending to make it an essential item of fleet equipment. Thus the debate has been given new impetus.

Meanwhile development of new concepts, such as the specialized anti-submarine ships, the sea control ship and the through-deck cruiser; and the emergence of the practical V/STOL aircraft, have all taken over some, but by no means all, of the conventional carrier's tasks. This book reviews these new concepts and describes the fascinating processes of evolution that will assure the future of the aircraft carrier.

CONTENTS

AIRFIELDS AT SEA

MISTRESS OF THE OCEANS

THE NUCLEAR ERA

AIRFIELDS AT SEA

From foredeck to flightdeck

Previous page: Fairey Flycatcher fighters on the deck of HMS 'Glorious' on exercise in the Mediterranean in 1933.

Below: The Short 184 seaplane was the first aircraft to be built in quantity for carrier use and the first aircraft type to destroy an enemy ship by torpedo, at the Dardanelles. No 166 was one of the seaplane complement of the first 'Ark Royal' (bottom), the first ship fully converted for aircraft duties when she was completed in 1914.

During nearly two years of war the people of the shores of Fife and Midlothian had become accustomed to the great grey ships of the Royal Navy moving silently and unobtrusively to sea on their various missions. But on this clear evening in late May 1916 something special was obviously afoot, with columns of smoke rising from the massed funnels of the destroyers at Port Edgar framing the battlecruisers as they slipped under the brooding mass of the bridge and into the gathering gloom to the east. The northern dusk still lay clear on the water as, shortly before 22.00, the slim forms of the cruiser squadrons followed in their wake. With the four 'Towns' of the 3rd Light

Cruiser Squadron was another vessel, whose form was anything but warlike, a hull slim and low with a graceful counter and twin well-proportioned funnels. At her after end was an unlovely box-like superstructure and a pair of cranes that totally marred her appearance. She was the *Engadine*, late cross-channel packet, now temporary seaplane carrier to His Majesty's Grand Fleet. She was about to make history, as the dispatch reproduced below records.

Enclosure No 24 to Battle Cruiser Fleet Letter No BCF01, 12.6.16.

HMS 'Engadine'
2nd June 1916

Sir,

I have the honour to make the following report on this Ship's movements on 31st May and 1st June 1916:

When in company with the Battle Cruiser Fleet, Seaplane No 8359 was hoisted out at 3.7pm with Flight Lieutenant F. J. Rutland

Above: The need for faster and more-nimble wheeled aircraft led to the British scheme for getting them airborne at sea illustrated here. It was to tow a fighter on a long barge at speed, behind a destroyer, as this Sopwith Camel flown off by Lt Stuart Culley during trials in 1918, after a first attempt by Col Sampson had failed to get airborne.

RN as Pilot and Assistant Paymaster G. S. Trewin RN as Observer, with orders to scout NNE for hostile Ships, in accordance with your signal received on board at 2.40pm. Their reports are attached.

The delay in hoisting out (the) Seaplane was caused through the Ship having to keep clear of the Cruisers.

After the Seaplane was hoisted out, the Ship proceeded in an ENE direction, (the) same direction as the Seaplane and Light Cruisers.

The following signals were received from the Seaplane:

15.30 Three enemy Cruisers and 5 Destroyers, distance from me 10 miles bearing 90°, steering course to the NW.

15.33 Enemy's course is South.

15.45 Three enemy Cruisers and 10 Destroyers steering South.

15.48 Four enemy Cruisers and 10 Destroyers steering South.

The last signal was not received in the Ship, which I think was due to the Seaplane descending at the time...

The last sentence of the captain's report was indeed correct as, to quote from that of the pilot:

At 3.45pm (GMT) a petrol pipe leading to the left front carburetter broke and my engine revolutions dropped from 1,200 to 800 and I was forced to descend. On landing I made good the defect with rubber tube and reported to the Ship that I could go on again. I was told to come alongside and be hoisted in. I was hoisted in at about 4.0pm (GMT)...

In this somewhat undistinguished manner the one-time channel packet *Engadine* made history by being the first warship to employ aircraft in a naval action. HMS *Galatea's* sighting report was confirmed and the Battle of Jutland joined.

This, however, is to anticipate, for although still primitive, naval aviation had already advanced far. Through history the planning of a successful attack depended greatly upon good intelligence of an enemy's strength and disposition; such knowledge benefited also a weaker force, enabling it to retire without being brought to action or to track and report until more powerful assistance was to hand. Even in conditions of good visibility, the horizon from a flagship's bridge was somewhat limited and, with the size of an early twentieth-century battle fleet, back markers of a column were barely in sight, a situation aggravated by volumes of funnel smoke that spread slowly downwind like a pall. Fleet admirals relied heavily on light cruiser squadrons scouting far ahead and on the flanks, analogous to cavalry ashore. Even these eyes could be dimmed by the conditions on a small heaving bridge in a seaway. How many commanders down the years would have traded their souls for an eye in the sky, all-seeing and remote, reporting dispassionately on an opponent's movements and correcting one's own fall of shot.

With the opening of the twentieth century it even began to look feasible. The long summer of the late Victorian years drew to its close but left as a legacy a spirit of inventiveness, a drive towards new

The first-ever aircraft landing on a ship by Eugene Ely in January 1911, in a Curtiss biplane on a 120ft-long platform fitted with wire-and-sandbag arrester gear over the after end of armoured cruiser USS 'Pennsylvania'.

technologies and their application. As early as 1903 the Royal Navy had begun experiments with the towing of large kites behind fast ships. It was not until 1908, however, that a man was added to complete the combination, due to the fact that an airship equipped with the newly developed wireless set seemed more promising. Dedicated men were, of course, tinkering with heavier-than-air machines but these contraptions of string and baling-wire could not yet be seriously considered for duty at sea, although the first serving officers learned to fly them privately in 1909.

Thus, in 1911 the Royal Navy's first rigid airship was completed for evaluation. Her unofficial name of *Mayfly* was all too prophetic for her life was short indeed with her back being broken by the weather after only four months' service. Having learned little of value, the Admiralty lost interest and turned its attention toward manned observation balloons. Traditionally, it reacted to developments rather than initiating them but, in the challenging new field of aviation, this leisurely approach was denied it. Both the French and the Americans had been investigating from the beginning the possibilities offered by powered flight and the fleet of Tsarist Russia, having exercised with airships as early as 1907, was seeking to procure aircraft of its own. The benefits had been demonstrated of aircraft working *with* warships; it remained to capitalize on that

experience by operating aircraft *from* warships.

First take-off and landing

The Germans had a bold plan to launch an aircraft from a ship to speed express mail delivery, the news of which spurred the Americans to try to beat them to it. They did. In November 1910 a notable 'first' was scored by a civilian pilot, Eugene Ely, when he flew a Curtiss biplane from a temporary platform erected over the bows of the cruiser *Birmingham*. The fact that the weather was calm and misty and that the ship was at anchor led initially to the erroneous belief that a platform's place was aft where it would not detract from the fighting efficiency of the ship and a newly airborne pilot would not be run down if forced to 'ditch'. Within two months the intrepid Ely completed his double by successfully landing a similar aircraft on to a platform on the after end of the armoured cruiser *Pennsylvania*. This structure was only about 120 feet in length and the aircraft had a conventional wheeled undercarriage. In order to bring the aircraft to a halt inside this limited distance a series of transverse arrester wires were erected, their ends weighted with sandbags, and the aircraft was equipped with several hooks.

The British were some way behind and it was not until early 1912 that a similar experiment was undertaken. In spite of American beliefs it seemed common sense to use the forward motion of a ship to generate extra lift to an aircraft. After a trial run using the battleship *Africa*, anchored off Sheerness, successful take-offs were made underweigh in the English Channel from structures built forward in the battleships *Hibernia* and *London*. The flights were made by Lieutenants Samson, Gregory and Longmore, the privately tutored pupils of three years before; their Short S27 was a strengthened Boxkite aircraft modified with airbags to enable it to land in the sea to be recovered by crane, unlike Ely's which used an airfield for one end of each flight.

At about the same time service flying was put on a regular footing by the establishment of the Royal Flying Corps (RFC) in April 1912. The intention was that this central body should administer a wing serving the needs of each of the three services but the spirit of independence was strong and the naval wing of the RFC soon became known as the Royal Naval Air Service (RNAS), a title confirmed shortly before the outbreak of war.

After Ely's successes, the Americans — the majority of whom were not happy about the large afterdeck — sought to use compressed air to catapult a seaplane into the air, a nice space-saving compromise. The first successful launch was made ashore and a catapult was then installed on the cruiser *Huntington*, on the quarterdeck pointing aft. This was followed rather later by a forward-facing structure on the USS *North Carolina*. In both cases half the main gun battery was impaired and the modifications were regarded as temporary. The British were slower in developing the catapult and it was 1917 before a converted hopper — renamed *Slinger* — was used for experiments. They were active in other directions however; in 1911 a patent was filed for a system whereby a seaplane could be mounted on a trolley and launched along a track, followed in 1913 by the introduction of a satisfactory folding wing.

Wireless link established

These two developments made possible the Admiralty's conversion of the 5700-ton protected cruiser *Hermes* to carry three aircraft forward. One was a Short Folder and marked the beginning of a long association between the Short company and naval aviation, although the first flight was made by a French-built Caudron GIII, which was recovered from the sea after its flight. In 1913 also, a Short floatplane from the ship demonstrated that it could transmit information to the ship by wireless, a notable advance. Although most of the *Hermes* flights were made by seaplanes lowered over the side, she showed sufficient promise to stimulate their Lordships to

make the necessary appropriations for the acquisition of an 'aviation vessel'.

A ship was purchased on the ways, a typical five-hatch three-island dry-cargo carrier of the time. She required great modifications for her new role and it was then mid-1914, with Europe rumbling ominously; as it would obviously take time before she could commission, other measures were taken to get aircraft to sea. The 'moth-balled' *Hermes* was reactivated (only to be sunk shortly after the outbreak of war) and the first three of many cross-Channel ferries were taken over. Such narrow-gutted ships might appear a strange choice, but, in that age of great railway competition, fast ships were good business and these turbine-driven packets were well able to make fleet speeds. Thus, the *Empress*, *Engadine* and *Riviera* were each given a large hangar aft, together with handling cranes but no flightdeck. They had belonged to the South Eastern & Chatham Railway Company and were soon joined by three more from the Isle of Man service, *Ben-my-Chree*, *Manxman* and *Vindex*, and later by the larger short-sea passenger ships *Nairana* and *Pegasus*. Each carried four seaplanes but it was found that they were very susceptible to weather conditions.

While the Royal Navy thus made preparations for a war, the US Navy became the first to use naval aircraft on active service. Much of their naval aviation effort had gone into the establishment of stations ashore but, when a crisis developed with

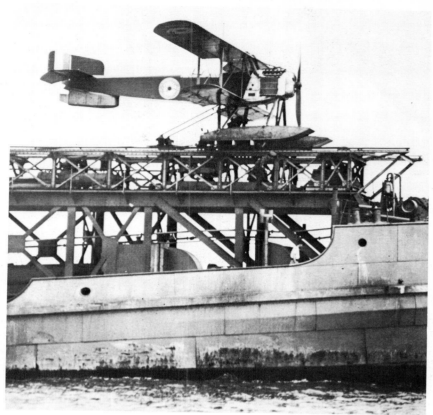

The Americans originated the catapult to get seaplanes airborne without the lengthy business of first craning them into the water. The British followed in 1917 with the converted hopper 'Slinger', here seen with a Short floatplane on the catapult about to be hauled back to the starting position.

Mexico in 1914, A3 and C3 aircraft were put aboard the battleship *Mississippi* and the *Birmingham* and were used to reconnoitre troop movements near Vera Cruz and Tampico.

Events in Europe progressed rapidly towards war, which finally broke out in August 1914. Neither Germany nor her partner Austria-Hungary, in spite of their sizeable fleets, showed much interest in operating aircraft at sea. Both of them were essentially land powers and developed naval forces built around capital ships of generally excellent design but geared to short-range forays to counter any effort by enemy fleets to impose a blockade. They were, therefore, planned primarily to react to events rather than initiate them and their operations could be covered from the shore by their strong force of Zeppelin airships.

The seventy or so British naval aircraft at the outbreak of war were reinforced, albeit at a distance, by over 50 Curtiss flying-boats of the Russian fleet. The Russians are highly innovative by nature and were seeking from an early date the best ways of integrating aircraft with their large fleets, particularly those in the Baltic and Black Sea. With neighbouring Turkey entering the war against them, the Russians also were stimulated to conversions of merchant ships for the operation of seaplanes. The largest of those put in hand were the 9000-ton *Imperator Nikolai I* and *Imperator Alexander I*. Each could carry eight aircraft which had to launch from the sea, although it was proposed that they be suspended by electro-magnets from booms, engines running, while the parent ship steamed at high speed into the wind to generate enough lift to enable the aircraft to rise away upon being released. There is no evidence that his precarious arrangement was ever tried in earnest!

First Ark Royal

The other major allied fleet was, of course, the French but, although well ahead of most in the development of aircraft they were in no hurry to get them to sea. A depot ship, *Foudre*, was in the process of conversion for the operation of seaplanes, and was, in fact, completed before the British had their first purpose-built seaplane carrier ready, in December 1914. She bore the proud Elizabethan name of *Ark Royal* and had little resemblance to the freighter from which she sprang, with the well-decks filled in to make a high-freeboard hull and all accommodation and machinery moved aft. Where the *Foudre* had a hangar on top, however, the *Ark* had space below for ten aircraft, together with workshops etc, access being through flush-fitted hatches plumbed by steam cranes. The foredeck was kept clear for projected use as a flight deck. This rather odd-looking

ship was a great step forward but, unfortunately, she was still working up when the Royal Navy launched its first air strike on Christmas Day 1914.

Cuxhaven raid

The plan was to bomb the Zeppelin sheds at Cuxhaven, near the mouth of the Elbe, in the hope that it would goad an enemy force to sea from nearby Wilhelmshaven into a submarine trap. Tyrwhitt's Harwich Force of destroyers and light cruisers escorted *Empress*, *Engadine* and *Riviera* deep into the Bight where, in spite of perfect conditions, only seven of the planned nine seaplanes, a mixture of Short Folders and Types 74 and 135, managed to get airborne. Unfortunately, the warm sun offshore had had the effect of raising a dense fog over the damp flats of the North German coast and the aircraft were totally unable to find their target and their bombs were released on an opportunity basis. Their orders were to overfly the Schillig Roads on the return flight to report the presence of German fleet units in the stream.

There was, indeed, a squadron present and the effect of the unknown threat from enemy aircraft was sufficient to make each ship weigh anchor in a panic reminiscent of that off Gravelines in 1588 when the Armada sighted the English fireships bearing down. Several minor collisions resulted but this small success was tempered by the fact that only two of the seven aircraft made it back to their parent ships. The remainder ran out of fuel and alighted, their crews being picked up by various ships. Enemy aircraft tried to bomb the returning force but it returned unscathed, frustrated and richer for the experience.

Even if she had been present, the *Ark Royal* would have made little difference to the outcome and she sailed early in 1915 to support the Anglo-French adventure at the Dardanelles. A feature of the early days of this campaign were the repeated attempts by pre-Dreadnoughts to force the strait and open the way to Constantinople, in the teeth of numerous fortifications and the dicta of Alfred Thayer Mahan. The waterway was narrow, winding and steep-to, giving the ships little chance of outranging the forts with their powerful main batteries. Only indirect fire could achieve this and, as the armies had not succeeded in occupying the necessary high ground, techniques were soon improvized for using aircraft to spot fall of shot. Even the great *Queen Elizabeth* came to calibrate her new 15-inch guns by firing blind across the Helles Peninsula.

This use of aircraft would have advanced farther had not the free use of the Dardanelles approaches become hazardous with the arrival of the first U-boat, whose

To provide larger warships with ability to fly off wheeled aircraft for reconnaissance and interception, the British fitted take-off platforms on gun turrets. Here a Sopwith 1½-Strutter is taking off with only the turret turned into wind.

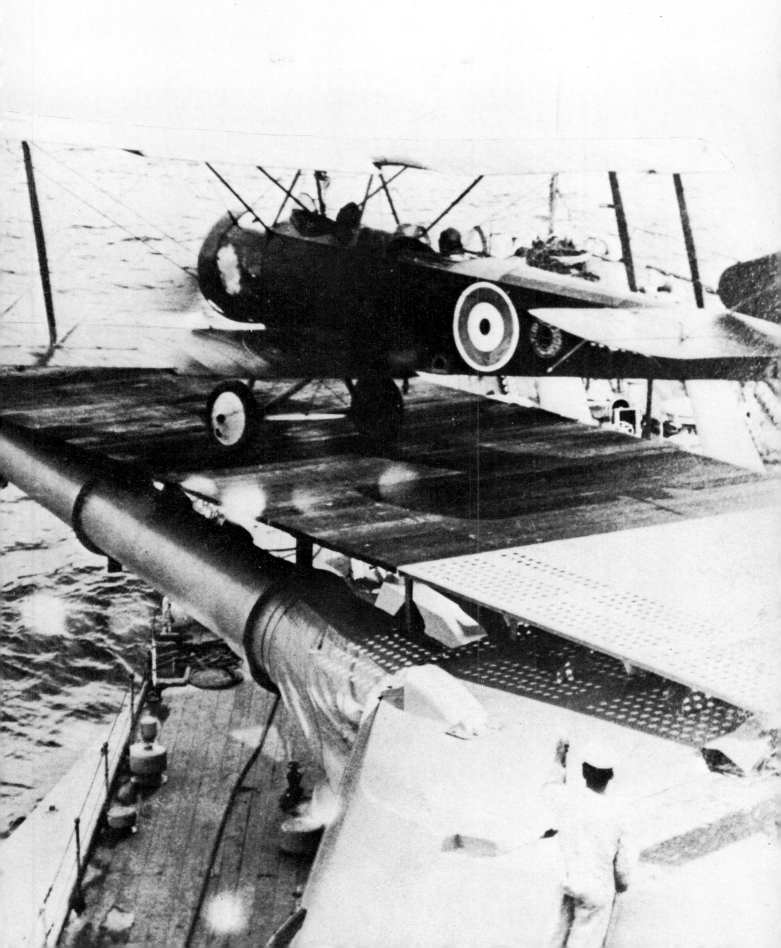

The seaplane carrier 'Ben-my-Chree' in action at the Dardanelles in August 1915 with one of her Short 184s in the water alongside. The seaplanes sank one Turkish merchantman and damaged two more with torpedoes.

presence was announced by the rapid loss of two old battleships. *Ark Royal*, whose speed could best be described as lacking, was considered far too vulnerable to work in the forward area and was pulled back in June 1915 to the more secure waters around the fleet base at Imbros, her place being taken by the more agile *Ben-my-Chree*. The lower capacity of this converted packet meant that greater reliance needed to be placed on ballon observation.

Only days before the outbreak of war, Lt Longmore had demonstrated that a 14-inch torpedo could be successfully dropped from a short Folder. In August 1915 *Ben-my-Chree* applied this example to good effect, loading a similar-sized weapon under an improved Type 184 seaplane which lumbered over the craggy spine of the peninsula and discovered a good-sized Turkish supply ship. The torpedo ran true from under a quarter-of-a-mile and destroyed its target, the first ever to have been thus sunk. A few days later the attack was repeated with a pair of aircraft and again remarkable accuracy was achieved with both torpedoes finding their mark. Unfortunately, the 14-inch torpedo carried too small a warhead to guarantee success and both ships survived, damaged.

The Admiralty was slow to realise the potential. Instead, the policy of cautious growth was pursued with the acquisition at the end of 1914 of the *Campania*, an ageing Cunard record-breaker still capable of about 22 knots. With a length of 620 feet she was long enough to have a sloping 200-foot flying-off deck added forward (this was done in two separate stages) and at a height which gave the most ponderous of seaplanes a good chance of getting airborne directly by mounting them on trolleys and propelling them along rails. This great length of tracked deck served by an elevator from below meant that the forward funnel had to be removed and the uptakes routed up a pair of casings which flanked the deck and did nothing for the ship's appearance. All of her 10 aircraft were seaplanes because no landing-on facilities yet existed and only recovery from the sea was possible after

flight. It was, of course, well recognized that the performance of conventional landplanes was far superior and, soon after the *Campania* became operational in August 1915, another pocket conversion, *Vindex*, launched one of a pair of wheeled Bristol Scouts, which had had to be dismantled before they could be accommodated aboard. By means of flotation bags secured beneath, the little aircraft was landed successfully in the water and recovered.

Early failures

One of the greatest contributions made by aircraft in the 1914-18 war was in the field of photo-reconnaissance and, before she left the Eastern Mediterranean, *Ark Royal* proved at Salonika that seaborne aircraft could also perform this task adequately. It was becoming increasingly clear that the airship was not liked in some high places (although non-rigids were being built for the RNAS to operate from ashore on coastal patrols) and that the aircraft was to be the chosen instrument of naval aviation. The wholly land-based German Zeppelins meanwhile were used to support the High Seas Fleet, among other duties, by virtue of which they developed a 'bogey' image that was largely unjustified. Nevertheless, they carried out bombing attacks on British warships as yet unused to a war in a third dimension. Only one airship was destroyed by high-angle gunfire and it was obvious that the only real answer was to launch a high-performance fighter aircraft; much thought began to be expended in this direction but, until a suitable method was available, more direct methods had to be used in the form of raids against the Zeppelin bases on the German coast.

In an attempt to eradicate the enemy at source a strike was planned against the Emden sheds early in 1916 but it was frustrated by a U-boat mounting an attack against the *Vindex* while she was engaged in the time-consuming task of hoisting out her seaplanes. Although the torpedoes missed, the operation had to be abandoned. A repeat attempt was made in March 1916, this time against Hoyer on the Schleswig coast, and covered by the Harwich Force. In deteriorating weather conditions this raid was also a failure, although it succeeded in bringing a powerful German squadron to sea to pursue the departing nuisance. British planning had, unfortunately, not catered for the immediate presence of heavy forces or submarines to capitalize on this eventuality and the hasty withdrawal in darkness and heavy weather was carried out in some confusion, resulting in several collisions as a result of which the British were fortunate to lose only one destroyer. Nevertheless, these unrewarding expeditions were not abandoned but were continued with another, equally unsuccessful, attempt at the same target in May.

At the end of the month, as already noted, the fleet action of Jutland was fought; its lack of conclusive result was a matter of bitter disappointment to the Grand Fleet, which had been trained to a fine pitch for such an event. The reasons for the failure were various but one was certainly the poor flow of intelligence available to Jellicoe with regard to enemy dispositions. *Campania* should have been present and conceivably her seaplanes could just have provided that last piece of information that the admiral sought, but she had been anchored at a distance from the main body of the fleet and received her sailing orders too late for her ever to catch up. In spite of *Engadine's* efforts, it was the Germans who benefited most from aerial support although most of the large force of Zeppelins involved were totally frustrated by poor visibility in the battle area.

First aircraft carriers

Jellicoe afterwards pressed the need for readily available aircraft of good performance; this ruled out seaplanes, whose every operation was hostage to the weather and whose losses were unacceptably high. What was required was a ship capable of launching wheeled aircraft and recovering them without the need of stopping. It was decided to purchase a pair of liners then building in the UK to Italian account and convert them into 'aircraft carriers' (as opposed to seaplane carriers). Their powerful machinery, length and freeboard made them particularly suitable for the purpose, which was the next logical step beyond *Campania*. In the event, caution tempered enthusiasm and only one hull was proceeded with for evaluation purposes; it was that of the *Conte Rosso*, renamed *Argus*, a name that suggests a role of observation rather than attack.

Even with full priority, however, she was not likely to be commissioned inside 18 months — a long time in a war. A stopgap

solution was resolved upon in a Campania-type conversion of HMS *Furious*, one of the interesting trio of 'tin-clads' pushed through by 'Jackie' Fisher as part of his grand plan for a major landing in the Baltic. For this operation, heavy gun support was deemed indispensable but battleships could not work inshore due to draught limitations and the purpose-built monitors were too slow. Two 22,700-ton 'light cruisers', *Glorious* and *Courageous*, were therefore built, carrying four 15-inch guns apiece, on a 22-foot draught, followed by a slightly larger sister, *Furious*, with two single 18-inch mountings. Where the first two had little practical value the third had absolutely none and the Navy, with its gift for the *mot juste*, christened the trio *Spurious, Curious* and *Outrageous*.

Withdrawal of Furious

With Fisher's fall from power, the still incomplete *Furious* lost her primary champion and half her armament to a sloping forward flightdeck about 230 feet in length and served from the hangar below by an elevator. It was mid-1917 before she joined the fleet and yet she offered little that the much earlier *Campania* could not, particularly in that her ten aircraft could not be recovered by landing-on. Officially, that is. One of the original band of naval pilots, Dunning, then a squadron commander, skilfully side-slipped a Sopwith Pup around *Furious's* superstructure and landed on her foredeck with the aid of braking provided by a

In August 1917 Cdr E. H. Dunning successfully landed a Sopwith Pup on the sloping forward flying-off deck of HMS 'Furious' by sideslipping round the ship's superstructure, and the help of a deck crew ready to grab straps fitted to convenient points on the aircraft. In a later attempt the aircraft went over the side and he was killed.

flightdeck party which literally pulled the aircraft out of the air as the throttle was cut back. A few days later when Dunning attempted a further landing to develop the technique, the engine cut prematurely and the aircraft went overboard and was run down by the ship; the Navy had lost a man of great ability. As a direct result of this incident *Furious* was withdrawn after only a few months of service to have a second, landing-on, deck added aft.

It was then late in 1917, the *Argus* was only at the launching stage and work had scarcely begun on the first purpose-built ship, based upon her and to be named *Hermes*. Once again a stop-gap solution was embarked upon in the conversion of the large cruiser *Cavendish* as a miniature version of *Furious* with separate flightdecks forward and aft. She was renamed *Vindictive* after the cruiser that had distinguished herself at the Zeebrugge raid but was not completed in time to see action. She was in fact preceded by *Furious* herself in March 1918 in her second guise with a 280-foot flightdeck aft, which was built on the level of the after end of the forward deck and connected to it by ways along each side of the still-complete superstructure. This rebuilding had resulted in the loss of the after 18-inch gun and the three existing barrels were mounted in monitors for their original bombardment purposes. The after deck was equipped with rudimentary arrester wires, laid axially but weighted with sandbags as in Ely's experiments so long before; if an aircraft's primitive arrester hooks did not succeed in engaging this arrangement, only a rope palisade was provided to prevent collision with the after end of the superstructure. This failing was not over-significant, however, as the violent eddies downstream of the superstructure made landing difficult to the extent that it was abandoned as impracticable.

As a consequence it was ordained that the still-building *Argus* and *Hermes*, together with a third and larger carrier to be converted from the appropriated hull of the battleship *Almirante Cochrane*, under construction in the UK to Chilean account, should have no superstructure at all.

It was *Furious* in July 1917 that mounted the first really successful strike against the Zeppelin sheds in Schleswig. Seven Camels were launched, each armed with small bombs. They proved more than adequate to pierce the thin roofs of the giant hangars and two of their occupants were destroyed by fire. Less happy was the fate of the aircraft; none was shot down but five crashed from mechanical failure or lack of fuel and the two that made it back were ditched and lost because of the continuing inability of *Furious* to recover wheeled aircraft.

The need to get high-performance aircraft to sea led to other strategems. It was reasoned that even a small ship could fly off a biplane if she had the speed to generate sufficient wind-over-deck to give the necessary lift. The light cruiser *Yarmouth* was, therefore, fitted with a short flying-deck extending from the lower bridge deck to a point over the forward gun. Trials with a Sopwith Pup were successfully completed in early 1917 and other cruisers were put in hand for similar modifications. On 21 August the experiment was triumphantly vindicated when *Yarmouth's* Pup destroyed a shadowing Zeppelin off the Danish coast. Short platforms were also added over turret and guns of major warships, fittings which had the added advantage that they could be trained in azimuth to allow flying-off without so much changing of course. Later seaplane carrier conversions were also fitted with a flying-deck forward for wheeled aircraft.

Another, very English, innovation was the High-Speed Sled. This was little more than a 58-foot lighter, designed to be towed at up to 32 knots with an aircraft on top. The system worked reasonably well and much. effort was put into it but it arrived late in the war and was responsible for the destruction of only one Zeppelin although, to be fair, it was designed primarily as a reconnaissance aid. The impetus of war had advanced the aircraft of 1918 to a weapon of some potency — the drawback was the lack of suitable decks from which to operate it.

Argus commissioned

Torpedo attacks from the air inspired great enthusiasm in some quarters after the success of the *Ben-my-Chree* at the Dardanelles, and it was seen as a means of attacking a German Fleet reluctant to seek action. Sopwith designed the Cuckoo, a landplane capable of carrying an 18-inch torpedo, which was built by various manufacturers to expedite the creation of a large force. Even so, the first squadron became operational only in October 1918, a month before the Armistice and just in time for the commissioning of the *Argus*.

Early in 1918 the fledgling air arm of the fleet had had a real chance to prove itself when the German battlecruiser *Goeben* and her light cruiser escort *Breslau* made a long-expected foray out of the Turkish waters in which they had spent the war. British forces in the area were powerful but not concentrated and the enemy easily dispatched two monitors, surprised off Imbros. In a dramatic reversal of fortune the Germans ran into a minefield, losing the *Breslau* and heavily damaging her formidable partner which successfully made the Dardanelles, only to run aground.

Bombing attacks had been made by a pair of Sopwith Babies landed previously by *Ark Royal* but their bombs were too light to inflict damage and both aircraft were lost. Further similar attacks were frustrated and a race developed between the Germans, trying to refloat, and the British, who brought in both *Ark Royal* and *Manxman* to the very gates of the Dardanelles with Short seaplanes that had been hastily converted to carry 14-inch torpedoes. The failure of the aircraft to get airborne even with these modest loads ended the affair, which was given more poignant force in the loss of the submarine E14 when it attempted to force the strait to finish the job.

This frustrating end of the last real chance that the RNAS had to prove itself seemed to be typical of the times. In April 1918 it lost its separate identity when the newly formed Royal Air Force combined both RFC and RNAS under one command, with the result that the Navy lost control of its air arm and became rapidly a poor relation in the queue for aircraft. Then, a week before the war's end, the already-doomed seaplane carrier acquired an epitaph in the loss of the *Campania*, never the luckiest of ships. Dragging her anchors during a gale in the Forth, she fell across the stem of the battleship *Revenge*; after a further collision with *Glorious*, she sank. The arrival of *Argus*, too late to be of any use, was in like vein. Had she been earlier, her effect on an enemy totally unprepared for air attack at sea could have been far-reaching. Raw and untried she was but, in that particular country of the blind she might well have been the one-eyed man. As it was, progress on *Hermes* and the later conversion, *Eagle*, were slowed to await her evaluation as the first true aircraft carrier.

Sopwith Camel taking off from HMS 'Argus', the world's first carrier with completely flush deck (and therefore nicknamed 'The Flat Iron'). She was finished too late for service in WW1 but provided the basis on which many realistic carrier operations were evolved and continued in use mainly as a training and ferry carrier during WW2. Note the steam 'windsock'.

The carriers came forth

At the close of hostilities in November 1918, Britain was pre-eminent in naval aviation. *Argus*, with a 549-foot clear flightdeck was active and gaining experience with an admixture of torpedo, fighter and reconnaissance aircraft. There existed nothing like her elsewhere and the results of her early operations were being ploughed back into the slow construction of *Hermes* and *Eagle*. With the imminence of the true carrier's arrival, the majority of the converted seaplane carriers had been retired and practically all seaborne aircraft in the Grand Fleet, over one hundred, were carried by conventional warships, two to a capital ship and one on many light cruisers. All of this capacity was, however, undermined by the fact that the greater number were wheeled aircraft which were unlikely to be recovered after a flight. It was, nevertheless, a fine start and one which was being observed closely by all other major fleets — but the decline had already set in with the loss of Admiralty control of its air arm to the RAF. The fight to regain it was to last the next 20 years; it was finally won in 1937, just in time for another war.

The French Navy had operated seaplane carriers during the later stages of the war and were interested in developments without committing themselves. The Germans had been satisfied with shore-based aerial support but had converted the Hapag ship *Stuttgart* for the evaluation of seaplane operations. The Americans had been largely preoccupied with the shore-based seaplane and the development of the necessary paraphernalia to carry aircraft on major warships. Significantly, the loudest demand for specialized US seaplane carriers was from Admiral Sims, who commanded American naval forces in European waters and had seen at first hand the possibilities afforded by aircraft. By early 1918, his requests for four seaplane carriers — notably directed toward A/S warfare — seemed to be making an impression, followed in mid-1918 by the glad news of a Navy Board recommendation for no less than six 33-knot aircraft carriers with unrestricted 700-foot flightdecks. But the end of the war was obviously in sight and the plans were put in abeyance as it was not considered possible to produce any results in the limited time left.

Clearing the superstructure

Which left the Japanese. As an ally of the Entente, Japan's Imperial Fleet had played a rather minor role in what was primarily a European war. Her interests and ambitions were in the vastness of the Pacific and the ability of aircraft to cover distances quickly was immediately apparent to her. As the British proceeded leisurely with the construction of the *Hermes*, the Japanese laid down the 7500-ton *Hosho* at the end of 1919 and commissioned her in December 1922 as the world's first purpose-built aircraft carrier. She was small but marked the beginning of a long series of carriers that were to provide the Japanese fleet with a formidable cutting edge. Japanese fleet traditions were based upon those of the Royal Navy and it was no coincidence that the hull of the *Hosho* resembled that of *Argus* with the marked difference topsides of a diminutive bridge and three downward-hinging funnels. The bridge was subsequently removed, establishing the pattern for the greater number of carriers that followed her. A 12,500-ton running-mate, *Shokaku*, was authorized under the 1922 programme but was never built, for reasons to be mentioned later.

Britain's *Eagle* was brought to trials condition by late 1920. She was of 22,500-tons but was not fully completed for a further four years, being used to gain experience for the final casting of *Hermes*, commissioned in 1923, as a 10,900-tonner with a useful flightdeck almost 600 feet in length. One feature finally resolved by these experiments had been the form of the island superstructure, placed to starboard and of a basic layout that has remained ever since.

The Americans meanwhile, after the stillbirth of their earlier ambitions, were far from inactive, commencing the conversion of the fleet collier *Jupiter* in 1920 into what was to become their first carrier, *Langley* (CV1). She was commissioned early in 1922 and, with hangar and flightdeck built on top, earned the nickname of Covered Wagon, more from affection than derision for she taught them much. Her 534-foot flightdeck was almost devoid of

Facing page: From a painting by Henry Rushbury in the Imperial War Museum depicting an aircraft carrier under construction during the war years.

America's first and second carriers illustrate a striking advance. CV1 USS 'Langley' (top), the converted fleet collier commissioned in 1922, displaced 11,050 tons, had a 534ft flightdeck and a speed of 15 knots and could operate up to 34 aircraft. The 'Lexington' (CV2), here seen launching Martin T4M torpedo carriers in the late 1920s, displaced 33,000 tons, had a length of nearly 890 feet and a speed of over 33 knots and operated a normal complement of 80 aircraft, though she could stow up to 120.

superstructure and, having the machinery aft in collier fashion, the two diminutive folding funnels were well back.

During *Langley's* construction another great issue relating ships and aviation had been fought out in the USA. In spite of British experience to the contrary, there were hawks who maintained that large warships could not survive co-ordinated modern bombing attacks and that no more should be built. None was more forceful on the subject than Brigadier-General 'Billy' Mitchell of the US Army Air Force and with ceded ex-German warships available as targets it was decided to carry out bombing trials, off the Virginia Capes, in 1921. The technique used was to place the bombs close aboard, exploiting the concussive effect of the explosions to sink the targets by breaching their plating. A submarine and destroyer were disposed of in short order followed, with slightly more resistance, by the light cruiser *Frankfurt*. Their final target, the battleship *Ostfriesland*, was dispatched after a couple of days with methods that engendered acrimonious exchanges with the US naval observers. Mitchell claimed that his theories had been proven but the opposition pointed out that he had shown only that it was possible to sink ships by bombing and this under ideal conditions from low level with the targets anchored and not firing back.

Stimulus of Washington Treaty

Developments in the evolution of the aircraft carrier would probably have continued at a leisurely pace but for the unexpected stimulus offered by the Washington Treaty, signed in 1922. The origins of this agreement lay in rivalry between the late partners of the US and Japan, with the former determined to retain their newly won place as a front-line naval power and the latter, which considered herself mistress of the Western Pacific, equally determined to acquire the naval power to underline the claim. Successive building programmes were rapidly instituted, with each nation seeking to out-trump the other, so that as early as 1919 both were laying down 43,000-ton capital ships armed with 16-inch guns. Half-a-world away, Great Britain still considered herself *the* naval power and had no intention of letting any upstart fleets get the better of her. Thus the 1921 Estimates provided for a class of 16-inch battlecruisers of 48,000-tons, to be followed by even larger 18-inch-gunned battleships. To nations lately weakened by war this new naval race was total madness and the growing financial recession was greatly responsible for forcing the American President, Wilson, out of office on the strength of his policies. His successor, Harding, called a halt and brought the rival factions to the conference table, together with France and Italy, each of whom had a sizeable fleet and interests in the Mediterranean balance of power.

Although the main objective of the treaty was the reduction in major gunned ships — and many fine vessels found a premature end at the breakers as a result — it would seem that the full potential of naval aviation was not fully appreciated in view of the generous tonnages that the Powers allowed themselves as maxima for carrier construction. These were 135,000 tons each for Britain and the US; 81,000 tons for Japan; and 60,000 tons each for France and Italy. The first figure was geared to the tonnage operated and planned by Great Britain and the rest arrived at by a simple 9:5:4 ratio agreement. A 'scrap-or-convert' clause enabled incomplete capital ships to be rebuilt as carriers and the sudden availability of a quantity of large hulls with high-power machinery spelled the end of the earlier cautious development.

Astronomical cost

The advances in size were indeed great. Whereas the American CV1 was the little *Langley*, CV2 and 3 were commissioned in 1927 as the *Lexington* and *Saratoga*, 33-knot monsters with a length of nearly 890 feet (and already exceeding the agreed individual ship maximum of 33,000 tons).

At a then astronomical total cost of 90 million dollars, they could house between 70 and 80 aircraft in hangars built British-style, with the walls and flightdeck an integral part of the hull. Their bow plating was also continuous from waterline to flightdeck, a feature subsequently abandoned and then reintroduced after WW2 as the 'hurricane bow'. A heavy armament of no less than eight 8-inch and 12 5-inch guns was carried but hull protection was confined to side belts of horizontal armour below hangar deck level; a thick-skinned flightdeck was precluded by stability considerations and the thin deck subsequently persisted in American carriers as a feature that was to prove a real Achilles heel. Their funnel casings were of magnificent proportions, encompassing the five uptakes of the earlier battlecruiser design.

Japan, meanwhile, abandoned plans for the *Shokaku* to rebuild two of her four available battlecruisers as the carriers *Amagi* and *Akagi*. The conversion of the former was started in mid-1923 but within months the hull was damaged beyond repair by earthquake while still on the ways. The other pair of battlecruiser hulls had already been scrapped, so her place was taken by that of the battleship *Kaga*, shorter, beamier and, at 27 knots, four knots slower than *Akagi*. Completed in 1927-8, they continued the earlier precedent of having no island superstructure. The flightdeck terminated some distance short of the bows and the lower hangar deck continued forward on to the forecastle through large doors; the upper hangar deck could also be opened at the forward end and extended to a

point midway between the other two. This system theoretically allowed take-offs from three levels simultaneously but was not a success; later reconstructions boxed in the forward ends, increasing hangar space and extending the flightdeck right forward. Islands were also added, portside in *Akagi* and starboard in *Kaga*. Like the two Lexingtons, they had two elevators but a capacity of only 60 aircraft and their 690-foot flightdecks did not compare.

Although Great Britain viewed these developments with a wary eye her lead was not yet really challenged, with *Eagle* finally becoming fully operational in 1924 and the unhappy *Furious* emerging in 1925 with a full flightdeck after her final four-year rebuilding. With *Argus* and *Hermes* this represented a considerable force, but the *Furious's* two sisters were also put in hand, *Courageous* completing in 1928 and *Glorious* in 1930. Unlike the *Furious*, they had a full island superstructure but had an increased aircraft capacity of about 42 in their two hangars. Where the *Eagle* had a full-sized flightdeck, however, both of these later conversions reverted to the arrangement of an open-ended hangar extended as a sloping forecastle from which fighters could, theoretically, operate directly. The *Eagle* had only a battleship's 50,000shp or so but the three ex-battlecruisers could muster about 90,000shp for a speed of 31 knots.

By 1930, therefore, Britain had a half-dozen carriers but still only about 150 aircraft with which to equip them. The backbone of this slender force consisted of such aircraft as the Fairey Flycatcher and IIIF, sturdy biplanes with open cockpits, limited performance but few vices; they had

In 1925 HMS 'Furious' at last appeared with a full flightdeck, though it stopped short of the stem to provide a short flying-off deck over the bow section as an extension of the hangar. This picture shows a Fairey Flycatcher fighter on the flying-off deck and an interesting close-up of the two bridges, captain's to starboard and flying commander's on the port side.

a seeming ability to be converted for any desired role and were much loved by those who flew them. The Blackburn Dart, used as the standard torpedo aircraft in the 1920s, began to be phased out in 1929 in favour of the Ripon from the same manufacturer.

The inefficient system of longitudinal arrester wires was augmented in the mid-1920s by a series of transverse wooden flaps which, in being knocked down by the aircraft, were supposed to absorb its energy and slow it. Not surprisingly, the arrangement caused much damage and was taken out; incredibly nothing was available to take its place and, for the next five years, aircraft landed with no arrester gear whatsoever. Mercifully, a new method of transverse wires led over braked drums was introduced on *Courageous* in 1931 and formed the basis for design of the hydraulically damped wires used successfully ever since.

During this flurry of activity from the major fleets, the Washington Treaty's other signatories seemed largely unimpressed by the possibilities of naval aviation. France remained land-orientated and directed her naval energies mainly to outpacing the rival Italians but did convert one battleship, *Béarn*, into a carrier. She had been originally laid down in 1914 and finally commissioned in 1927 as a 25,000-tonner but her low-power machinery was good for barely 21 knots and she was a failure. The Italians had few colonial interests and their main

sphere of interest, the Mediterranean, could be covered by land-based aircraft.

A parallel existed in the Soviet Union, recovering from the trauma of revolution and with few resources to devote to her fleet. The official view was that aircraft were a means of *projecting* power and that Russia, not being an aggressor nation, had no need of them. At the same time it was considered that a naval air arm, operating from frozen areas of sea and in conjunction with submarines, could destroy any enemy fleet approaching the coast. Thus, by 1925, the Morskaya Aviatsiya could boast nearly 400 aircraft, all land-based.

As allowable aircraft carrier tonnage was still available, Japan laid down the small carrier *Ryujo* in 1929, for completion in 1933. Of about 10,000 tons, she could operate up to 37 aircraft and her modest 29 knots belied her name, best translated as Galloping Dragon.

Compressed-air catapult

Between 1931 and 1934 the US Navy had constructed its first purpose-built carrier, *Ranger* (CV4). At 14,500 tons she could not be called large, yet a measure of her good design lay in her astonishing capacity of 76 aircraft, typically including Douglas T2Ds or Martin dive bombers and Boeing F2F fighters. She had an island but uptakes exhausted through six small hinged funnels aft, three to a side and interconnected to minimize smoke nuisance. *Ranger* had only

Of the five Washington Treaty signatories, the French and Italians showed little interest in carriers. The French did convert the battleship 'Béarn' into a carrier in the middle 1920s but she was not a success. Here Béarn is pictured in 1927 with Levasseur biplanes on the flightdeck.

one catapult where her larger predecessors had two. Even the little *Langley* had a couple of early examples, which had previously seen service in USS *Seattle* and *Huntington*. The Americans had continued their interest in the catapult beyond the war and had a prototype turntable version powered by compressed air on the battleship *Maryland* in 1921. Attempts to perfect a flywheel-powered model were abandoned and by 1924 the *Mississippi* was evaluating the first version to employ powder as a propellant; it proved successful and was developed with a turntable for use on major gunned warships and as a flush-tracked device for aircraft carriers. This latter fitting enabled a carrier to launch aircraft using only the forward portion of the flightdeck and opened up the possibility of recovering them aft at the same time (with a palisade erected level with the bridge to prevent overshoots from careering into the aircraft ranged forward ready for take-off). At one stage consideration had been given to installing no fewer than six catapults in *Ranger*, three forward and three aft

The modest size of *Ranger* resulted partly from British and Japanese experience, which had already shown that more aircraft could be kept at sea if available tonnage was devoted to a larger number of small carriers rather than a few large ones. The capabilities of the smaller carrier in AS warfare were also being explored, but *Ranger* exposed the weaknesses of small decks compared with those of the giants that had preceded her and two new carriers authorized in 1934 were tailored to the 20,000 tons by then considered a minimum for effective operations. They were the *Yorktown* (CV5) and *Enterprise* (CV6)

commissioned in 1937 and 1938. Their extra size allowed a small increase in aircraft complement and four elevators promised more efficient flying operations. Their greater length was utilized in providing lines for a useful speed of 33 knots and the machinery uptakes exhausted through a conventional stack integral with the island structure. Worthy of note subsequent to the Lexingtons, was the American reversion to the hangar-on-top approach used by the Japanese. Horizontal protection was worked in at hangar deck level in preference to the flightdeck and the latter, together with the supporting side walls, was made a light structure which improved capacity and simplified stability calculations but at the cost of survivability, as will be seen.

The rival Japanese Navy was concurrently constructing its own pair, *Soryu* and, later, *Hiryu*. They echoed the *Kaga* and *Akagi* (then being modernized) in one (*Soryu*) having a starboard-side island and the other to port. It has been suggested that these curious arrangements were to allow the four ships to operate as a tight formation but this is rather hard to justify. They followed what had become standard Japanese practice in leading smoke aft in long trunkings, exhausting through bent-over casings of unlovely aspect. Although of a size with the American Yorktowns, their aircraft capacity of 50-60 in no way compared. At about 747 feet, they were also considerably shorter, suggesting that better protection had been provided.

A new Ark Royal

It may be recalled that the large number of British merchantmen converted to seaplane carriers had reverted swiftly to their peaceful occasions in the introduction of the aircraft carrier. Only *Ark Royal* and *Pegasus* were left, used frequently for the transport of RAF aircraft and personnel to the points of upset that peppered the imperial harmony of the period. Over a short

Some landings-on were spectacular, particularly on early British carriers which had indifferent arrester systems, or none at all, until the system using transverse wires running over braked drums was introduced on HMS 'Courageous' in 1931. Perhaps the wind-indicating steam jet provides the clue to this Fairey 111F's ground loop.

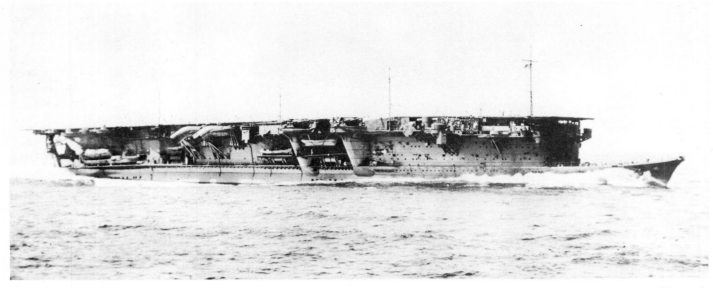

The 10,000-ton Japanese carrier 'Ryujo', completed in 1933, was an early example of the intention of the Washington Treaty working in reverse, that is, the signatories building up to the maximum tonnage allowed. Although small, 'Ryujo' had two lifts and could carry 12 aircraft in reserve as well as a normal operational complement of 36. This picture shows her in 1934 after modifications (hull bulges, removal of some guns and other top weight) to improve stability.

space of time the *Ark* appeared successively in the Black Sea, off British Somaliland, the Sea of Marmora, the Persian Gulf and the Levant coast, efectively demonstrating the flexibility of sea power. A closely similar ship, *Albatross*, was built in 1926 for the Royal Australian Navy and, shortly afterwards, *Ark Royal* became a floating testbed for catapults and developments in floatplane techniques. *Pegasus* was scrapped in 1931 and in 1934, rather confusingly, *Ark Royal* adopted her name. The reason was that, in 1935, a new carrier was to be laid down, a new *Ark Royal*, the first since the commissioning of *Glorious* and *Courageous* and destined to become one of the Royal Navy's best-known fighting ships.

The new *Ark Royal* was completed in 1937 and was a major step forward, setting the pattern for all succeeding classes. Her aircraft capacity of up to 72 demanded fuller lines that required a 15 per cent increase in power to match the speed of her predecessors, with their lean battlecruiser hulls, but advances in machinery design enabled this to be effected with a triple-screw layout and without much space penalty. Two hangars were provided, giving a high silhouette, but their walls and flightdeck were built integrally with the lower hull to provide a stout protected box whose shell plating featured a pronounced flare to bow and stern and gave a maximum width along the full 800-foot sweep of flightdeck. Three elevators were included and 16 dual-purpose 4.5-inch guns were mounted in twinned gunhouses, two 'at each corner'. She followed a general practice in that, subsequent to the Lexingtons, carriers did not carry heavy surface armaments but relied on their aircraft for protection.

Exceptions to the practice would have been the pair of 23,000-ton Graf Zeppelin-class carriers planned by the rapidly expanding German Navy of 1936. Through centuries of war between England and France the latter had continually exploited the vulnerability of the island kingdom's mercantile trade in *guerres de course*, a type of war taken up with great success by Germany's U-boats during WW1. Great Britain had been close to suing for peace in 1917 because of the submarine war and the new German regime appreciated the fact fully. Its new warships were designed with an eye to commerce raiding and the new carriers were, in reality, large cruisers with flightdecks. Aircraft capacity was low for their size but an armament of 16 6-inch and 12 of the excellent 4.1-inch guns was mounted around a hull with vertical protection designed to withstand gunfire. They had a designed speed of 34 knots (very fast for a German warship) and, interestingly, two Voith-Schneider cycloidal propellers were installed forward for absolute control during flying operations. The forward end of the flightdeck was built out over the forecastle and terminated in two catapults.

Only 40 aircraft were planned to be carried on each, 28 Ju87C versions of the famous Stuka dive bombers for strike purposes and 12 Messerschmitt Bf109T fighters for defence. Had the ships ever been completed they would have provided a nightmare for any convoy escort commander but, fortunately for the Allies, they were doomed by the inter-service rivalries that bedevilled German war production. No priorities were accorded them so that the second hull was broken up in 1940 without even being launched. The construction of *Graf Zeppelin's* specially modified aircraft had to compete with the demands of Goering's Luftwaffe and the production of vital equipment such as arrester gear progressed at a snail's pace. Fitting-out was suspended in 1940.

At about the same time that the *Graf Zeppelin* was laid down, the US Navy was locked in battle with Congress over a requirement for another carrier. Only 15,000 tons were left out of the agreed Treaty ceiling of 135,000 and strenuous efforts were being made to downgrade the old *Langley* to a training role, thus releasing the necessary tonnage. This ploy was not sanctioned and the limit was rigidly enforced, resulting in the *Wasp* (CV7) of 1936 displacing only 14,700 tons. She could still stow 80 aircraft but, like the *Ranger*, suffered from her lack of size. An innovation on *Wasp* was a side elevator, running on its inboard edge up vertical tracks on the hull and transferring aircraft from hangar to flightdeck through an aperture in the shell plating. Its inboard edge was also hinged so that it could fold against the ship's side when not in use. It has proved very popular in subsequent American carrier designs, contributing to their large aircraft capacities by not impinging on hangar space like the more conventional elevator. The type has not been widely adopted elsewhere, largely because it weakens the hull.

War looms again

By the time the *Wasp* was laid down it was becoming increasingly obvious that another war was but a matter of time and the major naval powers began to construct beyond Treaty limitations; where the Allies were concerned it was none too soon as Japan's increasingly aggressive postures in the Western Pacific showed that her support for the Axis cause was not merely a paper exercise. With the completion of the *Soryu*

in December 1937 the first of a new pair was laid down. *Shokaku* (Flying Crane) and her later sister *Zuikaku* (Lucky Crane) were to belie their poetic names by proving themselves doughty opponents. They were of about 25,700 tons and their fine 846-foot hulls could be driven at 34 knots, although they had the endurance at lower speed to keep the sea for extended periods, vital in the vast Pacific theatre. In appearance, they were very similar to the smaller *Hiryu* but they could operate more than 70 aircraft; like their American contemporaries they bought these statistics at the expense of protection.

Japanese plans for a Southeast-Asian *lebensraum* called for an extremely rapid takeover of the salient island groups, after which, it was reasoned, the Western Powers, presented with a fait accompli, would accept the position as being preferable to war with a battle-ready power half a world away. These operations called for numerous carriers, as overwhelming air power was to be employed simultaneously at widely scattered points. There was no time to build from scratch and the Japanese reverted to conversion, rebuilding a pair of 28-knot depot ships as the little 11,200-ton *Zuiho* and *Shoho* in time for the outbreak of the Pacific War.

Great Britain fortunately recognized both the continuing great importance of the aircraft carrier and her own weakness in modern units. Materials were diverted from the planned battleship programme for the four-ship Illustrious class authorized in 1936. They were slightly shorter than the *Ark Royal* and had a lower silhouette by

As the 1930s moved towards their close, and war loomed again, the British still relied on dated biplanes on their carriers. Meanwhile the Japanese embarked the world's first monoplane carrier fighter, the A5M 'Claude', in 1937, to be shortly followed by the A6M 'Zeke' (the legendary Zero), and the Americans were well on the way with the production Wildcat, the Grumman F4F-3, which entered squadron service in 1940 — and with the RAF as the Martlet 1. This picture shows a developed F4F-4 Wildcat.

virtue of having only one hangar deck; their displacement was greater, however, a measure of the extra protection worked in. They were designed to take punishment, a feature that was to serve them well. Started in 1937, the group was augmented two years later by the pair of Implacables, which were a development reverting to a double hangar arrangement and absorbing up to 150,000shp on quadruple shafts in place of the earlier ships' triples.

Debilitated British force

Although the line-up of British carriers looked impressive, it was no better than the means available to man it — the men and their aircraft. There lay the great flaws, for the debilitating effects of the years of RAF control had created an almost unbridgeable gap between the relative efficiencies of seaborne aviation in Britain and abroad.

The RN knew what it wanted (although some of its requirements were overdemanding); it just could not get sufficient allocations in competition with an RAF that seemed sold completely on the hypothesis that a major war could be won by aircraft alone.

By the early 1930s the US strength in naval aircraft was six times that of the British and the Japanese nearly three times; even at the beginning of the fateful year of 1939 the Fleet Air Arm could dispose of barely 250 aircraft, increasing to about 340, of which two-thirds were carrier-borne, at the outbreak of war. More important, they were of greatly inferior quality to either their American or Japanese counterparts. US carriers had striking forces composed of excellent SB2U Vindicator reconnaissance/dive bombers and TBD Devastator torpedo bombers; the Japanese had the formidable D3A 'Val' and B5N 'Kate' equivalents. Compared with these fast purpose-built monoplanes the FAA could muster the first

few Blackburn Skuas (its first specialist dive bombers as well as its first monoplanes) and the ubiquitous Swordfish for torpedo and reconnaissance duties. The 'Stringbag', as the Swordfish was universally known, was an obsolescent biplane by 1939 but went to war for want of something better and lived to prove that, sometimes, performance is not everything. For fighter strength the Navy was to have received the Skua's first derivative, the Roc, but the design was a failure, leaving a serious gap until the arrival of the Fairey Fulmar in mid-1940. In contrast at this time, the Japanese were getting the Zero fighter and the Americans the F4F Wildcat.

In 1938 the Americans went beyond Treaty limits for the first time in starting the *Hornet* (CV8); to save design time she was essentially a repeat of the Yorktowns but still could not be expected before late 1941. The design effort was, in fact, being expended on a new-style carrier that could be produced in series; in making doubly certain of every requirement in her construction, her laying-down was delayed until April 1941, but in the *Essex* (CV9), the US Navy was to get the forerunner of a protracted series of excellent ships. Their

main parameters were fixed around the operation of the equivalent of one squadron each of bomber, fighter, torpedo and reconnaissance aircraft but aircraft strength was kept to 83 by amalgamating the bombing and scouting roles in one aircraft and carrying 25 per cent spares of all types. A full-sized deck-edge elevator was fitted and there were two catapults, one sited at hangar-deck level in the first 11 units, which were also credited with the ability to launch and recover aircraft from either end of the 872-foot (some had 888-foot) flightdecks. No fewer than 32 ships were funded, of which 24 were eventually completed; they gave excellent war service and went on to extensive postwar modifications. During the programme, the early planned displacements of about 27,000 tons went up gradually to around 34,000 tons.

With neither Russia nor Italy indulging in carrier construction, the only major power yet to build was France. The unsuccessful *Béarn* hardly fired the French with enthusiasm and they lacked the geographical stimuli of the other great fleets. Not until 1938, therefore, did they lay down their first purpose-built carrier. She was to have been named *Joffre* (to be followed by a second, the *Painleve*) but she was still on the ways when France was overrun in 1940 and was dismantled there.

HMS 'Ark Royal', pride of British carriers when WW2 broke out. She was laid down in 1935, launched in 1937 and completed in 1938, when this picture was taken as she exercised her Swordfish multi-role carrier aircraft. She was a well-armed 22,000-tonner with a normal complement of 60 aircraft and a maximum capacity of 72 and could steam at 31½ knots. Points of interest are her integral construction (compare with 'Ruyjo' p26 and 'Ranger' p33), seaboat swung out ready to recover ditched crews and neutrality markings (for the Spanish Civil War) on forward gun mounting.

MISTRESS OF THE OCEANS

The cutting edge bites

Previous page: USS 'John F Kennedy' (CVA67), the ultimate in conventionally powered carriers. Displacing around 61,000 tons and over 1000ft long, she can make 34 knots and operate 90 jet aircraft.

Below: An oil painting by Charles Cundall of a British escort carrier recovering Swordfish aircraft.

The conflict that broke out in September 1939 began as a European war with the combined Axis fleets of Germany and Italy no match on paper for those of Great Britain and France. That of Germany was not geared to defeating the Royal Navy in straight combat but, essentially, to tying it down by a 'fleet-in-being' policy (and, it was hoped, wearing it down by attrition) while Britain was destroyed economically by the elimination of her merchant fleet through every means possible. Until the enemy had made clear his strategy however, the Admiralty made its fleet dispositions for the prosecution of war in the time-honoured fashion of putting the opposition out of business by the slow strangulation of total blockade and the instant destruction of such elements of his fleet that dared to put to sea. That it did not work quite as simply as this was due largely to the arrival of the aeroplane in its first sea war.

With the old *Argus* by then relegated to training and ferrying duties, six front-line carriers were available. *Ark Royal* and *Furious* were based at Scapa with the main body of the Home Fleet to block any German movements through the Scotland-Norway gap. The Western Approaches, important because of their mercantile traffic, were the responsibility of the Channel fleet, to which were attached *Courageous* and *Hermes*. *Glorious* was with the Mediterranean Fleet and *Eagle* in the Far East.

Aircraft had shown themselves to be effective in A/S warfare and, when the enemy's U-boats swung immediately on to the offensive, it was decided to carry the war to them by means of carrier-borne aircraft operating beyond the range of available shore-based forces. The philosophy was later to be proved triumphantly correct, but the methods of 1939 were no more suitable than

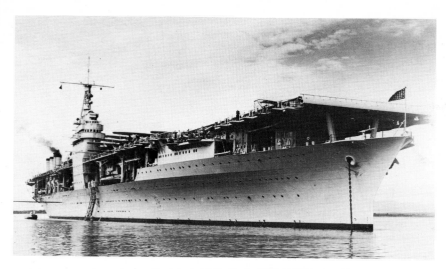

Top: With their fourth (and first purpose-built) aircraft carrier CV4 'Ranger', completed in 1934, the Americans adopted the relatively low displacement of 14,500 tons but still contrived to provide about 750ft of flightdeck and accommodation for up to 80 aircraft and a speed of 29.5 knots.

Above: Pictured through the struts and bracing wires of a Swordfish, the veteran HMS 'Eagle', 22,600 tons, escorting the August Convoy to Malta. 'Eagle' was torpedoed and sunk by a German submarine in the Mediterranean within a few days of this picture being taken.

from anti-submarine duties. For the next few months carrier operations were confined mainly to the interception of German merchantmen trying to reach home and searching for raiders and their supply ships which had been put on station before the war started. At the end of the year *Ark Royal* went south as part of Force K to watch over the armoured cruiser *Graf Spee* cornered in the River Plate; the raider declined further action and scuttled herself.

The period of the 'phoney war' was ended dramatically on the European mainland by a massive series of invasions by the Germans, commencing with Norway on 9 April 1940. While the war at sea had hardly been relaxing to those taking part, it now livened up considerably as the greater part of the enemy's forces necessarily had to be seaborne. While the conventionally gunned ships of the Royal Navy had a busy period with the heavily committed Kriegsmarine, naval aviation was absent when it mattered; *Furious* did not arrive on the scene until the 10th but she made an abortive Swordfish strike on enemy destroyers at Trondheim the following day. *Ark Royal* was exercising in the Mediterranean but, fortunately, her Skua dive bombers from 800 and 803 Squadrons had been flown to the UK. Using a staging airfield in the Orkneys they flew to Bergen where the damaged German light cruiser *Königsberg* was lying. This stationary thin-skinned target had the misfortune to become the first major warship sunk by air attack in war.

On the 24th the lone *Furious* was reinforced by the *Ark Royal* and *Glorious* and, while the older ships were used mainly to ferry short-range RAF fighters to Norway, the *Ark* endeavoured — unsuccessfully — to establish a measure of air superiority. But the locust years told and no amount of dedication on the part of their pilots compensated for the inherently poor qualities of the FAA fighters.

Glorious goes too

The carriers were forced farther offshore but remained active, watching over a forlornly hopeless campaign that could have but one conclusion. By early June the inevitable evacuation was started and *Glorious* skilfully recovered a force of RAF Hurricanes and Gladiators which were landed aboard in spite of their total lack of arrester gear. On 8 June, while on the short return passage to the UK she had the bad luck to run into the fast German battleships *Scharnhorst* and *Gneisenau*. Unable to operate her own Skuas or Swordfish because of her cluttered flightdeck, she was destroyed by long-range 11-inch gunfire. Her two escorting destroyers perished with her

the means. As early as 14 September *Ark Royal* was narrowly missed by torpedoes from U39 in the NW Approaches. Her assailant, one of the large Type IX boats, was summarily dispatched in a highly professional manner by the *Ark's* escort of five F-class destroyers but the warning was writ large, underlined later on the same day by a brush with a second submarine. In countering the latter, two of the carrier's eminently unsuitable Skua dive bombers were lost.

Early loss of Courageous

Three days later the lesson was brutally rammed home by the U29, which put two out of three torpedoes into the *Courageous* while she was engaged in recovering her aircraft west of Ireland. The encounter fortuitously coincided with a temporary reduction in her escort and she sank rapidly with a heavy loss of life. Her absence was to be keenly felt and carriers were withdrawn although *Acasta* succeeded in covering the shell-torn sea quickly enough to put a torpedo into *Scharnhorst* before succumbing.

These grievous losses were partially offset — at least materially — by the completion of *Illustrious*; in addition the American Wildcat fighter was being acquired (and renamed Martlet) and the new Fairey Fulmar began to replace the unsuccessful Rocs.

The evacuation of Norway coincided with that from Dunkirk, whereupon Italy, with an eye for easy spoils from an apparently stricken Great Britain, declared war. The hitherto quiet backwater of the Mediterranean became overnight an active theatre and as many Royal Navy units as could be spared were sent out including *Ark Royal*, whose Skuas, in a valedictory raid on Trondheim, succeeded in hitting the *Scharnhorst* with a 500-pound bomb — which failed to explode.

Britain's Mediterranean Fleet was outnumbered by the sizeable Italian Navy, but, fortunately, in its C-in-C, Cunningham, it had one of the navy's finest fighting admirals. He had trained it to a fine pitch of efficiency and it was rarin' to go! *Ark Royal* was soon to be reinforced by the *Eagle* from the Far East; *Argus* was also present but she was used to ferry fighter aircraft to Malta. A very busy phase ensued in which the British occupied themselves in establishing an ascendancy over the Italians, who, although without carrier support, enjoyed continuous air cover from plentiful airfields in Sardinia, Sicily and North Africa.

French fleet neutralized

Hoped-for support from the French fleet was not forthcoming owing to its country's collapse, a situation made doubly unpleasant by the Oran affair of 3 July 1940. A powerful force of the French navy was based on Mers el Kebir, its political affinities unknown; should it have sided with the Vichy regime it could have been taken over by the Germans. Britain, faced already by a situation bordering on the desperate, could not permit this and pre-empted the issue by sending a powerful naval contingent with an ultimatum which gave the stark choice 'be interned or be sunk'. French pride was not yet dead and their ships prepared to fight. They were hopelessly caught inside the harbour, however, and aircraft from the *Ark* had the sad task of directing 15-inch salvos into ships that were so recently close allies. Although the whole business was totally abhorrent, it demonstrated Britain's total resolve to continue the war at a very bad period. The new French battleship *Richelieu*

was shadowed by the aircraft of the little *Hermes* into Dakar, a place where she could do no harm for the moment.

Success for Force H at Taranto

This particularly bleak period was made brighter by the renewal of the ancient British art of applying seapower. *Ark Royal* operated with a powerful balanced squadron from Gibraltar; it was known universally as Force H and was the forerunner of the later fast carrier groups. *Eagle* acted more in the role of fleet carrier, rapidly acquiring expertise in the operation of continuous air patrols and anti-submarine strikes. A regular feature of the Mediterranean scene was Italian high-level bombing which, in spite of legend, was frequently unpleasantly accurate. A welcome newcomer in August was the freshly worked-up *Illustrious* with a Fulmar squadron and a score of Swordfish torpedo aircraft. Constant pressure was maintained on the Italians by the flexibility of the carriers. Thus the submarine *Iride* and her depot ship were sunk by *Eagle's* Swordfish while in the act of transferring 'human torpedoes' in an anchorage near Tobruk. *Illustrious* struck Benghazi in a night raid, sinking a destroyer and two freighters by torpedo and sowing mines which later claimed another destroyer.

On 28 October 1940 Italy invaded Greece; help was immediately offered by the Allies, resulting in a great increase in convoy activity in the eastern basin of the Mediterranean, from the main British bases of Malta and Alexandria to Greece and Crete. On 10 November two such convoys effected a junction of their separate heavy escorts and were joined by further fleet units including *Illustrious*. The latter's aircraft complement had been topped up with some transferred from *Eagle*, then undergoing repair of bomb damage. As soon as fighters had disposed of the inevitable enemy reconnaissance aircraft the force turned westward, towards Taranto, the main Italian fleet base in the south. Within that fine harbour, surrounded by defences powerful enough to engender a level of complacency, lay the main enemy force, confirmed only that morning by aircraft out of Malta as including no fewer than six battleships and six heavy cruisers. In the event that the British force be reported and the Italians put to sea to seek battle, *Illustrious* had four battleships and four cruisers in company (with a further cruiser force that was to conduct a simultaneous sweep of the Strait of Otranto).

Just after dusk, about 170 miles short of the target, 21 Swordfish were flown off, 11 with torpedoes, six with bombs and four with flares for illumination. An interesting comment on the FAA aircraft of the time

HMS 'Victorious', one of six Illustrious-class carriers that introduced radar and improved AA guns and armour to flightdeck and sides. 'Victorious' joined the Home Fleet in 1941 and in May that year, with a scratch complement of nine Swordfish and six Fulmars, joined in the attack on the 'Bismarck', registering one not-serious torpedo hit. In June she accompanied 'Ark Royal' in ferrying 48 badly needed Hurricane fighters to Malta before returning to the Home Fleet duties in the North Atlantic and Arctic of bottling up potential German shipping raiders and Russian convoy protection. Of interest is the raised deck barrier.

In the still peaceful Mediterranean in 1937 HMS 'Glorious' stems a rough sea for the celebrated photographer Charles E. Brown. About three years later 'Glorious's' crew demonstrated their skill by landing-on RAF Hurricane and Gladiator fighters entirely without arrester gear during the Norway evacuation. With a cluttered flightdeck and unable to operate her own aircraft, she was destroyed by long-range German gunfire while returning from that operation.

was that even a flight of such modest distance required an auxiliary fuel tank; it was a 60-gallon drum placed in the rear cockpit in place of the third crew member! The Italians had no radar to observe the Swordfish as they lumbered in at less than 100 miles per hour in two waves. Flares were dropped to perfection, enabling the slow-flying aircraft to manoeuvre around the numerous barrage balloon cables and pick their silhouetted targets. The first wave torpedoed the new battleship *Littorio* twice and the modernized *Conte di Cavour* once. As the Italians recovered from their shock, they were hit by the second wave, *Littorio* being hit again, as was the *Caio Duilio*. For sheer economy the raid would be hard to beat; for the loss of two aircraft, *Cavour* would never sail again and the other two would be immobile for half a year. The remainder of the heavy units were immediately transferred north where they could neither harm nor be harmed.

Thus the sea lanes were secured and the fragile flower of Italian morale dealt a severe blow. It was an object lesson in both planning and surprise and one whose potential was well observed by other eyes in a still-peaceful Pacific.

Enter the Luftwaffe

The total domination being established by the British in the Mediterranean had an unfortunate repercussion in that the

Germans, previously uninvolved in the theatre, had to step in to stiffen their ally against total collapse. Rommel's Afrika Korps was formed to buttress the reeling Italian armies in North Africa, but they still had to be transported there with their transport, armour and supplies across a Mediterranean very much under British control. The Luftwaffe had proved already during the Norwegian campaign that even a powerful fleet could not operate without air supremacy and this they resolved to establish with the transfer to Sicily of the anti-shipping Fliegerkorps X. Its striking force of Ju87B (Stuka) dive bombers and Ju88 multi-purpose medium bombers was covered by Me110 long-range fighters, about 150 aircraft in all. Its weakness in high-performance fighters was soon countered by the addition of a wing of Me109Fs.

On 6 January 1941 the Royal Navy began a complex operation to pass a convoy from Gibraltar to Malta while simultaneously reinforcing the island with troops carried by cruisers from the Aegean. The convoy, covered by Force H, had repulsed Italian air attacks successfully with the *Ark Royal's* fighters but, as was customary, the heavy warships turned back again before the narrows between Cape Bon and Sicily due to the high risk of that area. With only its close escort for protection the convoy was attacked by Italian torpedo-boats which were repulsed, with the loss of one of their number. For their final approach to Malta, the still-intact merchantmen were met by the main body from Alexandria, with *Illustrious* providing the continuity of air cover.

Stukas hit Illustrious

All seemed well, but the enemy had been keeping close watch. On the afternoon of the 10th a carefully co-ordinated series of attacks was mounted. While Italian torpedo aircraft and high-level bombers occupied the attention of the carrier fighters and ship's gunners, two groups of German Stukas arrowed down from 12,000 feet, singling out *Illustrious*. Holding their dives to below 2000 feet they succeeded in putting six 500kg bombs into the carrier. She had been built to withstand punishment, with several inches of armour at flightdeck and sides protecting her vitals; even so, she was put totally out of action but, saved only by her tough hide, she staggered into Malta, preceded by such of her aircraft as had been in the air at the time.

Under constant attack as the enemy tried to finish her off, Malta dockyard patched her sufficiently to make Alexandria, and, then the US for permanent repair. Even the Americans marvelled at the injuries that she had survived, and, if the argument for protection 'up-top' was ever in doubt, it was at last settled. The new generation of American carriers (later termed the Midways) were still in the planning stage and they were extensively re-worked to include protection on a vastly greater scale.

As if to demonstrate that the *Illustrious* episode was no isolated incident, one of the Stuka groups, II/St G2, had been homed-in the following day by a reconnaissance He111 on to the British eastbound force. Again, the

Anatomy of the Fairey Swordfish, mainstay of Britain's early carrier offensive operations. Key: 1 top ailerons, 2 leading-edge slots, 3 pilot's seat, 4 .303 machine-gun, 5 top centre plane, 6, 7 & 9 fuel tanks, 8 oil tank, 10 fireproof bulkhead, 11 engine control shaft, 12 Bristol Pegasus radial engine, 13 oil cooler, 14 wing locking catch, 15 bottom stub plane, 16 bottom wing hinge, 17 18in torpedo, 18 rear catapult spool, 19 arrester hook, 20 bottom aileron, 21 folding wing restraining strut, 22 .303 machine-gun.

technique of swamping the defences was successful and the cruiser *Southampton* had to be sunk by her escort after being immobilized by a 500kg bomb in the machinery space. The arrival of the Luftwaffe had shifted the balance of power overnight. If they could maintain air superiority it would be Malta that would be isolated and the Axis armies in North Africa could be freely supplied and reinforced by sea.

Formidable's arrival checked

This bleak situation was recognized and *Illustrious's* sister-ship *Formidable*, completed only the previous November, was sent around the Cape to restore the balance at the eastern end of the Mediterranean. Ironically, having arrived at Suez, she was unable to transit the canal after German aircraft had blocked it with magnetic mines. She was therefore used to good effect in concert with the veteran *Hermes* in strikes against the Italians in Eritrea and Italian Somaliland. This sudden influx of airpower was largely responsible for the reduction of Italian surface forces in the Red Sea and the collapse of their forces ashore.

The eventual arrival of *Formidable* in the Mediterranean was timely as the situation there was changing fast. Italy's adventure in Greece had all the makings of a first-class disaster and had prompted German forces to move into neighbouring Bulgaria during early March 1941. British reaction was swift; powerful Army forces were moved into Greece in a rapid succession of convoys from Alexandria, and were challenged only half-heartedly by the Italian submarines and aircraft from bases in the Dodecanese. Strong German pressure on the Italian High Command persuaded it to commit major fleet units to intercept one of the British convoys and preliminary movements to this end were noticed by British Intelligence on 25 March. Cunningham had anticipated this type of operation and immediately cleared the whole eastern basin of mercantile traffic simultaneously with stepping up reconnaissance effort by both submarines and aircraft.

An RAF Sunderland out of Kalafrana sighted an enemy cruiser about midday on the 27th, steering towards Crete and still about 300 miles distant. A British light cruiser force left Greece immediately with instructions to be off the south coast of Crete by .the following morning and the main force, including *Formidable* and three battleships, left Alexandria at dusk on the 27th.

The Italians had planned to sweep round both sides of Crete with heavy cruiser fleets backed up by the new 15-inch-gunned battleship *Vittorio Veneto*. They had been promised air cover by the German X Fl K but when it failed to materialize they

abandoned the Aegean leg of the operation and concentrated on the south side of the island.

By dawn on the 28th the British main force was close enough for *Formidable* to fly off search aircraft, which rapidly reported an unidentified force not far from the last known position of the British light cruisers. A sighting report from the latter confirmed the presence of the Italians and the main force worked up speed against a conflicting series of reports from the aircraft and the watching cruisers that confirmed only that the enemy was present in force, was not concentrated and included at least one battleship.

Italians surprised

Cunningham, only about 50 miles from the reported position of the battleship, immediately ordered off a torpedo strike of Swordfish and Albacores (the latter on their first major operation). The arrival of this force was a rude shock to the Italian admiral, Iachino, who had no inkling of the presence of the British main force and was assuming that he was in contact with a cruiser force covering another troop convoy. A heavy curtain of AA fire, including a 15-inch splash barrage from the battleship, met the attack and saved the Italians from damage by the still inexperienced *Formidable* flyers. Nevertheless, the Italians turned for home in their separate groups, their uniformly high speed leaving the hopefully pursuing British far astern. Unless the Italians could be slowed, action could not be joined and aircraft were the only hope. *Formidable* flew off four consecutive strikes and shore-based aircraft mounted

An alternative means of providing warships with the advantages of aerial reconnaissance and spotting the fall of shot was the use of seaplanes or amphibians, as illustrated by this Supermarine Walrus being hoisted on to its catapult aboard a Nelson-class battleship. They were also used offensively on occasions and in fact one such aircraft from HMS 'Warspite' bombed and sank U64 in April 1940 off Narvik.

separate attacks from Crete to Greece, but not until after 15.00 did a torpedo find the *Veneto*. The Italians slowed their pace but were back to 19 knots again by 19.00, concentrated into a powerful group with heavy cruisers in a separate force to the north.

Night action at Matapan

With the day wearing on, all hope of bringing the Italians to action seemed to be slipping away when a final strike flew out of the sunset through a desperate wall of flak. *Vittorio Veneto*, the prime target, escaped unscathed but one of the torpedoes meant for her struck the heavy cruiser *Pola* which slowed, stopped and dropped astern as Iachino bore on for home. With the cover of night approaching and believing his pursuers to be safely distant he directed two of *Pola*'s sisters, *Zara* and *Fiume*, to drop out of the northern force to escort her home. Cunningham, however, was a great exponent of night fighting and had long practised the Mediterranean Fleet in its ways; at the same time his enthusiasm was tempered by the knowledge that to be found in the area at daybreak was to invite full retribution from X/Fl K. He placed his light cruisers in a line of search ahead of the heavy units whose course he had resolved to maintain as long as possible. At about 21.00 a stopped ship was reported, her identification impossible to establish in the darkness.

The battleship *Valiant* made radar contact and reported her as being large and with hopes of it being the *Veneto*: imminent action was anticipated. Visual sighting of the mysterious stranger finally revealed that she was not alone; searchlights flicked on and 15-inch salvos crashed out simultaneously from all three battleships at under 4000 yards range. Illumination revealed not the hoped-for battleship but the unfortunate *Pola* and her escorts. Within minutes they were not so much destroyed as dismembered and the British turned to the northeast, leaving the final clearing up to the destroyers. Although the night's bag had been a good one it was a distraction which allowed the final escape of the damaged *Veneto*. Dawn found the British only about 40 miles from the Greek capes and, with increasing daylight and search aircraft reporting an empty sea, it was no place to linger. Cunningham turned for home and the action, to become known as the Battle of Matapan, was over.

Yet even all the gunpower that the British had would have been of little use had they not had a carrier present. Even with the weak striking forces that could be flown off at that time it was still possible to damage an enemy sufficiently to delay him until the

affair could be settled by the gun in the time-honoured fashion. The Italians, having virtually discounted any possible requirements for carriers, hastily reappraised the situation. They had, in fact, already put in hand the conversion of the liner *Roma* but the reconstruction had been proceeding in a desultory manner, aided by German spare parts from their abandoned *Graf Zeppelin*. She was renamed *Aquila* and re-engined with cruiser turbines for a planned speed of 30 knots and joined by the *Sparviero* (ex-*Augustus*). Neither was destined ever to be completed.

Crete abandoned

Repeating the theme of 'too little, too late', the British military expedition to Greece collapsed after the German invasion of 6 April 1941, as it had in Norway exactly one year earlier. For the Navy the result was similar, evacuation under a pitilessly hostile sky. Part of the force was used to garrison Crete in an effort to maintain a forward base but the island fell after an enemy invasion spearheaded by the largest airborne assault yet seen.

The Mediterranean Fleet worked around the clock until the crews dropped in their melancholy task of the final withdrawal to Alexandria. Losses were heavy as the available air cover diminished to a few shore-based aircraft (augmented by *Illustrious*'s Swordfish, left behind as 815 Squadron) and what could be provided by the lone *Formidable*. She was down to about a dozen patched Fulmar fighters, together with a handful of Albacores and Swordfish, when, in an effort to cure a problem at source, she struck on 26 May at the airfield at Scarpanto (Karpathos), base of the local 'Stuka club'. Unfortunately, the stick that had so enraged this particular hornet's nest was no weapon with which to dispose of its inmates once they took wing. In a series of attacks unpleasantly reminiscent of those which had hit her predecessor, *Formidable* was hit fore and aft with 500kg bombs by II/St G2 and near-missed by others that caused more damage. But again an armoured flightdeck saved the day, although she had to take the road to the US for full repair. Crete fell, as was inevitable, and the eastern Mediterranean fleet entered a long phase bereft of carrier support.

At the western end after the disabling of *Illustrious* only *Ark Royal* was left. She had a lesser ability to absorb punishment but this in no way inhibited her use, as in February 1941 when Force H bombarded Genoa. During the proceedings her Swordfish acted as spotters, minelayers and bombers on a variety of targets. Operating from Gibraltar, Force H was also well placed

In May 1941 the new carrier
'Victorious' faced her first
action with only one squadron
of Swordfish and six Fulmars
embarked, having been
hastily withdrawn from a
fighter delivery trip to
Gibraltar to take part in the
attack on the 'Bismarck'.
Here the nine Swordfish and
two Fulmars are being readied
for the attack, from which all
the Swordfish returned safely
after scoring one torpedo hit
on the German battleship.
The escorting Fulmars were
lost.

for Atlantic operations and participated in May 1941 in the long pursuit of the German battleship *Bismarck* which, with the heavy cruiser *Prinz Eugen*, had broken out on a planned commerce raid early in the month. Intercepted by the Royal Navy in the Denmark Strait, they sank the veteran battlecruiser *Hood* and forced the brand-new battleship *Prince of Wales* to break off the action. Determined to bring them to book, Admiral Tovey's Home Fleet placed itself over their lines of withdrawal. Present was the *Victorious*, the newly commissioned third unit of the Illustrious Class. She had been loaded with RAF Hurricanes for a maiden delivery trip to Gibraltar but they were hastily put ashore and she sailed with only the six Fulmars and nine Swordfish that she had on board for self-defence.

Swordfish versus the Bismarck

Yet, so great was the urgency and so slender the means available, this tiny force found itself the sole means by which

Bismarck could be prevented from reaching the umbrella protection of the French-based Luftwaffe before the Home Fleet could deal with her. *Victorious* was detached with an escort to use her high speed to mount a strike at the earliest possible opportunity. On the evening of the 24th, in conditions of low cloud, rain and heavy sea, all the Swordfish and a pair of Fulmars were flown off. In the gathering gloom they would probably have missed their quarry but for an early radar set in the leader and directions from two shadowing cruisers. The 825 Squadron Swordfish attacked from all quarters but the German ship was magnificently handled, evading all torpedoes except one which, while causing no great damage, started a leak from a ruptured fuel tank. Although the Swordfish returned unscathed, the Fulmars were never seen again, and shortly afterwards *Bismarck* eluded the shadowing cruisers and likewise disappeared.

While Force H pounded up from

After playing an absolutely vital part in the battle for control of the Mediterranean over a period of two years, facing constant attack as in the upper picture and being 'sunk' several times by German propoganda, the 'Ark Royal' was hit by a U-boat's torpedo in November 1941 and sank 15 hours later when the safety of Gibraltar was in sight. The lower picture shows her listing badly shortly after the torpedo struck.

Gibraltar, its target remained lost for 31 hours until contact was regained by a Catalina flying-boat of the RAF's 209 Squadron. *Ark Royal*, by then well placed, had a Swordfish overhead within the hour. Tovey's battleships, the designated means of execution, were still 130 miles distant and were unlikely to achieve a junction unless *Bismarck* could be slowed further. It was up to the *Ark*.

In appalling conditions and at extreme range a 15-strong Swordfish strike was flown off on the afternoon of the 26th. Unfortunately, the German was being close marked by the cruiser *Sheffield*, of whose presence the aircraft were unaware. Sighting her in conditions of low visibility, the majority attacked her in error; some of the sensitive magnetic firing pistols on the torpedoes detonated prematurely and the cruiser, patiently holding her fire, evaded the remainder. But more valuable time was lost as the chastened aircraft flew back to rearm and it was dark before they again took off. *Sheffield*, still in contact, vectored them in but, with the prevailing weather conditions, a co-ordinated attack was out of the question. In spite of this, *Bismarck* was again struck by a torpedo; again it was on her armour belt and caused little damage. Then another, almost missing, hit her right aft. It damaged both steering gear and shafts, and significantly, jammed the twin rudders. The ship was doomed from that moment.

All night *Bismarck* was worried by

destroyers which she kept at bay by accurate radar-laid gunnery. When 27 May dawned wild, faint hopes were roused in the Germans as her tormenters were totally unable to leave the *Ark Royal's* violently pitching deck. *Bismarck* ploughed doggedly on, making as good a course as possible, her weary gunners glimpsing from time to time through the murk the destroyers that marked her. *Rodney* and *King George V* awaited full daylight before closing in for the final act; there was now no hurry and within two hours it was done. The end was fittingly observed by the *Ark's* Swordfish which had at last been able to get airborne.

As at Matapan, air strikes had been on too weak a scale to decide the day but had injured the enemy sufficiently to force decisive action. But it had been a close-run thing as the first Luftwaffe units were already within extreme range; 216 sorties were flown by HeIIIs and Ju88s but in spite of some accurate bombing the *Ark Royal* emerged unscathed, although a destroyer was sunk. The lesson was clear. The British, with air power on the spot, achieved their aim; the Germans, operating from fixed sites ashore, did not.

The flexibility of the carrier was demonstrated in the following weeks by operations stretching from the Davis Strait to West Africa. Aircraft from the *Eagle*, *Ark Royal* and *Victorious* searched thousands of square miles of ocean for enemy shipping which was still at sea both to replenish the voracious U-boats and to run in vital cargoes such as rubber and industrially precious metals. It was imperative that both be discouraged and the unglamorous work disposed of about a dozen of the enemy's ships.

The Ark gives up

The year 1941 continued to be busy for *Ark Royal,* particularly as Force H covered several east-bound Malta convoys, often accompanied by *Argus* or *Furious* ferrying fighter aircraft to the beleaguered island. It was after one such sortie on 13 November, that *Ark Royal* was struck by one torpedo of a salvo of four fired by the U81. As she was not hit again and the weather was absolutely calm there seemed little reason to doubt her ability to reach Gibraltar, only 50 miles distant.

She had been hit on the starboard side in the machinery spaces, however, and rapidly lost all power. No efforts were made to take her in tow as her two escorting destroyers busied themselves on A/S duties and her list gradually increased. Damage control does not appear to have been well organized and the decision to wait for dockyard tugs was to prove fatal. They arrived after five hours, with salvage officers who corrected the ship's list by counterflooding. Lines were connected and, when steam was again raised in one boiler, things did not look too bad. Then, disastrously, a fire broke out in the boiler room and a race developed as the tugs strove to haul their charge to safety. But all to no avail; as though the great ship had lost her will to live she rolled over and sank in the early hours of the following morning, about 15 hours after being hit. She was within sight of the Rock, only one man had been killed and the majority of her aircraft had long since left. It was a strange affair, a short and violent career that ended on a note so muted as to be scarcely audible.

Materially, her loss should have been made good by the new *Indomitable*, but after her handing-over in October 1941, she was sent to 'safe' West Indies waters to work up and succeeded in stranding off Jamaica, suffering heavy damage.

The disasters did not stop here. In the Mediterranean the battleship *Barham* was torpedoed and sunk. Her running mates *Queen Elizabeth* and *Valiant* were mined by Italian frogmen and put on the bottom of Alexandria Harbour. *Neptune* and *Kandahar* succumbed to mines, *Galatea* and the famed *Cossack* to torpedoes. But even when it seemed that the news could not be worse it suddenly all paled into insignificance as a new name hit the headlines; it was that of a place totally unfamiliar to the average European. It was Pearl Harbor.

Pearl Harbor to Ceylon

The most famous and successful of Japanese WW2 aircraft, the Mitsubishi A6M Zero-sen, or 'Zeke', had the best performance of any carrier fighter of its day, though it lacked the protection provided by some of its contemporaries. The production A6M2 (Model 21) had a top speed of over 330mph, a ceiling of nearly 33,000ft, could reach 20,000ft in about eight minutes, was armed with two 7.7mm machine-guns and two 20mm cannon, and could carry two 130lb bombs or a drop tank for increased range. The Zero was not outmatched in the Pacific until 1943, by the Grumman F6F Hellcat.

Japan, like Great Britain, was an island kingdom supporting a large population. With few natural resources, she relied on international trade, employing a large merchant marine. But, where Britain had long since established her *lebensraum* through vigorous colonial expansion, Japan had retained her total insularity until the outside world thrust itself upon her in the shape of Commodore Perry's expedition of 1853. Once the Shogunate realized the advantages of Western ways, it adopted them with enthusiasm and the Western powers took full advantage of the trade thus generated. With their individual industry and zeal to learn, the Japanese caught up rapidly.

By the end of the 19th century, in a world already neatly parcelled up by the great colonial powers, Japan (like another emergent nation, Germany) observed that he who controlled the sea controlled the trade, and resolved to acquire a fleet to extend her influence. The example of Britain, apparently all-powerful, creating wealth from a worldwide empire while confidently resting on the shoulders of her fleet, could not fail to be understood. With an arrogant self-assurance, the Royal Navy was always on the spot to put down local troubles and provided much to be admired by an up-and-coming power; it was therefore to Britain, rather than the anti-colonial USA, that the Japanese turned for assistance in the founding of a fleet. Britain built her ships, trained her men and established the complex infrastructure inseparable from the efficient maintenance of a major fleet.

It was with a certain measure of pride that British observers with Togo saw their protégé break the heart of the Tsarist fleet at Tsushima in 1905, establishing Japan as mistress of the Western Pacific. With the build-up to WW1, the British became preoccupied with another major fleet on their very doorstep. Japan could by then cater for herself quite adequately and fought alongside the Allies during the war.

By 1918 Britain had suffered reverses and was weakened; to the East she no longer appeared unbeatable and had, to a certain extent, 'lost face'. It was not long before the first rumblings for self-determination were to be heard within the Empire and it seemed to a thrusting young power that the time for adventure was nigh.

New European dictators emerged and soon demonstrated that, faced with faits accompli, the great powers growled diplomatically and then accepted the situation rather than risk another war.

Japan takes to the carrier

Japan continued carrier development with expeditions in 1937 to Manchukuo and Korea.

To maintain the pretence that these actions were other than wars, efforts were limited in scale and hence were less than successful. A useful spin-off, however, was the need to use carrier-based aircraft as ground support due to the regular air forces' lack of experience in flying over the sea. Eventually, Japanese heavy bombers acquired the ability to range over China from their own islands and Formosa but carriers were still needed to provide fighter escorts as the latter were of limited range. The value of carriers was thus learned by hard-won experience and the Japanese gained confidence. Design effort was assigned to the production of a longer-range high-performance fighter aircraft; the first carrier-borne monoplane fighter, the A5M 'Claude', marked a big step forward in 1937 and led in 1940 to the Zero, or 'Zeke', which was superior to anything in the West at that time.

Requiring both space and raw materials, Japan cast envious eyes at the East Indies. To annex Indonesia, Malaysia and the Philippines would invoke the wrath of the great powers but, as they appeared to be avoiding war at all costs, it was reasoned that, if the takeover was accomplished with sufficient speed, the West would be forced to accept it from a weak bargaining position. Consolidation of this new empire would require also a vast ring of fortified Pacific islands and sufficient of the Asiatic mainland to protect the rear.

The essence of the plan was speed and the means of its execution was the fleet. Significant hindrance to seaborne operations could be immediately mounted only by the powerful US Pacific Fleet, based partly on the American West Coast and partly at the mid-ocean forward base at

Pearl Harbor in Hawaii. From Pearl Harbor it could intervene quickly and, possibly, decisively. It had to be neutralized but the audacity of such an idea created great divisions in the Japanese halls of power; once the decision had been taken, however, the plan was prepared in meticulous detail against 'the day'.

Oil the goal

Events leading up to the attack were closely geared to oil supplies. Japan had none of her own and had to import from the USA even for the limited Chinese war. The Americans fully appreciated its use as an economic weapon and, in turn, the Japanese realized that they would need guaranteed supplies for their ambitious plans of the future. Oil to spare was available in the Dutch East Indies and Holland was an occupied country in 1941. A logical first step in the move to the south was to annex French Indo-China in July of that year, relying on France also being in no position to act. America and nations still free to act did so, and rapidly, freezing Japanese assets abroad to prevent their acquiring oil on any market. It was a gamble; either the Japanese would climb down in the face of this united front or they would be forced to act. Not for the first time did the West misjudge the workings of the oriental mind.

Only in November 1941 was final permission given for a pre-emptive strike against Pearl Harbor, to be conducted simultaneously with the thrusts to the south. Concentrated on their Hawaiian base the Americans had nine battleships and two carriers (*Enterprise* and *Lexington*) with a third carrier (*Saratoga*) available at San Diego. Supported by 21 cruisers and 67

America's sixth carrier was the 'Enterprise', second of the three-ship Yorktown Class, which was completed in 1938. Third of the class was the 'Wasp' (CV7). With a displacement of 19,900 tons and length of over 740ft, the class could make 29½ knots and field up to 80 aircraft. 'Enterprise', and the other two Pacific Fleet carriers 'Lexington' and 'Saratoga', were fortunately away from Pearl Harbor when the Japanese attack came. The 'Enterprise' and 'Saratoga' went on to survive the Pacific war but 'Lexington' was lost to enemy action during 1942.

destroyers, this force was a very real threat to the Japanese, whose fleet would be fragmented on its various allotted missions. Indeed in major units they were hardly overwhelmingly superior, having 10 battleships, six large carriers and four small carriers. To turn the American concentration to their disadvantage by sudden heavy assault was an obvious move; history had shown in 1904 at Port Arthur that the Japanese could attack without formalities, and in 1940 Taranto had proved what prizes could be gained for small outlay, given sufficient resolution.

Carrier becomes capital ship

All six of Japan's large carriers were to be committed and in late November 1941 they moved to an advanced base in the Kuriles after months of exercise. By standards of the time their support was light; two battleships, two seaplane-carriers and a flotilla of destroyers led by a light cruiser. But existing standards were about to be upended; where previously the British had used carrier strikes to slow an enemy for other ships' guns to dispatch, the Japanese carriers were made the capital ships and accompanying forces were relegated to providing them with the freedom to operate. The 450 aircraft embarked on them made earlier British efforts look decidedly puny in comparison. There remained 3000 miles of Pacific to cross without detection.

The flagship *Akagi* led the way to sea on 26 November, followed by her half-sister *Kaga, Shokaku, Zuikaku, Soryu* and *Hiryu*. In addition to the escort there were eight tankers, essential for a long voyage, looping far to the north through mist-shrouded seas devoid of trade routes and their shipping. On 1 December, steaming at a leisurely pace, the force was halfway to its objective still unobserved. Back in Tokyo a final meeting of the cabinet committed the country to war and transmitted the now-famous code-signal 'Climb Mount Niitaka' to Nagumo, the Japanese commander. The raid had already been fixed for Sunday, 7 December, when the US fleet would be in harbour, so there was adequate time to top-up with fuel from the tankers.

Right: Massed 'Val' dive bombers and 'Kate' torpedo bombers warming up on a carrier deck preparing to take off for Pearl Harbor.

Below: The Aichi D3A 'Val' dive bomber was based extensively on German Heinkel designs. It had a top speed of about 240mph, could carry over 880lb of bombs and was armed with three 7.7mm machine-guns.

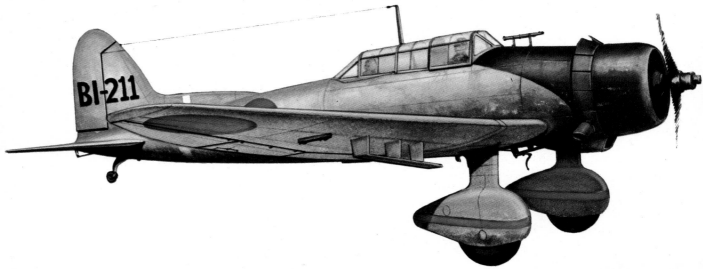

BI-211

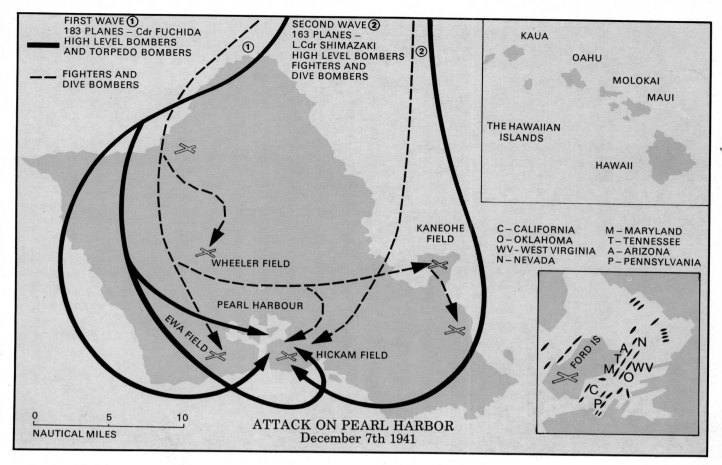

FIRST WAVE ①
183 PLANES – Cdr FUCHIDA
HIGH LEVEL BOMBERS
AND TORPEDO BOMBERS

FIGHTERS AND
DIVE BOMBERS

SECOND WAVE ②
163 PLANES –
L.Cdr SHIMAZAKI
HIGH LEVEL BOMBERS
FIGHTERS AND
DIVE BOMBERS

KAUA

OAHU

MOLOKAI

MAUI

THE HAWAIIAN
ISLANDS

HAWAII

WHEELER FIELD

KANEOHE
FIELD

PEARL HARBOUR

EWA FIELD

HICKAM FIELD

C – CALIFORNIA
O – OKLAHOMA
WV – WEST VIRGINIA
N – NEVADA

M – MARYLAND
T – TENNESSEE
A – ARIZONA
P – PENNSYLVANIA

FORD IS

0   5   10

NAUTICAL MILES

ATTACK ON PEARL HARBOR
December 7th 1941

On the 6th Nagumo learned of the latest American dispositions. Eight of the nine battleships were at their berths but the carriers were not present. In fact, both were away ferrying aircraft to other American bases; *Lexington* was off Midway Island having flown off a force of Marine SB2Us and *Enterprise* was about 200 miles to the west after delivering F4Fs to Wake.

As the Hawaiian naval city disported its way through a normal Saturday evening the Japanese force, blacked-out, parted company with its tankers and worked up to high speed for its launch point, about 275 miles to the north of the island. Before daybreak on Sunday a pair of 'Jake' floatplanes from the escort reported the area free of American ships and the first strike was sent off at a signal from *Akagi*, using the actual flag flown by Togo at Tsushima. There were 89 'Kate' torpedo bombers, half armed with shallow-running torpedoes and the remainder with 800kg armour-piercing bombs improvized from 14-inch naval shells. These aircraft were to attack the American ships; to neutralize reaction from the estimated 600 aircraft that were based on the island a force was detailed to make simultaneous strikes at all the airfields. Over 50 'Val' dive bombers were to pulverize the facilities with 250kg bombs, escorted by 43 Zeros to shoot out of the sky anything able to get airborne. Although

American radar detected these large formations, the echos were ascribed to the expected *Enterprise* squadrons and some Army B17s. The error was all too apparent at 07.55 on that clear Sunday morning when the perfectly co-ordinated attack knifed in, scything through the numbed and uncomprehending defences.

Battleships annihilated

It took around five minutes to reduce 'Battleship Row' to a shambles; after the time taken to fry a breakfast egg, *West Virginia* was blazing from at least six torpedo hits. Ahead of her wallowed the *Arizona*, whose forward magazine had been detonated, and astern the *Oklahoma* was slowly capsizing after taking at least five torpedoes. About a ship's length distant, the *California* had been put on the bottom in shallow water. *Nevada*, *Maryland*, *Pennsylvania* and *Tennessee*, shielded by their less fortunate compatriots, were damaged to a lesser degree. Above all rolled a pall of black oily smoke lit from within by a succession of explosions.

The airbases were also hit. Their aircraft, parked wingtip to wingtip, were raked to the extent that destruction was virtually total. Then, while the last aircraft exhausted their venom, the Japanese carriers launched a second strike — 54 'Kates', 78 'Vals' and 35 Zeros. They arrived an hour after the first strike as the bloodied Americans began to rally; a few fighters were getting aloft and AA fire was growing in intensity. Within two hours it was all over and the aircraft bearing the now all-too-familiar 'meatball' insignia were gone as suddenly as they had come, leaving the dazed island to take stock.

The Japanese could congratulate themselves on a most cost-effective raid. Of the 40 torpedoes dropped 18 had hit and the improvized AP bombs had been most effective. Most of the damage suffered by the battleships, however, although spectacular, was repairable and only two were total losses. For the loss of 29 aircraft the Japanese had destroyed 188 American machines, mostly on the ground. Damage to shore installations was extensive but not fatal. The main fuel store was not hit and the American carriers were still intact and this was to prove crucial.

Thrust to the south

Simultaneously the Japanese thrust southwards; to Siam (Thailand), Malaya, the Philippines and the East Indies. Automatically they were at war also with Great Britain and her allies. Surely never in history had a nation gambled against such odds; Japan, a modern Prometheus, had stolen the fire that was eventually to consume her.

As the two great fleets squared up for the combat ahead it was evident to both how vital a part the carrier would have to play, and here it is appropriate to pause to consider their relative positions. Although the CV9 (*Essex*) had been designed for series production, ships of this size could not be rolled off like Model T Fords. By December 1941 only five were in the early stages of construction with the prospect of just another four being laid down in 1942. A quicker method of producing flightdecks had to be instituted and the hulls of nine Cleveland-class cruisers were topped-off with open hangars and a flightdeck, a miniscule island and two elevators. They were known as the Independence Class (CVL22-30) and retained their original 100,000shp steam turbine machinery for 33 knots, exhausting through a characteristic row of four stumpy funnels cranked out to starboard. Although of only 13,000 tons full load, they had useful 550-foot flightdecks and each could accommodate 35 aircraft. In spite of the vigorous American programme, however, little could be expected before 1943 and the seven existing carriers (CV2 to 8) had to hold the ring for a year. The little *Langley* (CV1) had been converted in 1937 to operate seaplanes and was sunk early in 1942 off Bali while transporting aircraft.

The Japanese Navy had but little margin on the American in carrier strength and had laid down a large fleet carrier, *Taiho*, in July 1941. After the graphic lesson of the *Illustrious* bombing, *Taiho*'s 855-foot flightdeck was protected with up to four inches of armour, accounting for much of her 30,000 ton displacement. She incorporated also a British-style bow and rectangular stack. As she was to be three years abuilding, the Japanese, too, embarked on a crash conversion programme. Three submarine tenders of 1934 vintage became the 13,400-ton *Ryuho*, *Zuiho* and *Shoho*, rather slow and structurally weak but stowing about 30 aircraft. Interestingly, they reverted to the island-less profile but were not intended to be used for fleet operations.

Two slightly larger carriers, *Hiyo* and *Junyo*, were built from the hulls of a pair of NYK liners, under construction for the trans-Pacific service. They had been designed from the outset for such a conversion, incorporating deep double bottoms, extra bunker space and heavy stiffening in way of elevator trunks. Rebuilding was rapid and they were ready for service by mid-1942 but, although they could stow more than 50 aircraft apiece, their speed was not really sufficient for fleet use and, like other Japanese carriers, they did not have catapults.

Wake Island falls

About 2000 miles west of Pearl Harbor, in fact about midway between Hawaii and the Japanese islands, stood the tiny American outpost of Wake Island. The Japanese required the island as one of the strategic links in their planned outer defence chain and immediately staged a bombing raid on it from airfields on the Marshalls to the south. As has been seen, the American carrier *Enterprise* had just flown in a force of F4Fs and this timely reinforcement repulsed not only this exploratory raid but also an attempted landing a few days later. The fighters sustained high losses in the process and the American high command directed all three of their available carriers to the island's relief. There was little co-ordination, however, and they proceeded independently with none of the urgency that soon characterized Pacific operations; consequently the Japanese *Soryu* and *Hiryu*, diverted from their withdrawal from Hawaii, arrived first. With two preliminary strikes they virtually destroyed the remaining defences and on the following day covered a landing which carried the island with little further difficulty.

The simultaneous Japanese movements against the Philippines and East Indies took the form of a series of small landings at key points, following each other with bewildering rapidity and ably supported by their smaller carriers and seaplane carriers

A still from the 20th Century Fox film of the Japanese attack on Pearl Harbor 'Tora-Tora-Tora!', depicting a Zero working down a line of US Army P40s at Wheeler Field, Oahu.

converted largely from merchantmen.

The carriers *Ryujo* and *Zuiho* were equipped with 'Kate' torpedo bombers with only obsolescent 'Claude' fighters for cover; the seaplane carriers carried only 'Dave' and 'Pete' floatplanes. This scarcely formidable line-up was adequate for the job and demonstrated, not for the last time, that any air power is preferable to no air power.

End of big-gun era

Unwisely the British sent the capital ships *Prince of Wales* and *Repulse* to Singapore to deter the Japanese from a move in that direction, in spite of their lacking air cover due to the *Indomitable's* untimely stranding off Jamaica. The bitter experiences of Norway and the Mediterranean seemed to count as nothing and the two ships were swamped off NE Malaya on 10 December 1941 by no fewer than six waves of enemy aircraft operating out of newly acquired bases in Thailand. About 10 torpedo and numerous bomb hits were scored on the two violently manoeuvring ships; there was no shortage of expertise on the part of the Japanese pilots of this period and it was probably a blessing that *Indomitable* was absent, as her newly worked-up force of 20 Sea Hurricanes and Fulmars would have been overwhelmed to the extent that she, too, would almost certainly have been lost. As it was, coming so soon after Pearl Harbor,

the incident signalled the end of the big gun era at sea.

The Japanese worked remorselessly southward, island by island, using their air superiority to give the Allies no time for regrouping. By the end of January 1942 they were poised to strike at both New Britain and New Guinea and the small carriers, having proved invaluable in these operations, were reinforced by *Soryu* and *Hiryu*. Singapore fell in mid-February and Darwin in Australia itself felt the weight of a concentrated raid. Nowhere seemed secure and the Japanese were within sight of taking the chain of islands from Sumatra to Timor, destined to form the southern flank of their newly formed 'Co-prosperity Sphere'. It was becoming obvious to the British that the Japanese fleet would soon be free of their support role and be at liberty to extend their influence westward into the Indian Ocean, putting much of the Empire at risk.

Eastern fleet formed

India, East Africa, Western Australia — all were vulnerable and every effort was made to spare ships from the vital European theatre to form a new Eastern Fleet based on Trincomalee in Ceylon. The newly repaired *Indomitable* was hazarded in ferrying a cargo of 48 Hurricane fighters into Java; she then had to retire on Aden in order to recover her own aircraft. Ferrying was a vital

America's first aircraft carrier CV1 'Langley' after conversion to a seaplane carrier in 1937. After Pearl Harbor 'Langley' was employed in ferrying urgently needed aircraft to bases under Japanese attack and during one such mission in February 1942 she was hit several times by enemy bombs and finally dispatched by her own destroyer escort off Java.

service but best suited to older carriers which could be spared.

The *Indomitable's* escort on this occasion was Australian and a reminder that considerable Allied naval forces still existed east of Suez. There were cruisers and destroyers of American, British, Dutch and Australian (ABDA) origin but they suffered from lack of any real air support and lack of experience in working together. They were in constant contact with an enemy that seemed omnipresent and, in spite of scoring a few successes, were gradually whittled down in number. Finally, at the end of February 1942 in the Java Sea, the remaining units were pitted against the covering forces of a major landing. The Japanese had no carrier present but their 8-inch-gunned cruisers were formidable opponents and their excellent gunnery, together with a profligate use of the long-range 24-inch 'Long Lance' torpedo, won the day decisively. With this defeat, organized

Allied resistance at sea came to an end and, by mid-March, it was all over in the East Indies. The British fell back on Ceylon and the Americans on Hawaii to make urgent preparation to meet the next thrust of their victorious and, as yet, virtually unmarked adversary.

Ceylon threatened

The Japanese indeed, planned no less than to 'do a Pearl Harbor' on the British at Ceylon and, to this end, sailed the same formidable carrier group (less the *Kaga*) into the Indian Ocean late in March. Their strike against Ceylon was to coincide with an anti-shipping sweep by the small carrier *Ryujo* into the Bay of Bengal. With the modernized *Warspite* and four R-class battleships to hand, a combined broadside of no less than 40 15-inch guns was available to the British commander, Somerville, but it was no longer that sort of war and of more significance were the three carriers present.

Mainstay of the American seaborne attack forces during the whole of WW2 was the Douglas SBD Dauntless dive bomber, which was developed from the Northrop XBT-1. Here an SBD-3, the type that was being delivered to USN carrier squadrons from March 1941 and which could deliver up to a 1000lb bomb, circles its carrier.

One, the *Hermes*, was no longer a front-line unit but both *Formidable* and *Indomitable* were new and fully tuned.

Their weakness again lay in both the number and the quality of their aircraft. Although they had some Martlets (Wildcats) in addition to Fulmars, neither type was a match for the Japanese Zero which could really only be countered at low level by a Sea Hurricane. For strike purposes their Swordfish and Albacores, although radar-equipped, bore no comparison with the fully blooded 'Kates' and 'Vals', which also out-numbered them two to one beside being flown by crews with morale at a peak.

With the fall of Sumatra, part of the Japanese force that had taken Singapore undertook the long sea passage to Rangoon in Burma for its next landing. Such was the disorganization of the Allied cause that this very risky operation went unchallenged. For good measure, the enemy then took the Andaman Islands for use as a forward base.

Two battle groups

Somerville had organized his fleet into two battle groups, a fast force built around *Formidable, Indomitable* and *Warspite*, and a slow squadron whose nucleus was the little *Hermes* and the four R-class battleships. Intelligence indicated a strike on Ceylon by Nagumo's carriers about 1 April 1942 and the British ploy was to cruise to the southwest of the island in daylight and withdrawing to more sheltered waters each night, relying on a handful of Catalina PBYs for early warning. It was thus hoped that any Japanese reconnaissance around Ceylon would fail to locate the British force which, possessing radar and exercised in night-fighting, felt able to meet its enemy on something like equal terms.

When nothing untoward had occurred by 2 April, however, Somerville, who had obviously greatly underrated the muscle-power of Nagumo, expressed himself disappointed at not having had the chance of a 'good crack' and was obliged to send his fast division (unsupported by any auxiliary vessels) back to Addu Atoll in the Maldives to refuel. As a troop convoy was shortly expected at Ceylon, *Hermes* and other units including two heavy cruisers were sent north as cover. Then, on the evening of the 4th, a Catalina located the Japanese about 400 miles distant and approaching from the unlikely direction of southeast. The two cruisers *Dorsetshire* and *Cornwall* were hastily redirected to Addu, where frantic preparations were being made to get to sea.

Colombo and Trincomalee hard hit

Inevitably, the blow came out of the dawn as 90 bombers and dive bombers, covered by

36 Zeros, hit Colombo. Fully prepared, the British had sent all mobile shipping to sea but the fighter defences were still overwhelmed and heavy damage was inflicted ashore. In addition, a floatplane from the cruiser *Tone* located the retreating British cruisers and Nagumo vectored his reserve strike of 53 bomb-armed 'Vals' against them. Devoid of air cover, both quickly fell victim. By then Somerville's carriers were at sea and closing; their scouting Albacores actually contacted the enemy but were destroyed before getting off a sighting report. Both forces fell back and contact was never made. During the next five days the Japanese northern group centred on the small carrier *Ryujo* ravaged merchant shipping off the coast of India, sinking over 150,000 gross tons.

Nagumo, whose first strike against Ceylon had met with limited success, was not yet satisfied; on the 9th a scouting Catalina transmitted the dread news of the presence of the main Japanese force about 500 miles east of the island, steering northeast. Again the aircraft was shot down but its timely warning gave the likely target, Trincomalee, time to prepare. Shipping, including *Hermes*, was sent to sea but without the backing of Somerville's force which again was caught at Addu.

The Japanese mustered 91 'Kates' and 'Vals' for the strike, covered by 38 Zeros, and the sheer weight of the attack once again swept all before it. With the port all but devoid of shipping the damage was confined to base installations and would have been limited in success but for the chance sighting of *Hermes* close inshore to the south. The enemy's second strike was fully prepared and over 80 'Val' dive bombers put the little carrier under in about 10 minutes in a superb display of dive-bombing that scored at least 40 hits with 250kg bombs. Her own small force of 12 Swordfish were fortunately ashore. Shore-based aircraft of the FAA and RAF made contact with Nagumo's carriers which had to defend themselves for the first time, suffering no losses except for a few aircraft.

Well satisfied with their achievements, both Japanese forces retired independently through the Malacca Strait, knowing that American and British seapower had been dealt severe blows, both materially and to their morale. The British, indeed, fell right back on the base at Kilindini in East Africa.

US rebuilds forces

The Japanese had demonstrated conclusively the near-invincibility of a strong carrier group which could strike almost at will, reducing the opposition to the status of a man trying to fight off a swarm of bees with a cricket bat. By committing all his

The American battleship 'Nevada' making its famous sortie in an attempt to get clear of Pearl Harbor after the first Japanese attack; she was hit in the second attack and had to be beached.

power to the Indian Ocean however, the enemy gave the Americans a chance to recover from the debacle of Pearl Harbor. *Yorktown* was rapidly transferred through the Panama from the Atlantic to provide a fourth carrier but her addition was almost immediately nullified by the *Saratoga* being damaged by a submarine's torpedo. She, in turn, was replaced by the *Hornet*, leaving only the *Wasp* — attached to the Royal Navy — and the old *Ranger* in the Atlantic.

By the end of January 1942 the Americans had formed three fast groups, each built on one carrier. They were in contrast to the 'Schwerpunkt' approach of the Japanese and, although they mounted strikes against several of the enemy's outpost islands, it was soon apparent that a single carrier could not mount a raid sufficiently powerful to overwhelm the target. It was also hoped that this coat-trailing would entice Nagumo's main force out to battle, and it was perhaps fortunate at that stage that the ruse was unsuccessful.

Realizing the weakness of piecemeal attacks, on 10 March the Americans coordinated the resources of two carriers, *Yorktown* and *Lexington*, against the Japanese bridgehead at Lae in New Guinea. This enabled them to put up a force of 100 aircraft, SBDs and TBDs covered by F4F Wildcats. Whereas the enemy carriers were still left with a second-strike capability, however, the US carriers had just sufficient aircraft remaining to maintain a combat air patrol (CAP). The American pilots also yet lacked experience; with the advantage of complete surprise, a surfeit of anchored targets and no enemy fighters they sank only three transports. It was, nevertheless, a start.

Raid on Tokyo

Something far more spectacular had been planned by the Americans with *Hornet's* arrival in the Pacific. Still a new ship, she called at San Francisco en route and picked up 16 B25 Mitchell medium bombers of the 17th Bomber Group of the Army Air Force under Lieutenant Colonel James Doolittle. Experiment had shown that it was possible to fly the Mitchells off although they could not be recovered. In addition, being far longer than the elevators, they could not be struck below and were all stowed aft on the flightdeck in two echeloned lines, 'like an arrow with pinfeathers'. *Hornet's* own aircraft were, of course, inoperable and she and her escort rendezvoused near Midway Island with *Enterprise*, which was to cover on the raid that was to become legendary as 'thirty seconds over Tokyo'. The plan was nothing less than for 13 bombers to appear out of nowhere over the capital and one each over three other major cities; relying only upon surprise for their protection they would then have to fly on to friendly airfields in China.

With the Japanese by then in possession of an extended ring of outpost islands, chances of the carrier's approach being spotted were high and their course was arranged to take them well clear. Early on 16 April 1942 the Americans seemed to have slipped through successfully when they ran into the Japanese second line, a series of picket ships. Once they had been detected the Americans' only hope was to fly off the strike immediately, even though they were still well short of their planned closest point of approach. Heavy with bombs and fuel for their long passage (including 15 auxiliary 5-gallon cans of petrol carried inboard on each) the aircraft would have no easy task getting airborne, particularly as the weather was poor.

Two parallel white lines had been painted along the *Hornet's* flightdeck and the wheels of the B25s had to be kept between them to avoid the starboard wingtips hitting the island. Doolittle himself took off first and there was doubt in many minds whether he would make it but he 'hung his ship almost straight up on its props until we could see the whole top', according to one report, and with full flaps and throttle he was away, rapidly followed by the remainder.

Hardly were they out of sight when *Hornet* had her own aircraft ranged and combined with those of *Enterprise* against the only available target, the unfortunate Japanese pickets, several of which were sunk.

The B25s located and bombed their targets successfully but were too few to inflict more than token damage. They did, however, cause great dismay to the enemy who immediately doubled his defence measures and, even more important, caused tremendous jubilation in American hearts which had become conditioned to the acceptance of unrelieved bad news.

These beginnings were small but served warning on the Japanese that although their giant opponent was bloodied, he was not out and certainly was in no mood to accept any fait accompli in the Far East.

Three pictures recording the epic morale-restoring beginning of the American offensive in the Pacific war with the Doolittle raid on Tokyo in April 1942. Top picture shows Lieutenant Colonel James H. Doolittle and Admiral Marc A. Mitscher and some of their men aboard USS 'Hornet' (CV8) at the start of the mission and the others are of the hazardous take-off of the leading Army B-25 Mitchell medium bomber piloted by Col Doolittle.

The Woolworth carrier

A Dauntless dive bomber, hook extended, about to touch down on the deck of CV4 USS 'Ranger' in 1942. At the turn of the year 1941/2 all available American carriers except 'Ranger' were assigned to the Pacific. 'Ranger' was thought too slow and remained in the Atlantic where, even before America entered the war, she assisted in convoying troops between Canada and Europe; later she was active on various escort and aircraft ferrying duties until taking part in the North Africa landings.

The sea war in the Atlantic was a very different matter to that in the Pacific and developed around one overriding issue — the ability of Great Britain to keep open her sea lanes. To wage war or, indeed, even to sustain herself, she had to import vast quantities of raw materials and an ever-growing quantity of Lease-Lend goods; without a constant flow the efforts would wither and die. Traditionally, one of the prime tasks of the Royal Navy has been the defence of the merchant marine, and, however much ships and weapons might change, the importance of this duty cannot.

The value of the convoy had been appreciated over centuries but during the long years of the Pax Britannica it was one of the martial arts temporarily forgotten. During WWI the U-boat was developed as the major menace to British merchantmen. Operating at focal points of the trade routes it wreaked havoc; so much so that by 1917 matters were bordering on the desperate. Then after all too much deliberation, convoys were introduced and losses dropped dramatically.

It was so conclusive that a convoy system was fully defined and instituted immediately on the outbreak of WWII. Within the Royal Navy, with its traditions of taking the war to its enemy, there were naturally dissenting voices that argued that escorts should not be tied down in the defence of merchant shipping; if the U-boat had to be beaten, why not form killer groups and hunt it down? They were soon proved wrong as the sea is very large and the detection methods of the time were highly fallible. On the contrary, it was rapidly shown that it was far more economical in AS ships to place them with a convoy because, once detected, it attracted submarines as surely as a staked-out goat lured a tiger and search was unnecessary.

Wolf-pack tactics

Admiral Dönitz, the U-boat supremo, was a master of his trade and, with the fall of Europe, could deploy his flotillas from Biscay to the North Cape. His methods were brutally simple; string all available boats along the likely convoy route and one would

have a fair chance of an interception. The duty of the sighting boat was then not to attack but to track the ships and to act as a radio beacon, homing as many U-boats as possible to the scene for a co-ordinated attack which, all too often, swamped the meagre escorts available; the term wolf-pack tactics describes them perfectly.

The limited horizons of a surfaced submarine were extended by the use of long-range reconnaissance aircraft, Dornier Do18 and Bv138 flying-boats and, far more deadly, the four engined Fw200 Kondors, notably those of I/KG40 operating out of Bordeaux/Merignac and Cognac. They operated a veritable 'milk-run' with aircraft flying the northbound France-Western Approaches-Norway route one day and returning the next, reporting all shipping, 'zeroing-in' U-boats and attacking stragglers on opportunity.

The Royal Navy, meanwhile, depended upon the RAF-controlled Coastal Command for its long-range (LR) reconnaissance and the greater part of the strength of this force still consisted of Ansons, whose lack of performance had been recognized in 1937 but whose intended replacement, the American Lockheed Hudson, was only beginning to enter squadron service late in 1939. The excellent new Short Sunderland flying-boat was also becoming available to replace the many old Londons but only two squadrons had changed over by the outbreak of war. Thus the AS and general strike potential of Britain's land-based maritime aircraft was of a very low order and the good offices of Bomber Command needed frequently to be relied upon; although aircraft on passage frequently sighted surfaced U-boats, means and methods by which to attack them were still painfully inadequate.

Effect of air escort

Nevertheless, it was very soon apparent that the effect of the presence of an LR aircraft circling a convoy was greatly disproportionate to its actual capabilities; enemy snoopers were disinclined to approach and surfaced U-boats were obliged to dive — and a submerged U-boat had a speed and endurance too low to render it effective. By early 1941 the American Catalina flying-boat and Liberator bomber were coming forward in sufficient numbers to permit extended coverage of the North Atlantic by operations from either side and from new facilities in Iceland. The aerial cover over the centre of this particular pond was still rather sparse, even when bases in the Azores were added, and the situation was aggravated by the low bunker capacity of many convoy escorts which meant often that they had to leave their charges to refuel. Aircraft carriers were obviously required to accompany convoys to mount a continuous patrol/strike cover, but the few available fleet carriers were far too precious to be spared for any but the most important of operations and some sort of temporary expedient was of paramount urgency.

During the 1930s the ex-seaplane carrier *Pegasus* (previously *Ark Royal*) acted as trials and training ship for catapult operations, a vital function at a time when virtually every warship from light cruiser upwards carried one or more spotter seaplanes, usually a Seafox or the amphibious Walrus (nicknamed 'Shagbat'). The *Pegasus* provided the basis for the Admiralty's decision of December 1940 to accompany convoys with fighter catapult ships (FCS), converted from merchantmen. On the approach of a marauder an old high-performance fighter, typically a Mark I Hurricane, could be fired off to intercept. It

CVE 'Charger', originally BA VG4, was one of four early converted merchantmen of which three — 'Avenger', 'Biter' and 'Dasher' — were supplied to Britain. They were of 8200 tons and could operate up to 15 aircraft. 'Charger' was retained by the US for pilot training at sea.

was, of course, definitely a 'one-shot' system, with the aircraft carried already mounted on the catapult and with no means of recovery after flight. The unfortunate pilot, probably half-frozen on take-off after hours of readiness strapped in his cockpit, then had the prospect of 'ditching' alongside a friendly ship and hoping to be picked up before the inhospitable northern waters finished him off. (In between these events he had also probably been under fire both from his quarry and, all too often, from over-zealous 'friendly' gunners on his return!)

The *Pegasus* was already available with catapult and trained personnel for the operation of three Fulmar fighters and she was supplemented by the first three auxiliaries, *Ariguani*, *Maplin* and *Springbank*, by April 1941. Such was the urgency of the situation that the Admiralty did not wait for operational feedback but immediately ordered equipment for the conversion of another 50 merchantmen. They were termed catapult-armed merchantmen, or CAM ships, retaining both their cargo capacity and Red Ensign status, whereas the FCSs were commissioned as regular warships. Although a measure of success was achieved by their small band of courageous pilots, better means were to hand.

Enter the Merchant Aircraft Carrier

In February 1940 the Royal Navy had captured the new Hamburg-Amerika freighter *Hannover* as she crossed the Caribbean in a break for home. Set on fire by her crew, she was heavily damaged but

was kept afloat by a naval party and towed into a Jamaican port. With hull and machinery intact, she was a perfect candidate for a prototype conversion to a small auxiliary aircraft carrier through the removal of superstructure and the addition of a flightdeck. The idea was not revolutionary, having come from both British and American planners well before the war. In June 1941 therefore, HMS *Audacity*, ex-*Empire Audacity*, ex-*Sinbad*, ex-*Hannover*, commissioned with minimal facilities for the operation of six Martlet fighters.

She joined her first convoy, the Gibraltar-bound OG74, in September, breaking her duck with the destruction of a shadowing Fw200. Movements on this route were being particularly harassed by U-boats at that time and the next homeward-bound convoy, HG76, was held back until a powerful AS escort had been assembled for its protection. It sailed with *Audacity*, a week after the distant thunder of Pearl Harbor had subsided and the battle was joined immediately. No fewer than 12 submarines of the Seerauber flotilla were involved and they were adequately supported by French-based aircraft. A four-day running fight ensued in which *Audacity's* Martlets destroyed two more Fw200s and assisted the surface escort, under the command of the redoubtable Captain Walker, in the destruction of five submarines, including that of the ace Endrass (U567). The first major defeat for the U-boat was not accomplished without cost, however; the British lost two merchantmen, a destroyer

Left: The 350mph-plus Sea Hurricane was the main weapon of fighter catapult and CAM ships. Hurricanes were at first flown by Fleet Air Arm and later by RAF pilots, who needed a particular kind of courage knowing that, once launched, whatever the outcome of any encounter, they would almost certainly have to ditch or bale out over the sea, to be picked up by one of the ships if lucky.

Below: Two views of a Sea Hurricane on the catapult of a CAM ship, the means by which, before escort carriers were available, merchant ships and convoys could be given some air protection with minimal loss of cargo capacity.

and the *Audacity*, which fell victim to a torpedo from U751 when she had to leave the screen for the operation of aircraft. Her brief existence had proved the value of continuous aircraft cover, not only in the attacking of surfaced U-boats but also in the forcing of them to submerge out of torpedo range.

Fortunately her replacement was expedited as a programme of six further conversions had already been put in hand in the USA under the terms of Lease-Lend. It might reasonably be asked why the British themselves did not immediately embark on a similar exercise, but there was a great reticence to commit the high-quality mercantile tonnage necessary, probably born of concern for the high rate of loss being incurred in this class of ship and, moreover, shipyards were devoted mainly to the construction of warships. Five were, in fact, earmarked but their production was preceded by another typically British compromise, the MAC ship, or merchant aircraft carrier. With their reluctance to dispose of any available cargo capacity, the Admiralty's idea was to erect flightdecks on mercantile hulls, leaving the carrying space below intact. Obviously, cargo handling would have been very difficult for break-bulk goods so only bulk carriers were so converted, the grain and oil carried in them being handled by pumps.

Altogether there were six dry cargo and 13 tanker conversions. Most of them bore Empire Mac names, such as *Empire MacAlpine* and *MacMahon* but nine of the tankers were from the Shell fleet and carried their original names. Rebuilding was disappointingly slow and the first was not ready until May 1943; all, incredibly, survived the war.

The escort carrier

Fortunately, the Americans had no such ambivalence in approach; escort carriers were required and if hulls were needed for them then hulls there would be. The idea of the small carrier was not new to them; it stemmed largely from the conversion of the British cruiser *Cavendish* at the end of WWI. Although that remodelling had been a failure because the lack of a through flightdeck limited her to seaplane operation, the Americans saw her potential and suggested the conversion of a group of fast cruiser hulls with continuous decks suitable for wheeled aircraft. Protagonists of the plan envisaged these ships being used in close conjunction with cruiser squadrons in extending the reconnaissance power of the fleet, but when a board was convened to consider how the allowable Washington Treaty tonnage should be used, it was probably influenced by the large conversions already in hand abroad and could find no justification for their construction 'at this time'.

Despite intermittent lobbying, official approval was still lacking as the 1930s ran on inexorably to war and it was pointed out forcibly that small flightdecks could play an invaluable part in operations too minor to warrant the hazarding of a precious fleet carrier. The logic of this argument was inescapable and contingency plans were made for the rapid conversion of passenger liners. All was then brought to nought by the Secretary of the Navy who considered that the characteristics of then current aircraft would render the small flightdeck unsuitable. Valuable time was then lost until late in 1940, when the President himself took a hand, pointing out that large numbers of assembled aircraft were being sent to Britain and that the few carriers available could ill be spared for their transport. Suitably equipped merchant ships should, therefore, be acquired with the capacity, preferably, to fly off the aircraft being transported. (Why not, added the President, prepare also small flightdecks on other valuable merchantmen for the operation of helicopters?)

His authority was by then underlined by British experience in the value of aircraft in AS operations in the vicinity of convoys and things began to move. The helicopter, then very much in its infancy, was immediately discounted because of its lack of payload and the provision of full-length flightdecks was decided upon. Choice of a suitable basic hull was simplified by the existing standardization of cargo tonnage, a measure of official control being possible because of the necessity to manage the allocation of the Government subsidies which have always been so much a part of the American

The oddest flat-top of all was USS 'Wolverine', a converted Great Lakes paddle steamer of about 7000 tons fitted to train carrier pilots and flightdeck crews. There was a later similar conversion and the two ships survived the remarkable total of about 115,000 deck landings.

shipping scene. The US Maritime Commission divided standard designs into four main categories based on length, namely the C1 of under 400 feet between perpendiculars (bp); the C2 (which was to include the famous Liberty and Victory types) 400-450 feet; the C3 450-500 feet; and the C4 of over 500 feet. Individual owners could then specify variants of the basic types to suit their particular trading patterns. The C3 hull was selected for the escort carrier project and, although the greater majority of them were steam-driven, it was decided to change to diesel propulsion to reduce the funnel problem.

Long Island

Winston Churchill was of the opinion that such carriers could be 'improvised' in six months; Roosevelt said it could be done in three and he was right. Two of Moore-McCormack's diesel-driven C3s were appropriated in March 1941 and the first completed as the prototype escort carrier USS *Long Island*, classified AVG at first rather than the later more familiar CVE. She had a 362-foot wooden flightdeck served by one elevator from the hangar, which could stow 16 aircraft. Completion of the second was delayed until November 1941 and she was turned over to the Royal Navy as HMS *Archer*, the first of the six ordered by the Admiralty, whose requirements differed from the Americans. By the time of her completion the US Navy had thoroughly evaluated *Long Island* and, while satisfied with her speed, which the British considered inadequate, they decided to lengthen the flightdeck and speed up operations with a second elevator and a catapult.

The resultant programme was for 24 CVEs, and 12 CVLs built up from cruiser hulls (the Independence Class) capable of

fleet speeds. The CVEs were built on 20 available C3 hulls and four fleet oilers; the former were divided ten each to the US Navy (the Bogue Class) and the Royal Navy. Those built on oiler hulls were retained by the Americans as the Sangamon Class; with 503-foot flightdecks they were longer than the average CVE, could exceed 18 knots and possessed a second catapult. Much effort was put into the timely completion of this group to meet the deadline of the North African landings, planned for the end of 1942; with all American fleet carriers except the old *Ranger* fully occupied in Pacific waters the projected role of the Sangamons was of vital importance to the operation's success.

No captain's bath

It was understandable, therefore, that the first unit for the Royal Navy, *Avenger*, was not available until September 1942. The CVEs were functional in the extreme and worked well, although to the British seamen sent over to man them they possessed features that were definitely not 'pusser'. The captain, for instance, had to forego the accepted privilege of his own bath in exchange for a shower; the unpopularity of this was nearly matched by the fitting of bunks in place of the familiar hammocks, alleviated somewhat by the discovery of soda-fountains which dispensed six different flavours — for about the first three days out.

The *Avenger* was thrown very much 'in the deep end' with a maiden trip on the heavily contested Russian convoy route; many other CVEs were to follow on this grim and thankless duty. After the earlier loss of *Audacity* while operating alone outside the screen, it became standard Royal Navy practice to give a carrier a personal escort of a couple of AS or AA ships so that she could operate safely astern of the main body and retain full freedom of manoeuvre for the launch and recovery of her aircraft. American practice was at first to protect the carrier by placing her in a 'pond' in the

A typical deck view of USS 'Card' (CV11), one of a class of 11 'baby flat-tops' built 1941-3 on merchant hulls. As the escort carrier numbers increased the U-boat-v-convoy war gradually turned in the Allies' favour. 'Card' herself in 1943 received a Presidential Unit Citation for her part in record U-boat sinkings in the Atlantic.

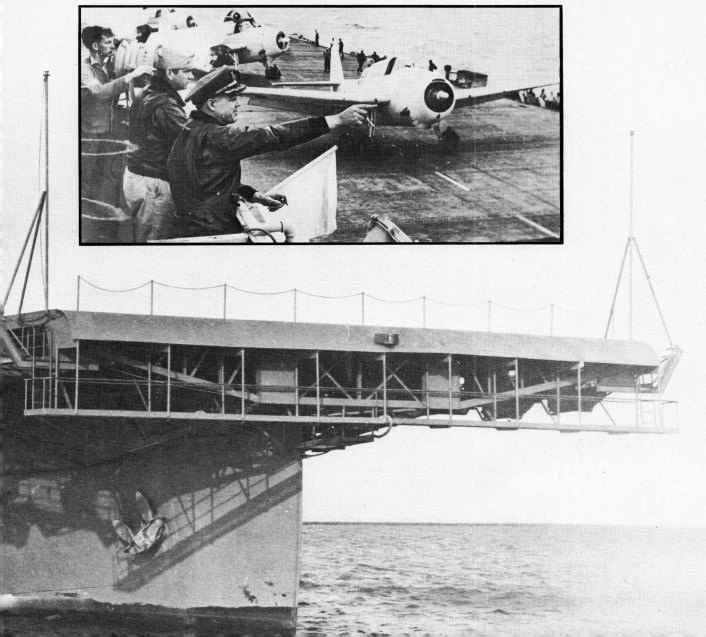

centre of the convoy. When this was shown to be too restricting on movement they too pulled her clear with her own escort to cover the main group from a distance, which was particularly useful if a second convoy was in the vicinity.

Through great effort the Americans succeeded in completing all four Sangamons on time for the North African landings, which took place to plan in November 1942. Together with three Royal Navy CVEs they were responsible for the greater part of the available air cover and their numbers enabled them to engage simultaneously a variety of widely spread targets, a strategy already successfully employed by the Japanese in the East Indies. Such was the need for flightdecks in the Pacific, where only two fleet carriers remained operational, that the American quartet was transferred immediately the North African bridgeheads were consolidated.

First CVE casualties

During the course of the operations, one of the British vessels, *Avenger*, was torpedoed, catching fire and blowing up with a heavy loss of life. This incident together with that soon after in March 1943 when *Dasher* was destroyed, highlighted the short cuts taken in their design and construction. Steps were subsequently taken to avoid the likelihood of further aviation fuel explosions but they inevitably led to delays in construction, causing some friction between the prudent British and the US builders, who considered that only justifiable wartime risks were being taken.

With the great expansion of Allied carrier forces it will be evident that a parallel effort was being made in the training of aircrews to man them. One of the CVEs building to British account, *Charger*, was retained by the US Navy for sea training purposes but so great were operational requirements that she was pressed into service. Fortunately, somebody had the happy idea of improvising a training carrier on the vast, but safe, waters of the Great Lakes. The result was the commissioning in the summer of 1942 of the oddest 'flat-top' to date — the paddle steamer carrier. She had begun life many years earlier in the excursion business as the sidewheeler *Seeandbee*. Given a 550-foot flightdeck, she became the USS *Wolverine*, the most imaginative Great Lakes warship since the days of Oliver Hazard Perry. There was no hangar so her freeboard was exceptionally low and her coal-fired machinery was good for only a basic 16 knots, features which could give the trainee pilots much to think about.

The *Wolverine's* record was, nevertheless, extremely good, with the passing-out of 400 qualified pilots in one period of only four months. She was therefore joined by a second 'carrier', the *Sable* (ex-*Greater Buffalo*) and between them they trained a quite staggering number of pilots and flightdeck crews. In spite of the severe Lakes winters, operations continued the year round and these unsung heroines of the fleet eventually survived a total of about 115,000 deck landings. The *Sable* claimed a record for one working day with 488 landings in 531 minutes!

Carriers in series production

By 1943 the American shipbuilding industry was fully geared to the series production of simple vessels, and yards that could turn out Liberty and Victory standard ships 'by the mile' could equally well produce mercantile-based escort carriers in the same way. Even so, the building of the first 50 of the new 512-foot Casablanca Class in exactly one year was a major achievement. The Casablancas had an improved capacity for up to 28 aircraft but were still very basic. Parallel with their construction, therefore, was designed a more refined follow-on class, known as the Commencement Bay type, which did not begin to enter service until late 1944, the majority being too late to see active service. Without doubt the great strength of American industry lay in its capacity for improvization; there existed many projects initiated by the warring nations that demonstrated that it was no use whatsoever producing a 'Rolls-Royce' design if it could not be built in time. The CVEs might have been the maritime equivalent of Model T Fords but they were exactly what was required; referred to variously as Jeep or Woolworth carriers or simply baby flat-tops, they were available when needed — and they worked.

The introduction of the escort carrier to the Atlantic war in March 1943 could not have been more opportune, as the battle reached its crisis with a supreme effort on the part of the U-boats. British shipping losses were enough to weaken the resolve of even the most ardent supporter of the convoy system; during the first three weeks of that fateful month nearly 100 ships of half a million gross tons went to the bottom. Of these 46 were lost from three Atlantic convoys whose escorts were swamped by concentrations of up to 40 submarines, which lost only one of their number.

Start of U-boats' decline

For the next eastbound convoy, the escort was augmented by the American CVE *Bogue* and one of the newly formed British escort groups. No ships were lost. Five such groups were formed and more British CVEs were made available; the long trial of strength reached a plateau from which the fortunes of Dönitz's boats began their

decline. They were not yet beaten and had major successes still to come but, from this point, their losses mounted steadily.

A major contribution was made by US hunter-killer groups, formed around CVEs such as the *Card* and *Core*, which became highly proficient in the sinking of the large supply submarines, so important to the extension of the average U-boat's endurance. Each German commander was in addition required to report regularly to his operation control, a habit turned by the Allies to their advantage by the development of improved high-frequency (HF) direction-finding equipment (Huff-Duff). Two escorts so equipped could obtain a fix on a transmitting boat, either running down the lines of bearing for an attack or, if they could not leave a convoy, directing an aircraft to the position.

This was the sort of task for which the small carriers were designed. Whereas a fleet ship could carry a balanced complement of aircraft for reconnaissance, strike and patrol duties, the CVE, with a capacity of under 30 aircraft, when allocated to escort duties tended to carry a mixed bag of only Swordfish and Sea Hurricanes, with the specialized communications for their control. As CVEs became more plentiful they were organized more frequently into groups for the establishment of air superiority in a required area, as pioneered during the North African landings. Towards the end of the war they were used in squadrons up to ten strong usually carrying TBF Avengers and F4F Wildcats.

Contribution to Victory

The secret of their successful employment was to use them within their limitations. They had little speed and negligible protection other than their aircraft. Designed for use in low-hazard combat zones they could be badly caught out if they became involved in fleet operations, as was to be amply demonstrated at Leyte Gulf in 1944. But this was a failing of the commander on the spot rather than the ship, which made a major contribution to the eventual victory at sea.

The auxiliary carrier was entirely an American preserve. Britain built four, *Activity*, *Campania*, *Nairana* and *Vindex*,

A major achievement of the American shipbuilding industry was the series production of functional aircraft carriers for escort duties. First of them was the Casablanca Class, which had improved aircraft capacity (28) over the earlier escorts; 50 were completed in a year and here we see the first, CVE55 USS 'Casablanca', shortly after her commissioning in 1943.

to a high specification and along the lines of miniature fleet carriers, including steel (unarmoured) flightdecks. The Admiralty's aversion to single-screw propulsion was reflected in their twin-screw diesel layout, with its superior 'get-you-home' capabilities in the event of heavy damage. In addition, the ex-Union Castle liner *Pretoria Castle* was rebuilt into a training carrier; with no equivalent of the Great Lakes available a high-performance ship was required for these duties.

British carrier construction then seemed to lose its way. Although faced with a need for strict apportioning of limited resources, the national tendency towards the construction of 'tailor-mades' asserted itself and conventional techniques were used in unconventional times to build over-complex ships that could not be completed in time. Where the Americans sacrificed all frills to get as many flightdecks as possible operational in the shortest time, the British — who had correctly allocated their major shipbuilding effort to the production of AS ships — used their remaining capacity to lay down in 1942 the first of a long series of light fleet carriers of the Colossus class to mercantile specification. In 1944, by which time it should have been apparent that each would take at least three years to build, a slightly enlarged type, the Majestic, was begun. Although these had little hope of completion before the war ended, it did not prevent the laying down of the even larger purpose-designed Hermes class. These ships were to prove useful in the postwar fleet but represented a useless waste of valuable wartime resources when they could least be spared.

Japanese light carriers

The Japanese, too, endeavoured to produce carriers rapidly from mercantile hulls. Three fast liners for the NYK Japan-Europe service were appropriated on the stocks and converted rapidly during 1941-2 into the 27,000-ton *Chuyo, Taiyo* and *Unyo*. With an overall length of 719 feet and a speed of only 21 knots, they could accommodate about 30 aircraft apiece. In the Allied fleets they would have been classed as escort carriers but the Japanese did not practise a convoy system on any grand scale and they were used for training purposes or independent missions.

Their German allies conducted a fickle affair with the carrier, as already shown by the stop-start progress of the two Graf Zeppelins. Enthusiasm seemed to be a function of the success or otherwise of the British with seaborne airpower at the time. Nevertheless, a series of four conversions was planned for 1942. Three were liners, the largest being Norddeutscher Lloyd's *Europa* which, with a gross tonnage of 49,750, was a slightly smaller mate to her Blue Riband partner *Bremen*. She had been lying idle at Bremerhaven since the beginning of the war and, had the conversion materialized, she would have carried a strike force of 18 Ju87 Stukas and a fighter wing of 24 Bf109s. With power for 28 knots, she could have been used on fleet operations and, suitably escorted, could have proved formidable.

German ghosts

Two other NDL liners, *Potsdam* and *Gneisenau* (not to be confused with the battlecruiser of that name), were also earmarked for similar treatment, each to have a capacity of 12 Stukas and 12 Bf109 fighters.

The last of the German 'ghost' carriers was the heavy cruiser *Seydlitz*. She and the *Lützow* were originally to have been sisters to the better-known *Prinz Eugen* but construction was intermittent because shipbuilding capacity was devoted largely to U-boat production. Finally, *Lützow* was sold to the Russians during the false honeymoon of 1940 and *Seydlitz* was never completed. Had her rebuilding ever taken place her planned capacity of eight Stukas and ten fighters compares unfavourably with the 45 aircraft stowed by the American Independence-class carriers, similarly converted from cruisers of slightly smaller dimensions.

All of the German auxiliary carriers would have had a single hangar deck, two catapults and a useful surface armament of up to a dozen of their excellent 105mm (4.1-inch) guns. That they suffered a like fate to their purpose-built sisters was not surprising in view of the capricious changes of attitude in the German High Command and inter-service rivalries. By late 1942 Hitler was of the opinion that surface ships were of little use to the pursuit of the war and his right-hand man, Goering, was vocal on the subject that 'his' Luftwaffe could tackle almost any task unaided; aircraft carriers were unnecessary irrelevancies that diverted effort from more cherished projects. In retrospect, the Germans would have done well to complete them; the resources thus committed would have made little difference to the eventual outcome but several fast enemy carriers, resolutely employed, would have given the greatly stretched Royal Navy some major problems.

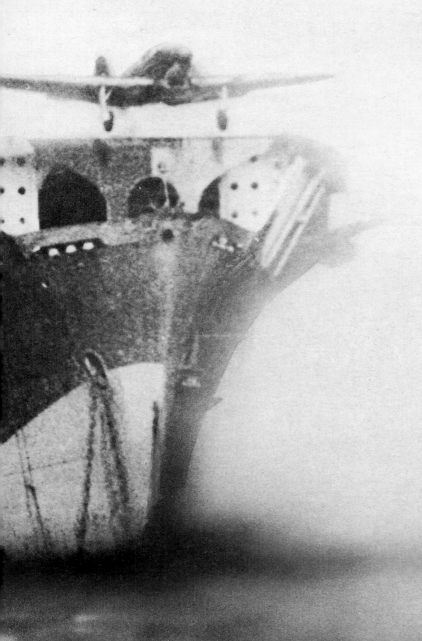

The auxiliary carrier 'Pretoria Castle', is shown with a Hurricane taking off while the ship was at anchor. She was first converted to armed merchant cruiser and then to escort carrier in 1943, with one elevator and a complement of 15 aircraft, and was used mainly on training.

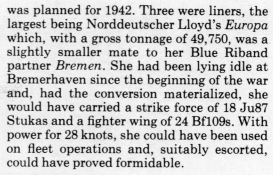

Fighting the convoys through

The close of Chapter Three saw the Royal Navy reeling from the succession of disasters of late 1941. Although the news of America's entry into the war after Pearl Harbor was cheering, it was tinged with doubts regarding her fleet's continuing ability to offer tangible assistance for the foreseeable future.

Indeed, for six months already, the Royal Navy had been faced with the problem of another newly acquired ally, Russia, which in June 1941 had been suddenly savaged by her erstwhile German bedfellows. Britain, in all conscience, had little in common with either but, being already at war with the one, had reluctantly to accept as partner the other. Having become embroiled in European affairs the problem was then — and not for the first time — how an essentially maritime power intervenes decisively in an issue between two major

landpowers. With the great length of the front almost totally land-locked, direct involvement would have been difficult even if men could be spared; however, it was not manpower that the Soviet Union lacked but the material to make them an effective fighting force. It was required quickly and in vast quantities, and could be transported only by sea — and this was Britain's business. Shipment via the Baltic or Black Sea ports was already impossible due to Germany's territorial gains. The ports on Russia's still-peaceful Pacific coast were far distant and all goods would have required transhipment over the Trans-Siberian Railway, a tenous link that could be severed all too easily. Persian Gulf ports lay in a politically unstable area, involved long sea routes vulnerable to attack and, again, transhipment by rail. The only viable proposition was the Arctic ports, close to the

This 1943 painting by Charles Pears, now in the Imperial War Museum, captures some of the drama and the high level of aerial activity that were regular features of the Allied convoys to Russia.

The Heinkel He111 torpedo bomber was the major scourge of the convoys to and from Russia whenever they came within range of German-held airfields and the precious carriers could not be spared to accompany them.

front where the cargoes were needed and involving the shortest sea routes.

Into the Arctic

Daunting disadvantages attended this choice in the enemy's occupation of Norway, whose coast flanked the approaches, and the weather, which ranged from summers of perpetual daylight when nothing could be concealed upon the tranquil face of the northern seas, to the winters capable of generating weather so unremittingly vile that friend and foe alike needed to abandon war to dedicate himself simply to survival. This, nevertheless, was the Admiralty's chosen arena and the means by which the somewhat primitive ports of Murmansk and Archangel could best be used were urgently studied.

Ice was a greatly limiting factor, closing Archangel for periods dependent upon the severity of the winter and advancing southwards in a continuous sheet whose edge was the limit of navigation and which left between itself and Norway's North Cape a bottleneck every bit as hazardous as the central Mediterranean narrows were to prove. Convoys endeavouring to enter the Barents Sea would have to do so under the hostile umbrella of the Luftwaffe, still powerful in spite of being weakened through transfer of units to the eastern front.

The logical answer to this form of opposition could lie only in carrier-based aircraft and the 'Via Dolorosa' that this route was to become was due mainly to a lack of them. Only *Victorious* and *Furious* remained based in the United Kingdom and the latter was shortly to be transferred to the Mediterranean. In order to remain a fully flexible force the Home Fleet needed to retain the *Victorious* to complement the remaining capital ships and this northern tragedy unfolded with naval aviation playing a role that was perforce a minor one.

Attack on ore shipments

The two vital Arctic ports were hazarded from the start by the close proximity of German-occupied Norway, buffered only by

the narrow Finnish corridor to the port of Petsamo. Finland was at war with the Soviet Union over territorial claims made by the latter and the enemy began to advance eastward along the Murman coast over Finnish soil. This operation generated a degree of coastal traffic, and there were outward shipments of iron ore of which the Russians quickly requested that the Royal Navy disrupt the flow. A carrier operation was therefore mounted at the end of July 1941, using both *Victorious* and *Furious*. Together with their escort, the carriers approached from the direction of Iceland (newly occupied by the Allies) and, in the long daylight of summer were spotted by a German reconnaissance aircraft while still well short of their launching point — a precedent for all too many later sightings.

In spite of the lost initiative, a total of 39 Albacores and Swordfish were launched, covered by 25 Fulmars and Sea Hurricanes. Most shipping had already been evacuated and the AA and fighter defences alerted. Even the cumbersome Me110s of 6/JG5 were too nimble for the low-performance FAA strike aircraft and mauled them, while Me109s took on the escorts. In this chastening encounter 15 aircraft were lost for minimal return and it set the tone for the grim struggles ahead.

With the transfer of *Furious* to the Mediterranean only *Victorious* was left and it was thought that she could best be utilized as part of a Home Fleet force acting as distant cover to the planned convoys, which would have their own close escort. In this manner it was hoped that the heavy force could interpose itself between the merchantmen and an attack by enemy surface units, although it was recognized that the carrier's aircraft could not normally act as close cover to the convoy.

Convoy PQ1

The first of a long series of convoys left Reykjavik on 21 August 1941. It was a small exploratory expedition and included the old *Argus*, ferrying RAF Hurricanes to Russia. Its passage was uneventful and the Home

Batmen on USS 'Wasp' directing its aircraft to touchdown on the flightdeck. In April and May 1942 'Wasp' made a notable contribution to the defence of Malta when she was loaned to the British Home Fleet and ferried over 90 Spitfires from Britain to the island, before returning to the US and thereafter to the Pacific to make a last heroic gesture at Guadalcanal.

Fleet covering force mounted another strike by aircraft from *Victorious* on Norwegian ports on the way home. Again results were meagre; much was yet to be learned.

On 29 September the ten-ship PQ1 convoy left Reykjavik and arrived without incident. It was followed before the end of the year by seven more northbound convoys and four southbound 'empties' totalling over 100 merchant ship passages for the loss of only one. This was due mainly to the enemy's pre-occupation elsewhere although there was ominous activity among the German surface ships that had survived the Norwegian invasion of April 1940. Particular anxiety surrounded the movements of *Bismarck's* newly completed sister ship *Tirpitz*. In January 1942, she moved north to Trondheim and additional U-boats were also moved up. Although these movements were naturally construed by the British to be a threat to the convoys, they did in fact stem from a conviction by Hitler that Norway was to be invaded by the Allies.

February saw the daring break up-channel from Brest by the fast battleships *Scharnhorst* and *Gneisenau* and the heavy cruiser *Prinz Eugen*. The *Eugen* was then dispatched to Norway in company with the 'pocket battleship' *Scheer*, which were hunted by a powerful Home Fleet force including *Victorious*. Aircraft from the carrier were defeated by the usual appalling weather and the German ships reached safety with no more than a submarine torpedo into *Prinz Eugen*.

Opposition mounted

Meanwhile, the merchantmen ground on almost unmolested, a further five convoys passing north by mid-February. Admiral Tovey, the Home Fleet commander, viewed the gradually lengthening daylight hours and the continuing enemy concentration with misgivings and surmised, correctly, that the blow was about to fall. Consequently he arranged for the northbound PQ12 and the returning QP8 to sail simultaneously so as to pass in the danger areas, where they would be concentrated and covered the more easily by the British heavy forces. Each sailed on 1 March and they were timed to pass on the 7th between Jan Mayen and Bear Island. The enemy, aware of their progress, sailed *Tirpitz* and three large destroyers from Trondheim on the 6th to intercept.

For Tovey the situation was working well, for he had two heavy forces well poised for cutting off the enemy and as yet he was undetected. With the *Duke of York, Renown* and six destroyers staying close to the convoys, his own group of *King George V, Victorious, Berwick* and six destroyers sought action. As usual, the weather closed in and the carrier was unable to fly off any reconnaissance aircraft. For a whole day the two convoys, the Home Fleet and the enemy milled around within an 80-mile diameter zone and, incredibly, virtually without contact, although the German destroyers did get close enough at one stage to sink a convoy straggler.

On 8 March, the day following, the enemy abandoned the search and headed back. The intentions of *Tirpitz* were deciphered from radio interceptions and, in clearing weather,

early on the 9th *Victorious* made contact with search aircraft west of the Lofotens. Without delay a torpedo strike of 12 Albacores was vectored in to catch the battleship, which was steaming hard for Narvik. As she was heading upwind, the low performance of the British aircraft caused them difficulty in overtaking and getting into position. A co-ordinated attack was mounted in the face of severe AA fire and it was bitterly disappointing that their violently manoeuvring quarry escaped into Narvik unscathed, destroying two of her assailants as she went.

Convoy losses begin

The convoys had passed safely but the operation underlined the fact that, in those days before long-range radar, a carrier was no better than her aircraft — and they were not good. On his part the enemy had had a fright; his narrow escape had demonstrated again the value of a carrier and there followed one of the periodic flurries of activity to complete *Graf Zeppelin*. Again, fortunately, it was not to last.

Weather damage forced *Victorious* into dock and, with the immunity broken, the following convoy PQ13 was assailed by aircraft, destroyers and U-boats, and was fortunate to lose only five of its number.

More-powerful close escorts had to be found and the Americans, by then stretched by the demands of their own war, generously loaned the *Wasp* (CV7) to the Home Fleet. Her well-trained outfit of TBDs, SBDs and F4Fs could have made their mark in the north, but Malta's need at the time was even more urgent and *Wasp* spent her short time in European waters ferrying Spitfires to the beleaguered island.

CAM ship success

With the lengthening daylight of the northern spring the enemy reinforced his Norwegian-based Luftwaffe with torpedo-carrying aircraft and, although PQ15 and QP11 at the end of April included AA and CAM ships in the close escort and the newly repaired *Victorious* in the distant covering force, these ships were unable to prevent the fast low attacks in half-light conditions which claimed several victims.

Political expediency enforced the sailing of PQ16 late in May. It was the worst time of the year, the convoy was the largest to date and it faced the threat of the German surface units reinforced by over 260 aircraft. With the Home Fleet cover too far distant to intercept any move on the part of *Tirpitz*, the convoy battled alone against a hail of bombs and torpedoes. One of the four ships lost was the CAM ship *Empire Lawrence*, whose lone Hurricane had broken up an attack by seven torpedo-carrying He111s, destroying one, damaging a second and spoiling the aim of the remainder. Not for the first time the fighter returning to 'ditch' was shot down by 'friendly' gunners and its gallant pilot was wounded.

PQ17

With the virtually permanent daylight of the northern midsummer, commonsense demanded a break in these awful pilgrimages until the shades of autumn offered their slight cover, but the demands of the Russians were incessant and another operation was risked. Accordingly, a 36-ship convoy sailed on 27 June 1942. Its code was

HMS 'Hermes' was the first aircraft carrier laid down as such, in 1917. Her building proceeded at a leisurely pace and she was finally comissioned in 1923, and set the pattern of the starboard island layout that with very few exceptions has remained standard throughout the world. 'Hermes' served with the South Atlantic group, helping among other things to prevent the French Fleet from aiding the Axis, until 1941, when she moved to the Indian Ocean. There, just after refitting in Ceylon, she was caught close inshore without her aircraft aboard by the second of the Japanese raids on the island and was sunk in a heavy dive bombing attack.

PQ17. The Admiralty in London was well aware of the enemy's intention of making this a trial of strength; from the outset it seemed uncharacteristically apprehensive. A powerful Anglo-American covering force included the *Victorious* and, using the convoy as bait, it was hoped that one of the two powerful enemy surface groups could be brought to successful action. What upset the equation was air power.

British respect for the Luftwaffe precluded the use of major warships much eastward of the line Bear Island-Jan Mayen and the Germans (unknown to the British) had ordered their major ships to keep clear of any convoy that included a carrier in its escort. Thus, surface action was but a remote possibility from the outset. PQ17 had passed Bear Island before it suffered its first loss on 3 July and things seemed to be going comparatively smoothly. Although the main cover was far to the west, a powerful cruiser force still augmented the close escort. This force had orders to withdraw on the following day and the Admiralty was very concerned about the *Tirpitz, Scheer, Hipper* and six destroyers which had arrived at Altenfjord, near North Cape.

Convoy shattered

At this critical juncture a spell of bad weather broke the continuous aerial surveillance and the tired operations staff in London assumed the worst, that the enemy had sailed to intercept the convoy passing to the north. In fact the German force did not move until the 5th and then only on a short foray, as it had been instructed not to approach PQ17 because the whereabouts of *Victorious* were uncertain. But the damage was done and the convoy escort was ordered to return and its charges to scatter on the evening of 4 July.

During the afternoon of the 5th an uncomprehending enemy reconnaissance aircraft reported the area southeast of the ill-named Hope Island alive with unprotected merchantmen. Ten U-boats and the whole weight of KG30 were brought to bear on the ships, whose lonely ends brought more distress to the men of the Royal Navy than almost any other incident. They felt that they had been forced to desert their charges, only 11 of which survived.

The main conclusion to be drawn from this sad affair is that control is best left to a commander on the spot and it was unfortunate that it was not realized that the movements of the *Victorious* were having the same bogey effect on the enemy command as those of the *Tirpitz* were having on London. PQ17's awful fate meant that, for the remainder of the summer, the non-stop clatter of Soviet demands were to fall on deaf ears in London and Washington.

Avenger joins action

It was 2 September 1942 before the next convoy, PQ18, sailed — a group of 39 merchant ships outnumbered by its escorts. The distant Home Fleet did not include *Victorious*, which had been sent to the Pacific but, significantly, the new escort carrier *Avenger* was present, positioned in the rear line where her 12 Hurricane fighters

Left: HMS 'Battler', one of the American-built CVEs, pictured shortly after commissioning with torpedo-armed Swordfish aircraft being brought up on deck.

Inset: Two of the first batch of American-built CVEs, 'Avenger' and 'Biter', pressing on in heavy weather in the Atlantic. 'Avenger' was in service in time to take part in convoy PQ18 in September 1942, when her aircraft took a heavy toll of the German attackers. She was lost soon afterwards.

and AS Swordfish could give direct assistance to the convoy itself. Also in the main group were two AA ships and a CAM ship, the whole surrounded by a 'fighting destroyer escort', which had proved successful in the Mediterranean. Having decided on air rather than surface attack, the enemy was initially successful in decoying the *Avenger's* fighters away long enough to allow a massed torpedo attack by the He111s of the 'Lion' Geschwader I/KG26. Forty aircraft sank eight ships but made the error of returning to attempt to sink the threatening *Avenger*. This time all was ready and the enemy attack was shredded. For the loss of 13 ships, grievous enough, the Germans paid to the tune of 41 aircraft and three U-boats; one was victim to co-operation between the *Avenger's* Swordfish and an escorting destroyer.

Having so dramatically demonstrated the value of even a small carrier, it was a tragedy that all available flightdecks were withdrawn from the northern convoys for the North African landings of November 1942, none being available again until the following February. Meanwhile, as if to wipe the slate clean, ensuing outward and homebound convoys were re-coded JW and RA respectively, starting with number 51.

Raeder resigns

His aerial strike forces already severely mauled, the enemy resolved to smite JW51B with a powerful surface force — fortunately, as the convoy had no carrier. Sherbrooke's immortal destroyer action in the defeat of the German *Scheer* and *Hipper* was the result, the little British flotilla ships worrying the enemy constantly until heavier relief arrived. The extreme timidity shown by the German ships would probably have ended in their loss had a carrier been present but their poor showing was sufficient to save the convoy and send Hitler into a rage during which he resolved to de-commission all major fleet units, in turn producing the resignation of Grand Admiral Raeder. A victory indeed.

The escort carrier *Dasher* sailed in February 1943 with JW53 but was forced to return with weather damage. Barely a month later she was destroyed by explosion in the Clyde and again the hopes of regular carrier escort were dashed. Again the Americans had plugged the gap in British Home Fleet carrier strength by the repeat of a loan, the absence of *Victorious* in the Pacific being offset partly by the little *Ranger* and a cruiser escorting force. As only the *Furious* was available in addition and the only CVEs available were needed on the Atlantic routes, Arctic convoys were discontinued until November 1943. Their resumption surprised the enemy and the first

movements passed without challenge; as they had been tracked and reported, however, surface attack looked a likely bet. Raeder's successor, Dönitz, was in fact planning to use *Scharnhorst* for the purpose, to recover some of the prestige so decisively lost a year before. Unfortunately, the *Ranger's* force had returned home in the November and the Home Fleet dispositions to cover the JW and RA55 movements were again without a carrier. The brilliant ambush and destruction of *Scharnhorst* in the darkness of an Arctic Boxing Day were, in any case, an affair to be settled by the gun. Its successful conclusion heralded better times for the northern trade.

The battle is won

Convoy JW57 sailed in February 1944 with the escort carrier *Chaser* in its escort. With their surface and aerial forces in the north very depleted, the Germans put no fewer than 14 U-boats into the effort against JW57 and the complementary RA57. Five of the U-boats were lost, three as a result of *Chaser's* presence. Appeals for Luftwaffe reinforcements to deal with CVEs in future could not be answered and, as ensuing convoys disposed of two carriers apiece as Allied strength grew, the battle was won; except for the high summer period, a monthly cycle was followed until May 1945.

The Arctic run could well be cited as one where carrier support would have made an incalculable difference had it been continuously available from an earlier date. On the Royal Navy's southern flank the weather was more clement, but there the advantages stopped, as the pitfalls were as numerous.

Mediterranean activity hots up

By early 1942 activity in the Mediterranean was at a low ebb. The fleet based on Alexandria at the eastern end was virtually blockaded by enemy air power after the withdrawal of *Illustrious* and *Formidable* through action damage, and the Gibraltar force was inhibited by the recent loss of *Ark Royal*. The latter's replacement by *Eagle* at the end of 1941 was therefore greeted with some relief, particularly as the enemy was stepping up his aerial assault on Malta. Already the operation of ships from the fleet base of Valletta's Grand Harbour was becoming more difficult; the fighter defences and essential supplies were diminishing through continuous attrition and an airborne landing of the type that had taken Crete seemed a very real danger.

In January 1942 a relief convoy had run to the island from Gibraltar comparatively easily. Its lack of carrier support was acceptable as air cover was available from facilities in Cyrenaica, augmented by

The carriers operating in the North Atlantic and the Arctic suffered dour conditions. Here crews are clearing the flightdeck of ice and snow before HMS 'Fencer's' Swordfish can get airborne.

fighters from Malta itself during the final phase. Rommel's Afrika Korps upset this arrangement by advancing rapidly eastward along the North Africa coast; not only were the airfields thus lost but they were available for the operation of the enemy's aircraft, a double misfortune.

With attention focused on the western basin, it appeared that a convoy quickly slipped through from Alexandria would stand an excellent chance. Accordingly, on 12 February MW9 consisting of three high-class freighters of the Clan and Union Castle Lines left Alexandria. In spite of a powerful cruiser and destroyer escort, German and Italian bombing sank two of the precious merchantmen and sent the third into Tobruk severely damaged. In addition, a powerful Italian force, including a battle-ship, was at sea to complete the job but they did not succeed in finding the compara-tively lightweight British naval escort. What was particularly galling to the Alexandria force was the arrival at about that time at the southern end of the Suez Canal of the

new carrier *Indomitable*. When she could have been so usefully employed in chastising an increasingly confident Italian fleet, she was merely calling for fighter aircraft to be ferried out for the disastrous affair in the Far East.

Malta reinforced

At Gibraltar, *Eagle* was reinforced by the old *Argus* for the first of a planned series of ferry runs to strengthen Malta's fighter defences. This became a frequent chore in the months that followed, assisted on a couple of operations by the American carrier *Wasp*. Between them they put a total of about 300 fighters into the island, indispensable not only for defence purposes but also to guarantee that merchantmen that successfully ran the gauntlet had at least a chance of discharging before being sunk at their moorings.

The fighter reinforcement was made as a matter of urgency after the fate of the four-ship MW10 convoy from Alexandria in mid-March 1942. Again, no air cover could be

The only remaining British fleet carrier available for service, the 'Eagle', with the old 'Argus', also put several loads of RAF fighters on to Malta. Here 'Eagle' is seen with fighters crowding her flightdeck in the Mediterranean with a Queen Elizabeth-class battleship as escort.

provided and the ships were soon spotted by an Italian aircraft which guided in a powerful surface force, including the battleship *Littorio* and three large cruisers. The convoy escort was under the command of Admiral Vian (of *Altmark* fame) and they encountered the enemy in the Gulf of Sirte soon after lunch on the 22nd under conditions of a rising gale. Best described as Nelsonian, the action that followed was a model of its kind and one of the finest of the war. The British ships could muster only 6-inch and smaller guns against the Italian's 15-inch and 8-inch, but they interposed themselves between the enemy and the convoy, laying smoke continuously and manoeuvring threateningly in and out of it. Without radar, the Italians were blind to Vian's actual strength and were unable to use their superior speed. For the span of a long afternoon they were probed, goaded and menaced; although they suffered little material damage from the light British projectiles, their spirit wavered and broke and, to the great relief of the escort, they retired.

But convoy lost

Yet again, however, there was to be no happy ending for the four cargo ships which, so far, had emerged unscathed. Delayed by the action, their final approach to Malta was during the forenoon and their close escort was by then perilously low on AA ammunition. Only two out of the four survived the ensuing heavy bombing by the German II/FlK and they too were quickly disposed of in the Grand Harbour before they had time to discharge half their cargoes. This was at a time when RAF strength was at a low ebb and the survival of the island obviously depended largely upon more fighters.

The *Wasp* flew in over 90 Spitfires in two runs (Operations Calender and Bowery) before she was recalled to join the Pacific fleet. Her efforts, together with those of the *Argus* and *Eagle*, resulted in the regaining of a certain measure of air superiority in the continuing trial of strength that had already reduced the island's airstrips to dusty craters and rendered the harbour virtually untenable. With Malta's striking forces brought to a state of near impotence, the enemy could run his desperately urgent North African convoys without challenge except by submarines. Without doubt, Malta could easily have been carried by a resolute airborne operation at that time but, incredibly, it was left alone by the Germans who preferred to take the strategically inferior Tobruk.

This cardinal error was compounded by Kesselring who, as commander of Luftflotte II, opined that the island was eliminated as an operational base, a statement the immediate upshot of which was the withdrawal of much of the Luftwaffe's Sicilian strength to the Russian and North African fronts. During May, therefore, the populace endured a much reduced scale of attack and the marauders themselves were surprised by an increasingly effective defence as the carriers reinforced the island's fighter strength.

Operation Harpoon

Nevertheless, the defenders existed at bare subsistence level and plans were made for a complex resupply operation to be run in

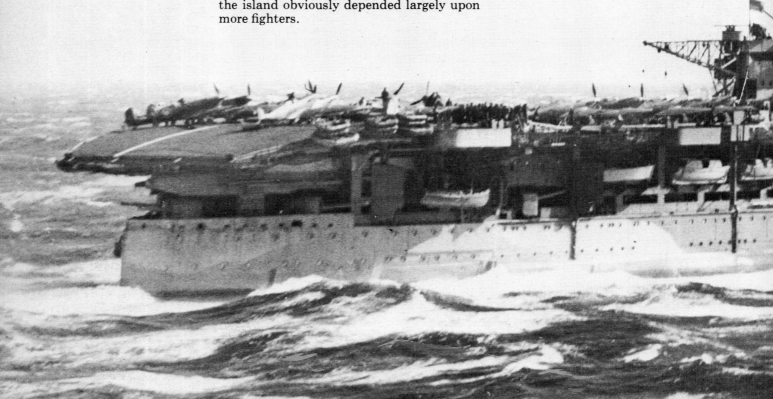

simultaneously from east and west. From the Gibraltar end came half a dozen merchantmen en route from the UK; they passed the Rock on the night of 11/12 June 1942, gathering an escort including a battleship, four cruisers and 17 destroyers and the carriers *Eagle* and *Argus*. The movement, codenamed Operation Harpoon, went well until the forenoon of the 14th when the ships came into the operational range of enemy aircraft based on Sardinia. With only a score of Sea Hurricanes and Fulmars between them, the old carriers were hard put to provide anything like a proper cover; what there was could be penetrated all too easily and Italian S79s, co-ordinating their attack with high-level bombers, succeeded in torpedoing and sinking the first of the convoy, and damaging a cruiser which was forced to return.

By evening the convoy was off Bizerta and approaching the narrows between Cape Bon and Sicily, and into range of the remaining Ju87s and 88s from their bases on the island. Until nightfall, the convoy spent some lively hours successfully dodging three separate air attacks, during which the heavy covering force pulled out and set a return course for Gibraltar, it being considered too hazardous to risk them any farther east.

In spite of the odds building up, things were still going to plan. Only one merchant-man had been lost and the other five now had about 24 hours steaming to reach Malta. Their cover was now restricted to the close escort of an AA cruiser and destroyers which proved inadequate at daybreak on the 15th, when the convoy, standing out from

the Tunisian coast, was attacked by two large Italian cruisers with destroyer support. Two British destroyers were soon disabled and the rest of the close escort was drawn to their assistance, leaving their charges an easy target for the Stukas of III/StG. One was sunk and another disabled and, during the long day as they crept closer under the protective fighter cover from Malta, a third was heavily damaged. Both lame ducks had eventually to be dispatched to allow the remainder to proceed. Two made the Grand Harbour out of the six that set out, losses that in other times would have been considered unacceptable but which were to be all too typical of the Malta run in 1942.

Operation Vigorous

Simultaneously with the arrival of the Harpoon ships in the Mediterranean, the other convoy, MW11 codenamed Vigorous, had been sailed in several groups from Alexandria, Port Said and Haifa. Eleven merchant ships were involved and their covering force included eight cruisers and 26 destroyers. Some of them had been withdrawn from the Eastern Fleet for the operation but none of its modern carriers — *Illustrious*, *Indomitable* and *Formidable* — could be spared from the more immediate challenge of the Japanese. The convoy had thus to rely on air cover from such bases as still remained at the eastern end of the North African coast, and Malta. In addition, the escort could muster nothing heavier than 6-inch and 5.25-inch guns to match any challenge by Italian surface forces and, as a pathetic gesture — and a measure of what

the fleet was by then reduced to — the old demilitarized battleship *Centurion*, long a target ship, went along as moral support.

Things did not augur well from the outset, even with the control in the hands of the redoubtable Vian. MW11 was reported by the enemy on 12 June, the day after it left, and it was soon attacked by Stukas of I/KG54 based on Crete. One cargo ship was damaged sufficiently to force her to make for Tobruk and a second, with machinery trouble, followed her the next day, escorted by two corvettes. This latter group had the misfortune to be spotted by a mixed force of 40 Stukas and Ju88s; the merchantman was sunk but it had taken the heat off the main convoy for a while.

For the whole of the next day the convoy kept doggedly on, losing another of its number to persistent bombing. That night a new form of pestilence arrived in the form of German S-boats out of Derna which struck at a most inopportune moment. A powerful Italian squadron, including two battleships, was known to be at sea searching for the convoy, the light composition of whose escort was well known to them. It was while making a feint to the eastward that the S-boats attacked, torpedoing two of the escort.

Vian gives up

In spite of the risk, a westerly course was resumed before dawn on the 15th and the Italians, by then a bare 200 miles distant, were heavily attacked by shore-based aircraft. A designed British submarine trap failed to spring and, with the enemy closing fast, MW11 was again turned east. After a report that both of the Italian capital ships had been torpedoed from the air, the convoy yet again reversed course toward Malta. The report was proved false and discretion was given to Vian to retire; although the faint-hearted Italians had reversed course, the convoy was under heavy and sustained air attack with no air cover and running low on ammunition. Damage was mounting and Vian decided to call it a day; to such a man as he the decision was more courageous than that to go on.

Thus, the Vigorous operation failed, at a total cost of a cruiser, three destroyers and two merchantmen. Without carrier support it was obvious that no more convoys could be fought through from the eastern end until the airbases on the North African coast were again available, and at the time the Afrika Korps was still pushing even farther east toward the Nile Delta. Things began to look gloomy for Malta's prospects of survival. Out of the three latest operations, seven high-quality freighters had been lost and only five had been fought through, three of which had sunk on arrival. Never was the need of a modern carrier more keenly felt.

The August Convoy

The meagre deliveries by the Harpoon convoy could not sustain the island for long. Knowing that the supreme test of strength was about to come, the enemy stepped up his aerial activity over Malta and reinforced Luftwaffe units in readiness. Small parcels of essential supplies were still run in by submarine and fast minelayers and *Eagle*, working from Gibraltar, succeeded in flying in another 60 Spitfires in two missions during July. Not until August had the Royal Navy assembled the escort necessary to fight through the next, all-or-nothing, convoy. It involved two battleships, seven cruisers and 32 destroyers, together with the three carriers *Eagle*, *Indomitable* and *Victorious*.

In addition, the old *Furious* went along with yet more fighters for the island. Both sides paused before the commitment, until on 10 August the 14-ship convoy passed Gibraltar eastbound. To the planners it was codenamed Pedestal, but it was to become immortal simply as the August Convoy.

By passing the Strait during the hours of darkness this great concentration of ships eluded the eyes on both shores and made precious ground eastwards as far as Ibiza without being reported. No attacks developed immediately and *Furious* began flying off her Malta-bound Spitfires late in the morning from an extreme range of over 500 miles and standing fighter patrols were put up. There was, as yet, no sign of an

aerial attack as the convoy was still outside the range of Sardinian-based aircraft but the calm blue sea concealed other dangers, a line of seven German and Italian submarines. One of them, Rosenbaum's U73, passed undetected to well within range of *Eagle* and put a full salvo of four torpedoes into her from 500 yards. Few modern ships could have withstood such massive injury and the tired old ship, twentieth bearer of an honoured name, rolled over and rapidly disappeared, meeting her death in the service of the island to which so much of her active life had been devoted. Later in the day the situation was almost repeated as *Furious* turned back, her mission completed, and

The fourth carrier of the Illustrious Class, HMS 'Indomitable', was assigned to the Eastern Fleet, but was active on occasions in home waters and the Mediterranean, including in Operation Pedestal (the August Convoy) in which she received heavy damage. Here she is seen in 1944 before departure for the Far East.

ran into the same submarine trap. Fortunately, her assailant was Italian and was promptly dispatched by the escort.

Heavy aerial attack

By dusk the enemy was in range and a heavy torpedo and bombing attack was mounted in the tricky fading light. This, like those of the following morning, was small in scope and met with little success as the carriers' fighters took their measure. Midday on the 12th saw the assembly south of Sardinia and the enemy mounted a full-blooded strike of nearly 100 bomber and torpedo aircraft with fighter escort.

In the face of a lively and resolute defence they succeeded in damaging only one of the convoy, which was forced to drop out. Soon afterwards a pair of the new Italian Reggiane 2001 fighter-bombers, each with a heavy bomb, made an immaculate strike out of the sun. Their target was *Victorious* and, in an attack strongly reminiscent of those later to be practised by the Japanese, they put their projectiles into their target and were away so suddenly that not a shot was fired. Fortunately the tough armoured flightdeck was well up to the task and both bombs, in shallow trajectories, bounced harmlessly off and broke up, but it could have been serious on a thinner-skinned ship.

Things began to hot up as the ships passed through a second concentration of submarines. They were all Italian and lacked sufficient resolution, achieving nothing for the loss of one of their number. Later in the evening, a well-synchronized attack was made by 14 Italian S79 torpedo bombers and about 30 Stukas with adequate fighter cover. Exhausted naval pilots and gunners put all they had left into the defence of their violently manoeuvring ships. As one of the torpedoes separated a destroyer from her stern the Stukas wheeled into one of their set-piece attacks, singling out the *Indomitable*. With the fighters lured away by the low-level S79s it was all too easy and three 500kg bombs found their mark. Pierced and burning she was out of the fight and only *Victorious* remained. Although 13 of the precious cargo ships still remained, the escort had suffered grievously and, with Cape Bon looming up and light fading, it was time for the heavy escort to turn back, leaving the merchantmen and close escort to pass on through the narrows on the last lap.

Heavy casualties

During the next two hours, as they wearily crossed the shallows of the Skerki Bank in the fading day, they suffered two submarine and one air attack. With the carriers gone and long-distance fighter cover from Malta withdrawn for the dark hours, the initiative was with the opposition; the price was a cruiser and two merchant ships sunk and two of each damaged.

Through the calm night the survivors kept close under the coast and by the early hours had rounded Cape Bon. But the darkness proved a false cloak; it concealed a 14-strong combined force of German S-boats and Italian MAS boats, poor radar targets and undetected under the looming land. Between 01.20 and 04.30 on 13 August the convoy, strung out as it threaded the coastal lane, was hit hard, losing four more of the precious merchantmen and another cruiser mortally damaged, without any reply on the small fleet marauders. So much had been achieved and now it seemed to be slipping away. Nevertheless, the ships regrouped and stood out from the Tunisian coast into the dawn and the final 12 hours of the ordeal.

With daylight appeared both fighters from Malta and the familiar enemy 87s, 88s and 111s, of which there seemed an inexhaustible supply. At what would have

been breakfast time had anybody remembered, a last merchantman was lost as her cargo of ammunition and aviation spirit detonated to a Stuka's bomb. Four more were damaged including the tanker *Ohio*, which finally made it, scorched and blasted, bearing the wreckage of an enemy aircraft that had crashed aboard.

Survivors arrive

To add wings to the last miles came reports of Italian fleet movements to the north of Sicily. They had no material effect due to the attentions of British submarines, and that afternoon three cargo ships and their escort entered the Grand Harbour before the massed populace of Malta; two more of the convoy were later assisted in. A carrier, two cruisers, a destroyer and nine merchant ships had added their remains to those already littering the route.

Never was an operation more fiercely contested, with both sides well aware of the fruits of failure. Much of its final success was due to the early efforts of the carriers, but in the final analysis, it was a result of the sum total of the courage and resolution of each who was present. Malta's survival was assured as it resumed the task of strangulation of Rommel's supply routes. With this slow attrition the enemy's power to continue was reduced and the North African campaign stalemated north of the Great Sand Sea before a place called El Alamein. As the enemy withered, the British — the canal at their backs — grew daily stronger. From November 1942 the Afrika Korps began the long trek westward, a trek that could have but one end. Rommel, a land animal, had been defeated by seapower as surely as had his predecessor Napoleon a century and a quarter earlier.

In that theatre at least the defensive phase was past; when the aircraft carrier returned to the Mediterranean it was as a sword rather than a shield.

A painting by R. V. Pitchforth, official artist to the Admiralty in 1944, now in the Imperial War Museum, showing HMS 'Brecon', a Type 4 Hunt-class destroyer, escorting an aircraft carrier off Algiers.

Carrier v carrier: Coral Sea and Midway

Having consolidated their occupation of Malaya and the East Indies, the Japanese set about the first steps in neutralizing Australia as a base for an Allied counter-offensive. They included taking the large island of New Guinea to act as an effective buffer and the occupation of those islands that commanded the vital sea routes by which American reinforcements could reach Australia. The twin operations were to start from the enemy advanced base at Rabaul, on New Britain in the Bismarck Archipelago, with the initial aims of landings on Tulagi in the Solomons and at Port Moresby on the southern side of New Guinea. Tulagi was a strategically situated island with a good deep-water anchorage and thought to be a suitable base for the occupation of the Solomons, from which the advance would continue in stages, probably as far as Samoa. Although the enemy already had a foothold on the Huon Gulf in northern New Guinea, the jungle-clad littoral of the Owen Stanley range inhibited any southward advance and the Port Moresby landing was designed to outflank the obstacle.

Aided by an excellent understanding of Japanese ciphers, the Americans knew of the enemy's intentions and fully understood their implications. The outcome depended upon air superiority. If the enemy possessed it, he would succeed; if he could be deprived of it, he would not. A first American move was the occupation of Espiritu Santo for use as a centre for counter-operations but little work had been carried out there when events overtook it with the news on 20 April 1942 of a major enemy fleet movement from its main base at Truk. Admiral Nimitz, C-in-C in the Pacific (CINCPAC), reacted by moving *Lexington* (CV2) and *Yorktown* (CV5) into the New Hebrides area. His other carriers, *Enterprise* (CV6) and *Hornet* (CV8), were still far to the north after the Doolittle raid on Japan.

Complacent Japanese

Possibly a little complacent from their unbroken series of successes, the Japanese had allocated only a small scratch force of minor warships for the occupation of Tulagi and its conversion to a base. For Port Moresby, a force of 11 transports was given a powerful close destroyer escort. Area cover for both groups was to be provided by the small carrier *Shoho*, moving independently with a four-cruiser escort, while to the north of the Solomons chain, a task group built around the formidable *Shokaku* and *Zuikaku* cruised to counter any major opposition.

American dispositions were complete by 1 May, with each available carrier forming the nucleus of a separate task force. Thus, *Yorktown* headed TF17 and *Lexington* TF11, each with cruiser and destroyer escort, supported by a mobile Australian/American force designated TF44.

BISMARCK ARCHIPELAGO

NEW GUINEA

NEW BRITAIN

PORT MORESBY

0800/8

SUPPORT GROUP
3 CRUISERS
2 DESTROYERS

AUSTRALIA

When the enemy eventually hit Tulagi on 3 May 1942, he appeared to have achieved surprise and quickly overran the small garrison. Reaction from Fletcher's TF17 was swift but it required a hard night's steaming to be in a position south of Guadalcanal at first light and close enough to launch a 40-aircraft strike. The mixed force of Devastator torpedo bombers (TBD) and Dauntless dive bombers (SBD) battled their way through the towering cloud masses of a tropical depression, emerging in bright sunlight just short of their target. All unsuspecting, the enemy was soon four warships the poorer, including a destroyer. *Yorktown* worked overtime to mount two further raids and, although the Japanese still held the island, they had lost their small craft, stores and, more important, the majority of the 'Mavis' flying-boats sent for use at the new base for reconnaissance. TF17 then rapidly withdrew to the south from the hornet's nest that it had stirred up and, by remaining under a band of frontal cloud eluded the enemy's depleted scouting forces. Simultaneously, the powerful Japanese carriers to the north, believing the *Yorktown* group to be alone, headed for the eastern end of the Solomons at speed to cut it off from a likely retirement on Espiritu Santo.

Lexington force unsuspected

By then the Port Moresby invasion force had sailed from Rabaul, being joined on passage by the surviving Tulagi group, and the big carriers, once having 'turned the corner' into the Coral Sea swept westward to cover them. They saw nothing of TF17, which was hardly surprising as it was well to the south, refuelled and in close company with the, as yet, unsuspected TF11. Back in business early on the 6th and aware of both the *Shoho* and Main Group's presence, the Americans put up dawn searches and narrowly missed sighting the enemy. The Japanese were keeping strict radio silence and relying on shore-based aircraft to pinpoint the *Yorktown*. Both sides were in fact sighted by

USS 'Yorktown' (CV5) pictured at her first anchorage in Hampton Roads, Virginia, in October 1937. 'Yorktown' was hit and badly damaged by dive bombers during the Midway action and sank three days later despite desperate attempts to save her.

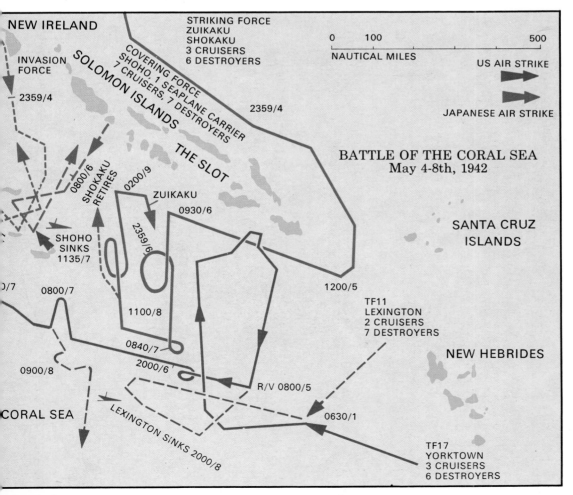

NEW IRELAND

INVASION FORCE

– 2359/4

SOLOMON ISLANDS

STRIKING FORCE
ZUIKAKU
SHOKAKU
3 CRUISERS
6 DESTROYERS

COVERING FORCE
SHOHO, 1 SEAPLANE CARRIER
7 CRUISERS, 7 DESTROYERS

2359/4

0   100   500
NAUTICAL MILES

US AIR STRIKE

JAPANESE AIR STRIKE

BATTLE OF THE CORAL SEA
May 4-8th, 1942

SANTA CRUZ
ISLANDS

THE SLOT

0800/6
SHOKAKU RETIRES
0200/9
ZUIKAKU
0930/6
2359/6

SHOHO
SINKS
1135/7

0/7
0800/7
1100/8
0840/7
2000/6
0900/8

R/V 0800/5

1200/5

TF11
LEXINGTON
2 CRUISERS
7 DESTROYERS

NEW HEBRIDES

CORAL SEA

LEXINGTON SINKS 2000/8

0630/1

TF17
YORKTOWN
3 CRUISERS
6 DESTROYERS

each other's aircraft during the day but neither sighting report was received and it was the American commander, Fletcher, who first obtained a 'fix' when Army Air Force B17s unsuccessfully attacked the *Shoho* group and saw the invasion force. The Americans took up a westerly course to be in a position to intercept the transports at dawn on the 7th, while *Shokaku* and *Zuikaku* headed southward but well astern.

Before first light on the 7th both forces vectored off the usual dawn searches and an SBD from *Yorktown* soon picked up part of the screen of the main invasion force. Its report, however, became garbled in transmission, giving Fletcher the impression that these were the large enemy carriers whose destruction he so desired. Seventy strike aircraft plus fighter escort were in the air before the mistake was realized but Fletcher let them proceed even though he knew the unsighted enemy main group could not be far distant.

His determination was rewarded when one of *Lexington's* aircraft came across *Shoho* in the act of flying-off a strike. The little carrier put a cover of fighters into the air but they were roughly handled by the F4Fs while the TBDs came in hard and low. Her defences swamped, *Shoho* staggered away blazing from the combined effects of up to 13 heavy bomb hits and possibly seven torpedoes. She lingered briefly before blowing up and sinking and, with the immortal signal 'Scratch one flat-top', the jubilant American flyers winged back, having lost only three of their number. Moreover, the invasion force wavered and turned back; it was never to return.

Mistaken identity

Curiously, meanwhile, the enemy's dawn search had an outcome much the same as Fletcher's. Missing the American carriers,

the 'Kates' spotted the fleet tanker *Neosho* with her single destroyer escort; fortunately, as already related, TF17.5 (as the combined force was now known) had already topped-up from her, or the ensuing events would have been serious. Reporting not what they saw but what they wished to see, the enemy scouts indentified the oiler as a carrier. Hara, the Japanese commander, responded cagily with a small strike of 15 'Kates' with bombs. It did not succeed in its object and neither did a second force, yet, although now aware that she was no carrier, the Japanese wasted even more time in mounting a major attack by 'Val' dive bombers. Blazing and holed, the tanker's sub-division still defied destruction and she was to drift for another four days before her crew was removed and she was scuttled.

During this affair TF17.5 was 300 miles distant dealing with the *Shoho* but remaining undetected under low cloud. Hara, chagrined by his lack of success and the incoming news, headed at full speed for the spot from which it was estimated that *Shoho's* executioners must have flown. Ahead flew a 27-strong mixed torpedo and dive bomber force but, unfortunately for them, Fletcher had no intention of hanging around and was pulling out fast to the south, recovering his own strike. The enemy formations overshot in the poor conditions and then wasted precious fuel in searching without success. Soon forced to return, they passed close enough to the Americans to be bounced by the CAP, whose Wildcats

The US Navy's main dive bomber throughout the Pacific war was the SBD Dauntless. Notes on the SBD's performance appear on page 49.

Below left: Mainspring of the Japanese aerial armoury was the B5N 'Kate' and a fleet strength of more than 400 was deployed by seven carriers at the start of the Pacific war. The 'Kate' was the world's first carrier-borne monoplane torpedo bomber and the first Japanese carrier aircraft with retractable landing gear. The main production B5N had a top speed of 164mph, a ceiling of over 25,000ft and could carry a 1760lb torpedo or three 750lb bombs.

earned their name in the tearing melee among the tropical thunderheads. Nine Japanese aircraft fell to the guns of the stubby F4Fs and the remainder were so scattered and disorientated that some even attempted to land on *Yorktown* in the gathering gloom; they were dissuaded! Only four made their own flightdecks and honours so far were with Fletcher as the opposing forces, aware of each other's close proximity, steered to open the range and prepare for the morrow.

Spoiling for a fight

Dawn on 8 May saw the two fleets only about 170 miles apart. Each was spoiling for a fight and had scouts in the air before first light. So certain were the Japanese of Fletcher's whereabouts that they searched only a 90-degree sector and actually had strike aircraft in the air before the first

sighting report was received at 08.20. Range to target was short enough to permit a powerful cover of Zeros.

Lexington, less certain, mounted searches in all directions out to a radius of 300 miles and the two sides made contact almost simultaneously when an SBD accurately defined Hara's force. Within minutes a 90-strong strike was winging a reciprocal course to the similar-sized enemy formations. Aboard the carriers, anxious eyes on each side looked for reassurance to the orbiting CAPs overhead. History was in the making as, for the first time, opposing fleets were to do battle without sighting each other.

In the heavy cloud the American formation lost cohesion, with the TBDs low under the murk and the SBDs necessarily up at 17,000 feet. Arriving first, the *Yorktown* dive bombers waited briefly for

The Japanese carrier 'Shoho' well alight after being torpedoed in the Coral Sea action in May 1942.

the remainder as, far below, the big enemy carriers chalked their wakes across breaks in the cloud. For freedom of movement they were about eight miles apart, with *Zuikaku* making for the cover of a rain squall while *Shokaku* was committed to an upwind course as shé launched further aircraft.

Shokaku afire

Patrolling Zeros began to take a close interest in the Dauntlesses and no further time was wasted; so precipitous were the dives that the pilots were half-blinded by the fogging of their canopies. Nevertheless, two 1000-pounders lanced the *Shokaku's* deck, one at each end, starting a serious fire and preventing further deck operations. As the 24 dive bombers drew the enemy fighters, the nine TBDs went in unopposed but, although they claimed 'three sure hits' on their return, no torpedoes had found a target.

Few of the *Lexington's* force made contact at all and those that did could not distress the burning *Shokaku* further. Nevertheless, it was still thought that the Japanese carrier was mortally injured and the worrying flight back on fast-emptying fuel tanks was the lighter for it. In extremis, some landed on *Yorktown's* deck and it was as well that they did, as things had happened fast in their absence with the enemy hitting TF17.5 only 20 minutes after its own blow had been delivered.

The American carriers, too, had separated in cloudless conditions and supplemented the standing Wildcat patrol by putting every available SBD up to 2000 feet with instructions to break up the enemy's formations of torpedoes. Nine 'Kates' made for each carrier while 33 unmolested 'Val' dive bombers flew high above. *Yorktown* was fortunate in being hit only once, even so, the 550-pounder sliced down to below hangar deck level before exploding. She was lucky not to be seriously damaged.

Lexington blows up

The large *Lexington* was the subject of a co-ordinated attack by six surviving B5Ns and the 'Vals'. Observers scarcely breathed as two torpedo tracks passed under the ship; as she steered to parallel two more, the final pair hit her, both on the port side. Two bombs had also found their mark, but as the damage control parties bent to their task, things did not look too bad, with fires coming under control and the ship's list neutralized by counter-flooding. A score of enemy aircraft had been shot down and *Lexington's* own aircraft were still being operated in spite of both elevators being temporarily knocked out. Unfortunately a more insidious danger lay in the fracturing of aviation fuel (avgas) mains and tank bulkheads. Being an early conversion, she had aviation fuel tanks built integrally with the hull, whereas later ships had separate

containments supported by, but not part of, the structure.

Although sited inboard of the bulges, tank seams were started by the shock of the explosions and fumes began to accumulate, resulting in a massive explosion an hour after the attack. From that point she was doomed, as fuel flowed freely to feed the fires. Still landing on aircraft and possessing full power, she was gradually paralysed by a series of detonations. Machinery spaces had to be shut down, power was lost, and hoses no longer had pressure. It was time to go. Evacuation was calm, with crewmen standing on the flightdeck eating 'salvaged' ice-cream from their steel helmets as they waited to transfer to a destroyer alongside. Shortly after sunset, deserted, the great ship received a *coup de grace* from the escort and the score was even.

The battle of the Coral Sea had been the first real setback to the Japanese; their invasion plans had been thwarted, New Guinea held out and the savaged *Shokaku* returned home as evidence of their enemy's resolve. But it was not a clearcut Allied victory. *Lexington* was the greater material loss and it set in train the requirements leading to the recall of the *Wasp* from the North Atlantic at a time when her presence could have been decisive on the Arctic route. It also highlighted — not for the last time — the awful susceptibility of American carriers to fire.

The Midway plan

A tenuous balance of power remained but it was to be weighted dramatically within a month. Yamamoto, the able commander of the Imperial Fleet's main body, had evolved a complex plan to take Midway Island, territory so sensitive to the Americans that it would inevitably provoke a major fleet movement, resulting in interception by a superior Japanese force and destruction after a showdown on the scale of Jutland. That the island could not subsequently be held was immaterial as it would have served its purpose.

Two pictures of USS 'Lexington' (CV2) after being hit by torpedoes and bombs in the Coral Sea battle show aircraft packing the deck as damage control parties struggle to control the fires and, inset, crew abandoning ship as the fire spreads, just before the explosion that finished her off.

One of the Japanese Shokaku-class carriers, either 'Shokaku' or 'Zuikaku', badly damaged and burning, turning abruptly in an endeavour to avoid the continuing American attack by torpedo and dive bombers.

Yamamoto's main concern was to get his major strength to a suitable ambush position without arousing American suspicions. To effect this he would have shore stations exchange W/T traffic with a fictitious fleet while the striking force took up its station under a cloak of total wireless silence. In addition, a feint operation was to be mounted against the Aleutian Islands; as the chain leads across the North Pacific to Alaska, it was hoped that the Americans' main strength would be divided in its reactions and priorities.

A plan on such homeric scale required the greater part of the Japanese fleet. Admiral Nagumo, the ravisher of Pearl Harbor, was returning with his carrier group (less the damaged *Shokaku*, and *Zuikaku* which had lost the major part of her aircrew at the Coral Sea). Supported by a pair of battle-ships and seaplane-carrying heavy cruisers, his task would be to reduce the island's defences to a point where the occupation force could go in. The force was borne in 16 transports, covered by two specialist seaplane carriers, two further battleships and eight cruisers. No fewer than 45 destroyers were allocated to the two forces.

Feelings of invincibility

Yamamoto himself, with the venerable *Hosho* and three battleships, would be so placed as to be a mobile reinforcement to either the Midway or the Aleutian oper-ations. The latter absorbed a further three carriers, four battleships and eight cruisers in two groups; they were intended to draw the Americans by hitting Attu and Kiska a full day ahead of the planned assault on Midway.

Any feelings of invincibility in the Japanese armada were understandable but misplaced, as the Americans, although materially inferior, had the tremendous advantage of having broken enemy codes to a point where the bulk of the Midway plan had been appreciated a month before. They who would surprise were about to be surprised.

Knowledge of the impending raid was one thing; what to do about it was something else entirely. Carriers obviously were the key to success and the Americans at that moment were reduced to only two, *Enter-prise* and *Hornet*. *Yorktown*, undergoing repair of her Coral Sea damage at Pearl Harbor, was cobbled together in 48 hours and fairly flew to sea, gathering her aircraft aboard as the went. The *Saratoga* was in dock at Bremerton after a torpedoing by an enemy submarine in January. She, too, was prematurely put to sea but in spite of her massive shaft horsepower and top speed of nearly 35 knots she was to arrive a day late.

Admiral Nimitz formed two task forces around his three carriers. Spruance took command of TF16, comprising *Enterprise* and *Hornet* with six cruisers and destroyers. Fletcher's *Yorktown* formed the nucleus of TF17 with a brace of cruisers and destroyers as escort. The lack of battleships was offset by the possession of Midway itself, whose airfields were reinforced until they fairly bulged with aircraft.

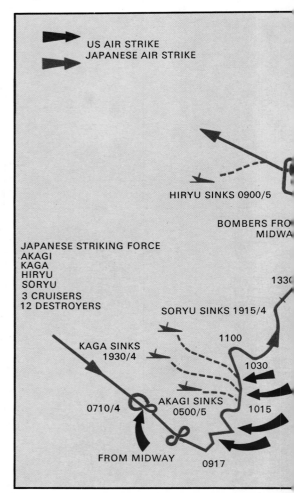

US AIR STRIKE
JAPANESE AIR STRIKE

HIRYU SINKS 0900/5

BOMBERS FRO
MIDWA

JAPANESE STRIKING FORCE
AKAGI
KAGA
HIRYU
SORYU
3 CRUISERS
12 DESTROYERS

1330

SORYU SINKS 1915/4

1100

KAGA SINKS
1930/4

1030

AKAGI SINKS
0500/5

1015

0710/4

FROM MIDWAY

0917

Aleutian anti-climax

All the Japanese formations sailed between 25 and 27 May, dependent upon their speed and passage length. They kept strict R/T silence and left from both Japan and advanced bases, causing problems to the Americans, who were relying for sighting reports on submarines and long-range B17 and PBY Catalina flights from Midway. By 2 June nothing had been reported and the US carrier groups had combined, marking time in a position about 350 miles northeast of the island and well placed to surprise any assault by the enemy. At first light on the following morning, in poor weather but right on time, aircraft from *Ryujo* and the new carrier *Junyo* attacked the Aleutians in a series of strikes that found very little to destroy. Some resistance was offered by American fighters but the carriers were not attacked and everything had an air of anti-climax. The Americans were obviously not falling for the ruse.

At about the same time that the defenders of the Aleutians were missing their breakfast a far-ranging PBY sighted a large group of ships about 700 miles southwest of Midway. Suspected as being the invasion force, it was left unmolested until mid-afternoon when, its identity confirmed, it was bombed by

B17s without result. This low-key reaction puzzled the Japanese, but Nimitz was after bigger game in the shape of Nagumo's carrier group, suspected of lurking under the thick overcast of a front coming down from the northwest. CINCPAC retained overall control from Pearl Harbor, leaving Fletcher in tactical command, with the general instruction that his operations were to be 'governed by the principles of calculated risk'. Fletcher's responsibilities were considerable, both sides being fully aware that the loss of his carriers would leave the Pacific wide open.

Softening up

As the passing hours of the night of 3/4 June brought no news of Nagumo's whereabouts, Fletcher cautiously closed the island and, as dawn flushed the eastern sky, was 200 miles to the northeast. About 250 miles west of his position the same light was catching the wings of over 100 enemy aircraft formating above their carriers cruising in the darkness below. Nagumo was moving in at 25 knots on his softening-up mission and, expecting resistance, one third of the strike were fighters. A PBY searching this likely sector fortunately missed this swarm and sighted the Japanese carriers at 05.30, one hour after

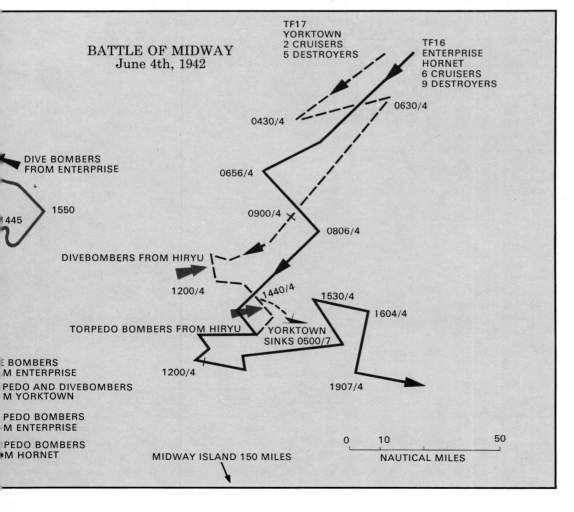

BATTLE OF MIDWAY
June 4th, 1942

TF17
YORKTOWN
2 CRUISERS
5 DESTROYERS

TF16
ENTERPRISE
HORNET
6 CRUISERS
9 DESTROYERS

0430/4

0630/4

DIVE BOMBERS
FROM ENTERPRISE

0656/4

1550

445

0900/4

0806/4

DIVEBOMBERS FROM HIRYU

1200/4

1440/4

1530/4

1604/4

TORPEDO BOMBERS FROM HIRYU

YORKTOWN
SINKS 0500/7

BOMBERS
M ENTERPRISE

PEDO AND DIVEBOMBERS
M YORKTOWN

1200/4

1907/4

PEDO BOMBERS
M ENTERPRISE

PEDO BOMBERS
M HORNET

MIDWAY ISLAND 150 MILES

0   10   50

NAUTICAL MILES

their aircraft had departed. Its sighting report, received both by Midway and Fletcher, was almost simultaneous with a ground radar report of the approaching strike, still 100 miles distant.

Things began to happen quickly. *Yorktown* recovered her search aircraft as TF16 closed Nagumo's reported position at utmost speed. Every aircraft on Midway took the air; about 20 Buffalos and Wildcats succeeded in intercepting the approaching enemy but were dismembered by the covering Zeros, losing 13 for five. Little damage was inflicted on the ground and further planes fell to the AA defences. It was obvious to Nagumo that his mission would require a second strike. He thought this of no great import as he did not suspect the presence of the American carriers, who were playing it craftily. Knowing that all of the Japanese aircraft had left Midway by 06.50 the Americans launched their own strike after 07.00 and timed it to arrive at the time when Nagumo's flightdecks would be cluttered with newly recovered aircraft, empty of fuel and unarmed.

Avenger debut

Nagumo was not entirely unprepared, however. Suspicious of American reaction so far, and suspecting that a surface force might be in the vicinity, he had held many aircraft back, mainly on *Kaga*, armed with torpedoes and armour-piercing bombs. The *Kaga* was also mounting the CAP, which came into action at 07.10 as ten torpedo-armed TBFs (the new Grumman Avenger in its first action) and B26 (Marauders) came in from Midway. Seven were shot down for no result but the raid underlined to the Japanese commander that a second strike on the island was necessary as the twin-engined B26s could not have been carrier-based. Thus it was that the *Kaga's* combat-ready aircraft were ordered to exchange their anti-ship weapons for high-explosive bombs for use against Midway.

Barely a quarter-hour later, with aircraft struck down and with munitions littering the deck, came a report from a floatplane launched from one of the accompanying cruisers that American ships were approaching. Incredibly, they were reported as a cruiser force although Spruance was in the act of launching his strike. Even so, Nagumo stopped the rearming of his aircraft and those 'Kates' still armed with torpedoes kept them. But then, between 08.00 and 08.30, came three heavy raids, from obviously shore-based aircraft and, although they were repulsed, Nagumo was concerned about which target needed neutralizing first.

His worries were not relieved by a salvo of torpedoes from an invisible American submarine. Any joy when they all missed

was extinguished by an incoming report at 08.30 — the American force included 'a carrier'. By then the full TF16 strike of 68 dive bombers, 29 torpedo aircraft and 20 fighters were formed up and on their way, with 200 miles to go.

Japanese confusion

Confusion hit the Japanese. 'Kates' recently stripped of torpedoes and AP bombs to take blast bombs started to have the operation reversed; they could not be ranged for take-off as the first aircraft began returning from the strike on Midway. Precious time was lost in their recovery and not until 09.15 was Nagumo able to turn to face the enemy. TF16's strike was only ten minutes' flying time distant, with a follow-up formation from TF17 a further hour astern. As usual, the Devastator TBDs were coming in low, in two groups from their separate carriers and each covered by Wildcats, although in the variable and layered cloud the *Enterprise* planes had become detached.

Between them, the Japanese carriers could muster over 80 Zeros and the greatest possible number had been scrambled. They hit a badly fragmented American force which, at that range, had no fuel to spare for reforming. *Hornet's* 15 TBDs went in against a wall of flak and unimpeded Zeros. All were lost, mostly outside dropping range. Unhesitatingly the 14 *Enterprise* planes followed them in. Ten more went down and the Japanese bored on, still unscathed. These proceedings had allowed the *Yorktown* contingent to catch up but, in spite of heroic covering by the few F4Fs still with them, they lost ten out of 12. Of 41 Devastators that had attacked 35 had been lost, for no result. They were experienced squadrons, over four years with the carriers, and, so brutal was the scale of these losses, the TBD was withdrawn from front-line service.

Nagumo was feeling better; his attackers had been virtually wiped out and, by superhuman efforts, his own strike was ready. The big carriers turned into the wind and, at 10.24 precisely, *Akagi* gave the executive order to launch. Even as they did so there was seen, far above, the glint of other wings as the American SBDs began their dives.

Lucky sighting

The attack should have been co-ordinated with that of the TBDs but the *Hornet* contingent missed its target altogether and, low on fuel, flew on to Midway or returned. The *Enterprise* aircraft also overshot but had the luck to sight a lone Japanese destroyer and realized that it was heading for the carriers. Following its projected course, they arrived over Nagumo at the

The Grumman TBF Avenger torpedo bomber, which made its battle debut at Midway, replacing the disappointing Devastator. Although the Avenger's showing on its first strike was also disappointing, it was 70mph faster (270mph) and could carry twice the weight of bombs or torpedo (2000lb) and it went on to make a major contribution to the outcome of the war.

Allowed to escape in the earlier successful attacks on 'Kaga', 'Soryu' and 'Akagi', the 'Hiryu' accounted for the 'Yorktown' before she too was dispatched by SBDs from TF16, two of whose bombs blew out the forward elevator. Note the portside island.

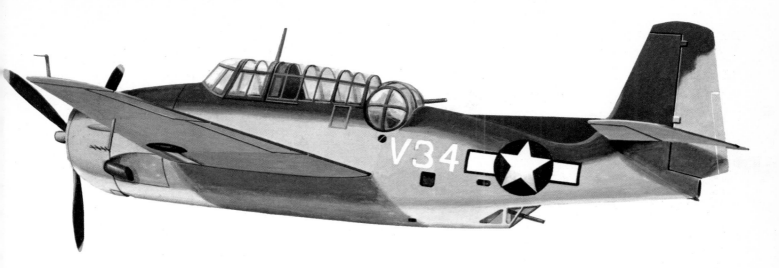

same time as *Yorktown's* group. All of the Zeros were low down, low on fuel and ammunition after their destruction of the torpedo bombers and the 55 Dauntlesses formed up without interference. Vengeance

for the TBFs was about to be exacted in full.

The *Hiryu* was some distance away and the other carriers took the brunt of the attack. Inside four minutes the flagship *Akagi* had her shell plating badly sprung by a near miss alongside the bridge. This was followed by the penetration of the flightdeck forward by a 1000-pound bomb which detonated among 40 armed and fuelled aircraft directly below. A second bomb, a 500-pounder, exploded topsides in the deck park. *Akagi* turned upwind to minimize the effect of the resulting fires but they took hold so rapidly that, within a quarter of an hour, Nagumo was forced to transfer his flag to a light cruiser. Had he had time to look, he would have been appalled by the wider scene.

Inferno

The *Kaga* had been hit about the same time on the forward elevator; although the deck was not pierced the blast caused severe damage to the bridge structure and killed, among others, the captain. Two more bombs, almost instantaneously, bored through the flightdeck and exploded in the midst of the combat-ready aircraft and the still-present discarded weapon stores, not yet struck down to the magazines. *Kaga* was instantly aflame and the effect of a fourth bomb hit on the starboard quarter was hardly observed in the vast smoke pall that shrouded the stricken ship.

The scene was repeated on *Soryu*, which was shocked to a standstill by three hits, two of which had wrecked the hangar, their explosions forcing out the forward elevator. Within minutes she, too, was an inferno above and below.

After an onslaught lasting a bare five minutes, the SBDs, virtually unscathed, hightailed it before their luck should change. If criticism can be levelled at so devastating an attack, it would be that the fourth carrier, *Hiryu*, was left unmolested.

Jutland parallel

Twenty-six years before, at Jutland, *Derfflinger* had been left unengaged by Beatty's ships, an error that led directly to the loss of the battlecruiser *Queen Mary*. A parallel was about to be drawn.

The *Kaga* was abandoned by all except those fighting her fires. Soon afterwards she was hit by a submarine torpedo that broke up on impact without exploding. It did not affect the outcome as she blew up and sank about seven hours after the attack. *Soryu* put up a game fight. Her fires were subdued to the point where she got under weigh, assisted by a tow from the battlecruiser *Kirishima*. Hopes were rising when three submarine torpeodes slammed home. Even so, it was another five hours before she, too, exploded and broke in two. *Akagi* fought on. Abandoned by both crew and Emperor's portrait, her hulk drifted blazing through the short night. Undamaged below the waterline, she showed no signs of sinking and was put down at first light by an escort's torpedo.

But this is to anticipate, for the *Hiryu*, at the time of the attack, resolved to sell herself dearly. In a neat reversal of fortune she saw the chance of hitting the American carriers during their delicate recovery phase. Due to losses sustained over Midway earlier in the day, only 18 'Val' dive bombers were available, escorted by a handful of Zeros. TF16 was being shadowed by a cruiser-based floatplane, so no searching was necessary and, although half their number were downed by Fletcher's vigilant fighters, the remainder pressed home their attack, singling out *Yorktown*. There was frantic activity aboard as the carrier stopped landing-on her aircraft and closed up for attack, all fuel systems being purged and made inert.

Once again, the dive bomber was to have the measure of the aircraft carrier, hitting her three times. Two went deep causing a severe fire and loss of steampower; it was now 12.30 and Fletcher's turn to shift his flag to a cruiser.

Burning Yorktown sails on

Within the hour, however, still blazing furiously, *Yorktown* was sailing at half speed and preparing aircraft for action. But *Hiryu* had not shot her bolt and further effort by her crew had her remaining ten 'Kate' torpedo bombers away, two hours behind the 'Vals' but ahead of the American riposte. *Yorktown* was an hour's flying time distant and the approaching enemy were reported at 30 miles' range. Only a few fighters could be put up by the injured

carrier and they could not be vectored efficiently because she had lost her air direction radar. Although her close escort had been augmented and put up a wall of flak the Japanese, with their usual disregard for losses, knifed in with a repeat of their Coral Sea tactics. In turning to comb one group of torpedoes, *Yorktown* exposed her flanks to the rest. Two struck her portside together and the ship again lost all power, developing a list so rapidly that she was abandoned as lost.

Spruance's TF16, undisturbed by the misfortunes that had beset Fletcher, ranged a further strike of 40 SBDs to nail the *Hiryu*. All were away by 16.00, flying in two groups. The range to target was short and she was found frantically turning round the aircraft lately returned from the first *Yorktown* sortie. Only a few Zeros were left in the air and they concentrated on the first formation, leaving the later group free to arrow down from near ceiling height through a sky blotched with flak. Four 1000-pounders pierced the flightdeck, two of them simultaneously alongside the forward elevator, which was uprooted and flung against the bridge structure. Like her late compatriots, *Hiryu* rapidly burned beyond control and having, like them, suffered all her damage topsides, drifted through the night. At 05.00 the following morning, 6 June, a destroyer took off the few weary survivors, drew off and put four torpedoes into the blackened derelict. Defiantly, she took a further four hours before finally plunging, taking with her Nagumo's second-in-command who had lashed himself to the ship as a final gesture.

Yamamoto frustrated

Throughout this day of intense activity, Yamamoto was making all speed to the scene with the Main Body and had ordered the Aleutians force to concentrate on the same spot. As the Americans were obviously still full of fight, the landing on Midway had been abandoned but the Japanese commander reckoned that the aircraft complement of Fletcher's carriers must have been weakened to the point where they were vulnerable to surface attack. Determined to offset his own disastrous losses, Yamamoto was to be frustrated because the American commander had a new interest.

Part of the complex Japanese plan had been the softening-up of the landing zone on Midway by four heavy cruisers. They had, in fact, been recalled before the event but, in the act of reversing course, they were attacked by an American submarine. Though all her torpedoes missed, she created such mayhem in the manoeuvring squadron that two cruisers collided heavily. It was these lame ducks that had drawn TF16 from the battle area; one of them was sunk and Yamamoto found a sea empty but for Japanese wreckage and survivors.

Chance then took a hand in the form of an enemy submarine which, in a rather bizarre little side-operation, had also been directed to bombard Midway. She had carried out a tiny cannonade and was then given a course to steer to intercept the maimed *Yorktown*. Listing, but far from sinking, the carrier had the fires under control by dedicated efforts of a skeleton crew and was under tow. It was a supreme misfortune to run into a four-torpedo salvo; only two of them actually hit, as a destroyer blocked the course of a third and the fourth missed. A desperate rearguard action to save her began but she had taken too much and at 05.00 on 7 June 1942 she rolled over. The Battle of Midway was over.

It had been an action of great significance, finally restoring American morale and demonstrating that the Japanese war machine was not invincible. Fletcher had been aided by good intelligence and a measure of good luck but had shown great flair in exploiting Nagumo's great mistakes — his preoccupation with taking Midway before he had ensured that he had the freedom to do so. As at the Coral Sea, neither fleet saw the other and the 16 great 14-inch guns of the battlecruisers *Haruna* and *Kirishima* that accompanied the enemy carriers were as useless as muskets. After June 1942 the great Japanese rampage across the Pacific was at an end; not only had four fine carriers been lost but also their full aircraft complement of 256 and, more important, half of their experienced aircrew. It started an irreversible trend for the Japanese who began to lose aircrew at a far higher rate than they could train replacements; it was the key to their losing the Pacific war.

Midway cost the Americans about 100 aircraft, most of whose pilots were recovered. From every angle they had won their most vital victory to date.

The Japanese heavy cruiser 'Mogami', one of two heavily damaged while withdrawing from Midway, first by collision and then by aircraft from TF16.

The Pacific regained

Midway had been disastrous for the Japanese cause but they were still left with a garrison in the Aleutians and had not been deprived of their foothold in the Solomons. The Americans were content merely to watch the former and to allow it to wither from boredom and impotence but the latter had the potential for acting as a springboard for operations deeper into the Pacific and it needed to be removed.

In spite of their triumph, the Americans had only two carriers available for action immediately after the battle, the *Enterprise* and *Hornet*. *Saratoga* was about to arrive from the West Coast and *Wasp* passed through the Panama Canal on 10 June 1942, four days later. These reinforcements were timely as the Japanese still had six operational carriers and were completing two more.

During July 1942 the enemy was observed to be establishing a permanent airstrip on an island at the southeast end of the Solomons chain. As its completion would

allow the Japanese to dominate the area with land-based air power, urgent action was required. The name of the island, Guadalcanal, was soon to acquire a bloody fame.

Amphibious force

A large force of amphibious transports was assembled in New Zealand waters and practised opposed landings during July. It should be remembered that this was then a new form of warfare; specialist craft were in short supply and personnel untrained. Speed was of paramount importance, however, and although the force that approached Guadalcanal on 7 August was considerable, it was still very raw. Evidently, the Japanese still expected an attack in the north for all their carriers had been accounted for in home waters. The Americans, therefore, took something of a risk in leaving only *Hornet* at Pearl Harbor and allocating the other three to cover the Solomons operation. As TF61, they were again under Fletcher's command and organized flexibly into three groups, each composed of a carrier and supporting ships.

Taking advantage of the dense frontal cloud masses so typical of the area, the great concentration of shipping arrived completely unsuspected by the Japanese and, after a heavy softening-up by ships and carrier-borne aircraft, the landings took place on Guadalcanal, Tulagi and adjacent islands at first light on 7 August.

By the next day it all seemed to be over, with TF61's F4Fs, nearly 100-strong, establishing total air superiority; the Japanese could neither move on the ground nor interfere in the air. Then, when all seemed to be approaching a satisfactory conclusion, Fletcher decided to pull out. He was clearly uneasy about hazarding his irreplaceable carriers further in such a tight operational zone. Despite protestations that the newly won airstrip could not hope to support sufficient airpower and, more serious, that seven Japanese cruisers had left Rabaul on the evening of the landings, TF61 withdrew southwards late on the 8th, justified mainly by a need to refuel.

Cruiser action

The enemy cruiser force, under the formidable Mikawa, was reported at least three times as it headed at full speed down 'the Slot' — the 600-mile long channel running along the spine of the double Solomon chain. Its 'Jake' floatplanes had reported the Allied force off the beachhead very accurately and Mikawa, whose ships were well trained in night fighting, resolved to attack in the early hours of the 9th.

A not-inconsiderable force of eight

Above: Fresh as paint soon after her commissioning, USS 'Saratoga' (CV3). She was sent to join the Pacific struggle in June 1942, when the American carrier force there had been reduced to only two, 'Enterprise' and 'Hornet', after the Coral Sea and Midway actions.

Left: CV6 USS 'Enterprise' bringing up her new TBF Avengers. The 'Enterprise' was still far to the north with 'Hornet' after the Doolittle Tokyo raid when the Americans shaped up to stop the Japanese advance but she and her aircraft were to have a decisive effect on the outcome of the Pacific war.

Waiting to join battle and keeping radio silence, one of the American carriers receives a message from a Dauntless returning from a scouting mission. The rear gunner drops the message as the pilot waggles the wings over the flightdeck.

assorted American and Australian cruisers was available that night in the waters around Savo Island, which controlled the approaches to the landing beaches, but sighting reports had been so garbled that no attack appeared to be anticipated, and the force was not concentrated. Shortly after midnight Mikawa slipped past an oblivious radar picket destroyer and caught the Allied force absolutely unprepared. In what was one of the worst defeats ever inflicted on the US Navy, four heavy cruisers were sunk in short order. The only saving grace was that his runaway success seemed to unnerve the Japanese admiral, who speedily withdrew when the helpless transports were ripe for destruction. Had he stayed the Guadalcanal bridgehead would have been no more.

During Mikawa's approach phase, Fletcher had both the information and the means with which to act. He did not. Fully informed of the night's events, Fletcher could have used *Wasp's* night-trained pilots to hit the Japanese as they pulled out. He did not. It was not too late to reverse course and mount a full strike, approach and withdraw without hindrance; even after the defeat of an Allied squadron, the means of overwhelming counter stayed in his hands. It was, and remains, inexplicable.

Results predictable

The resulting events were fully predictable. The offshore amphibious fleet, short of air cover and surface and anti-submarine support, was forced to withdraw leaving the American Marines stranded. They were in full control for the moment but ripe for an enemy counterblow; that the Japanese were not yet ready to follow up the initial success was purely fortuitous. When Yamamoto finally launched his operation on 19 August it had two aims; to put a force on to Guadalcanal and, by so doing, trigger an American response which would bring out their carriers to be destroyed.

Three Japanese carriers were available and the manner of their use was typical. Nagumo was back with his repaired and fully worked-up veterans *Shokaku* and *Zuikaku*, with a heavy escort and instructions to stay unobtrusively out of sight behind a diversionary force under Rear-Admiral Hara. The force included the small carrier *Ryujo* and the heavy cruiser *Tone*, converted for the operation of six reconnaissance floatplanes. Hara's job was scout and, if necessary, strike, but above all his duty was to be found easily by the American carriers. They, it was calculated, would inevitably mount an immediate attack and, once committed, they would be smitten by the unsuspected Nagumo.

Fletcher also had three carriers at sea, *Enterprise*, *Saratoga* and *Wasp*, organized as before in three separate groups. On 20 August 1942 they were sighted southeast of the Solomons on the very day that the first of the CVEs to arrive in the Pacific, the *Long Island*, ferried 31 fighters and strike aircraft to the beleaguered Marines on Guadalcanal. Nothing further occurred

until early on the 23rd when a PBY sighted the Japanese invasion force about 300 miles north of the island. Knowing that they had been reported, the enemy turned northeast into an area of heavy overcast, so that a mixed airstrike from both *Saratoga* and Henderson Field (as the Guadalcanal airstrip had been renamed) failed to find them.

Pre-invasion strike

It might reasonably be assumed that Fletcher would have appreciated that any serious attempt by the Japanese at landing would have been adequately covered and yet that evening he detached the *Wasp* group for refuelling. When *Ryujo* advertised her presence by mounting a pre-invasion strike, therefore, only two American carriers were present but Fletcher, fortunately, was not immediately drawn. He put up a series of air searches which, while they did not uncover Nagumo, revealed sufficient enemy activity to indicate the scale of the operation. Only a force from *Saratoga* was launched, consisting of 30 SBDs and eight TBFs; *Enterprise* remained uncommitted.

Almost immediately Nagumo's carriers were also sighted and a 'Jake' floatplane found Fletcher. Plans now became slightly unhinged, for the leader of the *Saratoga* strike intercepted the sighting report on Nagumo and, deeming the big carriers to be the more important target, over-flew *Ryujo* on his own initiative to find them. He was unsuccessful but had he done so he could well have surprised the Japanese at the vulnerable point of launching their 40-strong strike against Fletcher. As it was, he could not dally and reversed his course,

intercepting Hara shortly after 16.00. In spite of her standing patrol of Zeros, *Ryujo* still could not avoid four Dauntless bombs, topped-off with an Avenger torpedo. Blanketed by her own smoke, the carrier circled briefly with a jammed rudder and an increasing list. Her agony was brief.

All aircraft aloft

By then Fletcher had cleared his hangars of every strike aircraft that would fly in an effort to neutralize Nagumo and, shortly before 17.00, the situation was that the two separate carrier forces, virtually devoid of aircraft, awaited attack by three groups of aircraft. Two of these were a pair of Japanese forces steering a reciprocal course to the lately launched scratch American strike. To complicate matters, the aircraft that had just sunk the *Ryujo* were also returning.

Enough firepower was airborne for climactic results, but it was not that sort of day. It began promisingly enough for the Japanese whose dive bombers, in spite of being roughly handled by the *Enterprise* fighter cover, managed to hit the carrier three times. She burned but managed to contain her fires, only to have a steering failure as Nagumo's second strike appeared on the radar screens. With her defending fighters low on fuel and ammunition she would have stood little chance but the Japanese flight commander failed to locate her and cruised around close enough for the progress of his 18 dive bombers and nine torpedo bombers to be anxiously followed on the American radar screens.

In turn, Fletcher's strike also failed to connect although two of *Saratoga's* SBDs

USS 'Long Island' was the first of the CVEs to arrive in the Pacific and her first mission was to ferry 31 aircraft to the beleaguered Marines on Guadalcanal. Note the early CVE features of foreshortened flightdeck and identity letters.

came across the seaplane-carrier *Chitose* in the fading daylight of the 24th. Their 1000-pounders missed, but by so small a margin that the hapless ship nearly foundered from heavily started seams and was escorted away by the Main Force during the night.

The Americans pulled out to refuel and get the damaged *Enterprise* clear. Rejoined by the *Wasp* group early the next morning, it had been fortunate to move when it did, for the enemy swept the area that night with a heavy cruiser force. With the invasion frustrated, a carrier sunk and 60 irreplaceable aircrews lost, the Japanese had suffered another sharp reverse at the cost to the Americans of only a handful of aircraft. In what came to be called the Battle of the Eastern Solomons Nagumo was unfortunate in that his plan had worked as intended; only the actual strikes lacked the results he sought.

Guadalcanal a symbol

Guadalcanal thus became a symbol of each side's resolve — that of the Americans to hang on and that of the Japanese to throw them off — and a strange stalemate developed. At night, the Japanese ran in reinforcements by destroyer on so regular a basis that the Americans termed them the 'Tokyo Express'. Even without radar, they were formidable night fighters and, on the rare occasions when US naval units managed to intercept them, the Americans were usually worsted.

But, like the British destroyers at the time of the Tobruk siege, the Japanese had to be well clear by dawn for, by day, the arena was under American control. From carrier decks and Henderson Field, absolute air control denied the area to anything Japanese and enabled the Americans themselves to run in regular convoys. They were countered by the obvious means, enemy submarines, one of which put a torpedo into *Saratoga* a few days after the Eastern Solomons battle. With a boiler room flooded and all power lost, she limped away under tow, her second such ordeal. With *Enterprise* still under repair this left only *Wasp* to hold the ring, fortunately soon reinforced by *Hornet*.

Successful Long Lance attack

On 14 September 1942 both carriers were covering yet another Guadalcanal convoy when a patrolling PBY to the north galvanized the force with the news of Nagumo's 'big two' in the area, accompanied by the converted pair *Junyo* and *Hiyo*. A strike was rapidly mounted but, strangely, in spite of their close proximity, the enemy force seemed oblivious of the American presence. They had also been covering a 'milk run' and, their task completed, turned away with the result that the aircraft found only empty ocean.

The US carriers returned to their own duties and, on the following day, ran into an enemy submarine which fired a full salvo of the much-respected Long Lance torpedoes. At about 14.45 on the 15th, three of these weapons struck the starboard side of *Wasp* with terrible effect and the rest travelled on through the remaining force, over eight miles distant. One narrowly missed the *Hornet* and hit a destroyer and another

The Japanese heavy cruiser 'Furutaka' was one of a force of five ships assigned to shell Henderson Field on 11 October. The force was intercepted and attacked and in the action 'Furutaka' and a destroyer were sunk and two more of the force were hit.

heavily damaged the new battleship *North Carolina*.

Seldom was a salvo of torpedoes more effectively expended. *Wasp* was grievously damaged, her Avgas mains, normally dry and inert, had been in use and were full; fires developed instantly and were aggravated by the firefighting pressure lines being also ruptured and useless. Within a quarter of an hour a magazine below the hangar deck erupted, the explosion wave blasting out the light shell plating of the hangar walls together with the midships elevator. She was abandoned shortly afterwards and sunk by torpedo from an escort. Only *Hornet* remained operational and it was obvious that this rate of attrition could not be maintained.

Iron Bottom Sound

The see-saw struggle for Guadalcanal continued unabated, the waters around Savo Island earning the grim soubriquet 'Iron Bottom Sound' from the ships that littered its bed. On 11 October 1942 for instance, an American cruiser force capitalized on its radar on a very dark night and avenged their earlier disastrous reverse by badly mauling a powerful Japanese squadron off Cape Esperance. But the enemy was nothing if not persistent, saturating the zone with submarines to inhibit American movements and pushing through the nocturnal 'express' with total disregard of losses. The *Enterprise* returned in mid-October, which was fortunate, for the enemy now had the equivalent of two divisions ashore and the final push was imminent.

The better part of the Japanese fleet left its base at Truk accompanied by no fewer than five carriers, Nagumo's *Shokaku* and *Zuikaku*, together with the *Zuiho* for distant cover and the sisters *Junyo* and *Hiyo* to act as shore support. *Hiyo*, still a new ship, was forced to return with a machinery breakdown. As a curtain-raiser on the night of 13/14 October, two Japanese battleships audaciously penetrated to the island and offloaded the better part of 1000 rounds of 14-inch shells into Henderson, churning the runways to a Passchendaele-like consistency and destroying half the 90-odd aircraft present. The enemy then underlined his mastery of the silent hours by adding 2000 rounds of 8-inch from cruisers on the ensuing two nights. With their land-based air-power thus diminished, the Japanese confidently expected that the Americans would have to commit both their carriers, the destruction of which would be a prize more valuable than the island itself.

New American commanders

Another event of mid-October was the appointment of Admiral 'Bull' Halsey as C-in-C South Pacific and Fletcher's replacement by Kinkaid. The nature of the former was summarized by his nickname; of aggression he had plenty, of subtlety, little.

On 24 October 1942 the *Hornet* group met the *Enterprise*, coming from Hawaii, in company with the two new battleships

By the time the great carrier battles of 1942 drew to a close the Douglas SBD Dauntless bomber, of which nearly 6000 were built between 1939 and 1944, had emerged as the single most effective weapon in the American armoury. It had been adapted to a variety of bomber and reconnaissance roles and proved able to absorb considerable punishment, emerging eventually with the lowest loss rate of any US Pacific carrier type. This picture anticipates a little, showing a bombed-up Dauntless, photographed from a squadron companion as they formed for yet another blistering attack in the island-hopping campaign that followed Guadalcanal.

Top: The sky is blackened with flak from her two escorting cruisers as the 'Hornet' makes a tight turn under a concentrated attack.

Above: End of a Japanese dive bomber as the pilot misses his target in an apparent suicide dive alongside an anti-aircraft cruiser.

South Dakota and *Washington*. **Known** collectively as TF61, the combined force doubled the northern end of the scattered atolls of the Santa Cruz islands and entered the wide channel dividing them from the Solomons on the 25th. About noon came a report from one of the ubiquitous PBYs of an enemy group steaming south. It was a battleship force under Rear-Admiral Abe and its sighting was rapidly followed by that of Nagumo's group, later amplified by a second report from another PBY which nearly succeeded in torpedoing *Zuikaku*.

Following Halsey's simple dictum 'attack-irrespective', TF61 had been heading for the enemy at maximum speed but its own search aircraft had found nothing, because the Japanese had sagely reversed course on being sighted earlier and an optimistically launched *Enterprise* strike not only missed but suffered casualties in landing-on again after dark.

Americans outgunned

Neither side sought evasion, however, and each established contact by 06.30 the following morning. Only 200 miles separated Kinkaid from Nagumo, who had by then detached *Zuiho* from his main force, in a repeat of the tactic employed at the Eastern Solomons action. Just 100 miles further west was the *Junyo* and her group; the Americans were outgunned.

TF61 had its strike away by 08.30 but had been beaten to it by the Japanese by a full half hour. The latter had just relaxed slightly after this concentrated effort when they were rudely surprised by a pair of *Enterprise* SBDs. True to her name, she had armed her search aircraft with 500-pound bombs, in case they might be useful, and this pair drilled through the unsuspecting Zero cover and planted both into *Zuiho's* after end, rendering her inoperable for the action that was to follow.

A second Japanese wave was away within an hour of the first, flying such a close reciprocal course to Kinkaid's aircraft that several individual combats occurred. So many aircraft were in the air at the same time that the American advantage in early warning radar was largely negated by inability to separate friend from foe on the displays (IFF was in its early days).

Hornet lost

As the first Japanese attack came in, the *Enterprise* group was safely buried in a rain squall and *Hornet* attracted their individual attention. Her close escort included a couple

Right: Early in the attack on 'Hornet' a 'Val' that had scored a hit on the doomed carrier was itself hit by AA fire; it crashed into the funnel casing and exploded as it slid along the deck.

of specialist AA cruisers that blackened the sky with flak but again the CAP seemed divided on whether the dive bombers or torpedo bombers constituted the greater threat. Their choice was purely academic for the enemy put together a superbly co-ordinated attack that would have swamped any opposition.

The leading 'Val' hit the carrier aft, but winged by AA fire, it crashed into the funnel casing and careered down the flightdeck, exploding as it went. Even before the fire parties had time to react, the ship shuddered to the detonations of two torpedoes striking almost simultaneously to starboard. Yet again, an almost total power failure resulted but *Hornet* had barely started to lose way when she was hit three times by bombs, one destroying the deck park, the second exploding below and the third forward. The explosion of the last was within the hangar and its effect was immediately eclipsed by that of a 'Kate' torpedo bomber, its pilot dead or intoxicated by the glory of the occasion, coming straight through the

shell plating and exploding below the forward elevator.

At 10.20, as the few surviving Japanese aircraft left the shattered wreck that had been *Hornet*, the very disorganized American strike arrived to find itself having to fight through a very resolute Zero defence. *Zuikaku* was now some distance removed so that, with *Zuiho* obviously still well afire, *Shokaku* became the butt of the attack from the few aircraft that achieved contact. Bombing was very accurate and six 1000-pound bomb hits were to put her out of action for many months, in addition to *Zuiho*.

Enterprise survives hits

Shortly after 11.00 the Japanese 'second eleven' found the *Enterprise*. They paid dearly for the three bomb hits that left the carrier damaged but operational. During these events *Hornet* was crawling clear at the end of a cruiser's towline, destroyers alongside fighting the fires that ranged her length. But if any hopes had been kindled that she would be saved, they were dashed as radar screens were again painted by the blips of approaching enemy aircraft, this time mainly from the previously almost uncommitted *Junyo*. *Enterprise*, which had survived yet another attack, was both damaged and irreplaceable, and was ordered by Kinkaid to leave the area at maximum speed — a decision of great moral courage.

The *Hornet* and her escort now awaited the ordeal alone. Already partially abandoned, her towline was slipped as the enemy, untroubled by air cover, came in hard at about 16.00. So spirited was the AA defence that her damage was increased by no more than another torpedo hit, again on the starboard side. Her list increased by degrees and her last crewmen were taken off and a further, ineffective, bombing attack two hours later led to the order to scuttle. There was some urgency required as Abe's powerful surface force was approaching but the events that followed had an element of grim comedy. Two destroyers were detailed for the job and frantically fired nine torpedoes (a further seven missed) and about 400-rounds of 5-inch shell into the hulk, only too aware of two Japanese battleships and a pair of heavy cruisers bearing down. *Hornet* stayed stubbornly afloat, an embarrassing beacon as the two destroyers became ever more desperate in their efforts. In spite of their best efforts to live up to Lawrence's exhortation 'Don't give up the ship' on the *Chesapeake* so long before, they were literally chased away by Abe's destroyers.

Fortunately, *Hornet* was too far gone for the enemy seriously to contemplate salvage and two Japanese ships were left to finish the job. After five hours of custodianship, the enemy finally dispatched their unwanted prize in the early hours of 27 October with another salvo of torpedoes. She was the fourth American carrier to be lost inside six months and the setback of the Battle of Santa Cruz demonstrated that sheer aggression was not in itself enough when faced by an adversary that had no intention of being intimidated.

Carrier shortage

Apart from the little *Ranger* in the Atlantic, only the damaged *Enterprise* and the *Saratoga* remained and appeals to the British for the loan of a fleet carrier could not immediately be met. As a result, the Solomons campaign was prolonged as landings could now be made only within the range of land-based air cover. It was fortunate that the Japanese, too, were hampered by having lost six carriers in the same period.

More American surface forces were committed to causing discomfiture to the 'Tokyo Express'; it was an alien form of warfare but, to their credit, they stuck to it and made the enemy suffer in turn, climaxing in the sinking of two battleships.

Guadalcanal, the bloody catalyst, was finally conceded by the Japanese in February 1943 by which time the Americans had developed their land-based air cover to the point where it could dominate the area virtually without carriers. In the March, indeed, the Japanese lost an entire New-Guinea-bound invasion force in the Bismarck Sea.

By the end of 1942 the Japanese had lost the initiative. Their emergency carrier-

Two factors around the turn of the year 1942/3 spelled the beginning of the end of the Pacific war. The first was the delivery of CV9 USS 'Essex', first of a 24-strong class of 27,100-ton ships capable of nearly 32 knots and operating up to 110 aircraft. The first seven of the class and nine Independence-class fast 45-aircraft light carriers, were completed by the end of 1943.

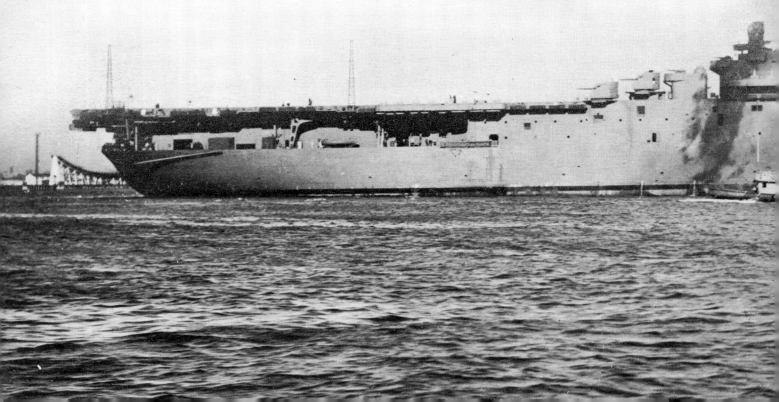

The second factor was the entry into service of the Grumman F6F Hellcat fighter. It was developed at great speed to counter the edge in performance of the Zero, which was a dominant factor throughout the earlier Pacific actions. With a top speed of 376mph and rapid climb, in the right hands the Hellcat could outperform the Zero and after delivery to Pacific squadrons began in January 1943 it proved so effective that it ended the war with a ratio of kills to losses of nine to one.

construction programme was hopelessly behind and the Americans took delivery at last of *Essex* (CV9), the first of the new generation. In addition, the large escort carriers arrived after release from the involvement in the North African landings. But the great carrier battles of 1942 were not to be re-enacted for the better part of a year as the two wasted fleets rebuilt their losses in ships and aircrew.

Mediterranean climax

The Year of the Carrier in the Pacific, 1942, had seen also the climax of the Mediterranean struggle. With Malta rescued by the August Convoy and secured by the Eighth Army's westward advance, after Alamein it remained to complete the undermining of the Afrika Korps by landings at the western end of the North African coast, in Morocco and Algeria. Codenamed Operation Torch, they were

mounted on the night of 7/8 November 1942 and relied on 12 carriers for initial air cover. As already briefly noted in Chapter Five, the American contingent, beside the little *Ranger* included the four Sangamon-class CVEs at a time when they were vitally needed to replace the heavy losses in the Pacific.

The Royal Navy had mustered all that it could and, besides the veterans *Argus* and *Furious*, had present the fleet carriers *Victorious* and *Formidable*, and the CVEs *Avenger*, *Biter* and *Dasher*. (It was this commitment that prevented loan of a carrier to the US Pacific Fleet until its crisis was past.) With such a large concentration of fighter strength, the Vichy French air forces were rapidly eliminated and the main function of the carriers was then to safeguard the large force of shipping offshore from German and Italian bombing attacks.

As no seaborne targets presented

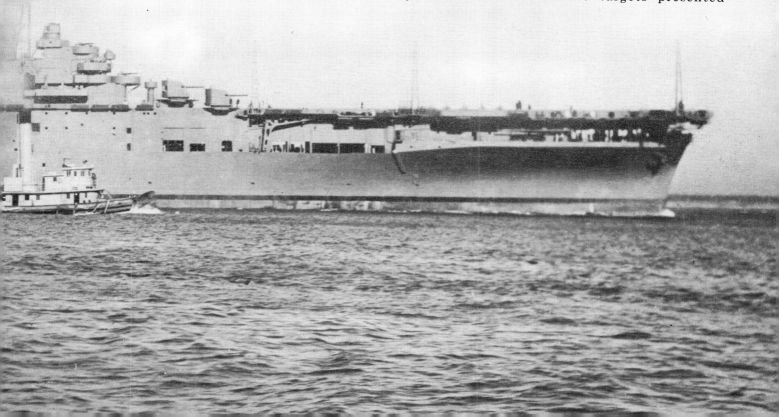

The carrier version of the immortal Spitfire fighter, the Seafire, was effective in providing the necessary high-performance air cover but, operated from CVEs in the Mediterranean, it was costly; many were lost in landing accidents brought about by a combination of the low speed of the carriers, absence of wind and the Seafire's high landing speed and narrow undercarriage.

themselves the Albacores kept their hand in by engaging targets ashore, covered by Sea Hurricanes but, as soon as airfields were secured, the American light carriers were withdrawn for more urgent duties in the Pacific, the Royal Navy staying on to 'sweep up'. It had been a 'soft' operation but yielded valuable experience in the use of seaborne airpower in the follow-up phase of a major amphibious landing.

Sicily landings

In May 1943, with the end of the North African campaign, the Mediterranean reverted to being largely an Allied-controlled lake, well covered by land-based air power and with a revitalized Malta again taking the war to the enemy. A still powerful Italian fleet remained strictly 'in being' but was expected to react to the planned landings in Sicily in July. No fewer than six RN battleships and the fleet carriers *Formidable* and *Indomitable* were available for this eventuality but were to be disappointed, even though Italian soil was being violated for the first time. Operation Husky went in on 10 July, the heavy naval units covering from a distance. So little organized resistance was encountered that a measure of relaxation set in, to be rudely disturbed as a lone Ju88 stole in completely unobserved, put a torpedo into *Indomitable* and escaped almost without a shot being fired. Recently recommissioned after a year's absence repairing the damage of the previous year's August Convoy, *Indomitable* returned for another — rather unnecessary — year in the dockyard.

Sicily fell rapidly and the Allied armies crossed the Messina Strait to commence the wasteful slog up the long Italian peninsula. No ports of any size exist between the strait and Naples, and it was considered that the latter's capture would enable enemy forces in the south to be cut off. To this end it was resolved to put an Anglo-American force ashore on the nearby flat plain of Salerno, a move well anticipated by the Germans.

Covered by a mainly Royal Naval force, bearing the proud title of Force H,

Operation Avalanche started smoothly enough early on 9 September. On its way north it had passed, on a reciprocal course, its old adversary the Italian Fleet, steaming to Malta to surrender. But their ally's defection only drove the Germans to greater efforts and resistance stiffened rapidly. *Formidable* and *Illustrious* were employed mainly in providing the air cover of off-lying ships and, until an airfield was available, shore forces were backed up by four British-flag CVEs and the *Unicorn*, recently purpose-built as an aircraft maintenance ship but pressed into service as an orthodox carrier. The latter force, under the capable Admiral Vian, was required owing to the landing zone's considerable distance from Sicilian airfields.

Expensive but effective Seafire

With close-in carrier support, the high-performance but short-range Seafire fighter could be deployed. It proved most unsuitable and the three days that the force had to operate before a landing strip was prepared was as much as it was able to function; there was high aircraft attrition due to a combination of the CVE's low speed and virtual absence of wind, together with the Seafire's high approach speed and fragile undercarriage. As a ground support exercise it was expensive but effective and drove the enemy to new tactics, by fighter-bombers and torpedo aircraft working in hit-and-run raids that were extremely difficult to counter. Another unpleasant innovation was the German radio-controlled glider bomb, which caused several casualties, not including carriers.

Though much heavy fighting was yet to be done ashore, the Mediterranean Sea area was at last secure, to the extent where most major units departed for other theatres. The last major operation in the area was the August 1944 landings in Southern France, the blow at the 'soft underbelly of Europe', covered by nine CVEs, including two American. Practice had shown these little ships to be capable of operations as a flexible and formidable force but, with the passing

In November 1942, when Operation Torch was mounted against North Africa, the F4F Wildcat was Martlet in FAA service. Here one takes off from HMS Formidable which had US-marked aircraft and flew the Stars and Stripes for the operation.

As the Mediterranean was progressively cleared of the Germans after the Italian surrender, HMS 'Illustrious' was one of the British carriers that provided air cover mainly to off-lying ships until shore airfields were established.

Below: The Fairey Barracuda was an awkward-looking aeroplane and was awkward to handle aboard ship. It came into service from about mid-1943 as a torpedo bomber and gradually replaced the Swordfish and Albacore in general-purpose work. With a maximum speed of about 230mph it was much faster than its predecessors but was still behind the performance of its American and Japanese contemporaries.

of the Luftwaffe in Southern Europe, they were used mainly in ground support and bombardment spotting duties. Finally there was a happy return to the Greek Islands where they terrorized the bypassed German garrisons into rapid capitulation. Simple ships they were, but they had been designed for such operations in low-risk environments and they proved superb.

Carriers move east

Early 1944 found the Italian fleet an ally and the Kriegsmarine eroded to the point where the Royal Navy's fleet carriers could better be employed east of Suez, where the Japanese were still far from beaten. To be true, the convoy war in the North Atlantic proceeded at a lively level; the CVEs there were now coming forward in numbers that assisted the escorts and long-range aircraft in getting the measure of the U-boat. With this hopeful background, Illustrious headed east early in the year, followed by Victorious and Indomitable.

Before the Victorious left home waters she took part in a final fling against her old enemy Tirpitz. An almost permanent feature of the northern scene, she seldom went to sea but exerted a widespread baleful influence. The threat of her presence had caused the PQ17 disaster, air attacks on her fjord hideouts had little success and powerful British naval forces were tied down by her mere existence. After her return in September 1943 from a rare foray against Spitzbergen, she was severely damaged in her Kaafjord anchorage by British midget submarines, which blasted her with large charges whose shock effect was enough to unseat vital machinery. She was gravely injured and had no access to a dockyard but, by the following spring, had been repaired sufficiently by local resources to raise steam for trials. These preparations were observed by reconnaissance aircraft and it was resolved to 'total' her with a massive carrier-borne air strike.

No fewer than 40 Barracudas were to mount the attack, some embarked in Victorious (which was also part of the heavy cover to the northbound JW58 convoy) and the remainder in the aged Furious,

accompanying four CVEs, which force was to rendezvous at the launch point. Three of the escort carriers, *Emperor*, *Pursuer* and *Searcher*, were to provide the necessary fighter cover to both the strike and the carriers and the fourth, *Fencer*, had a primary AS function with a complement of Swordfish.

End of Tirpitz

In the pre-dawn darkness of 3 April 1944, the leading aircraft began to formate about their carriers, flying into the Arctic dawn in two separate forces, about one hour apart. *Tirpitz* was actually weighing anchor at 05.30 when suddenly assaulted out of a clear sky by the dive bombers carrying a mix of 1600- and 500-pound bombs. As the fighters strafed the battleship's decks to hinder the manning of the AA guns the 21 Barracudas staged a set-piece attack, all releasing their bombs within one minute. Their target was smothered, receiving up to nine hits, and was moving back to her berth when struck by the second wave. In spite of a very alert defence at least five more hits were scored. It had been a model operation and was deserving of great success but, in their eagerness for accuracy, the FAA pilots had

pressed home their assault to too low an altitude for the armour-piercing bombs to be effective. Nevertheless, it was to be another three months before the ship was again mobile, after which the pattern of existence was resumed as before until the November, when RAF Lancasters finally destroyed her.

The *Indefatigable* and *Implacable* were the last fleet carriers completed for the Royal Navy in time for hostilities and, after working-up, headed east to join their four compatriots in the new British Pacific Fleet forming in Ceylon. Europe had by then become something of a backwater; convoys flowed freely, untroubled by the few remaining enemy surface ships and with a wealth of escorts and CVEs to counter the U-boats, which were suffering such a rate of attrition that few commanders survived long enough to be termed veteran.

The veteran *Furious* could now be laid up from sheer exhaustion as the little utility ships shouldered the burden; they cut enemy communications and allowed him no rest. Perhaps their greatest contribution was through their bringing of the war to the occupied lands, demonstrating to their oppressed peoples that the end of the tunnel was near.

HMS 'Implacable' was one of a pair of modified Illustrious-class carriers completed in 1944 and commissioned just in time to see active service in the Far East. Here, as if to symbolize the nearing end of the European war, she parades her men and machines as she comes to anchor.

Leyte: Carrier for bait

After the great carrier actions of 1942, both the American and Japanese fleets spent 1943 largely in the replacement of ships and aircrews and it was the turn of the fighting man on the ground to dominate the Pacific arena. Supported by a flexible fleet deploying an ever more-ingenious range of amphibious craft, US marines and soldiers earned immortality in an island-hopping campaign that both outflanked the enemy and met him in some of the most bitterly contested battles in the history of warfare.

Rabaul was the main Japanese base for the conquest of both the Solomons and New Guinea; it was approached relentlessly not only by an island route but also by a paralleled advance along the New Guinea coast.

Based on Hawaii, a series of operations relieved the enemy of the Gilberts and the Marshalls, establishing the axis of the long swing in the direction of the strategically important Philippines. These moves were conducted over open sea and invited a major fleet confrontation sooner or later and it may be appropriate at this point to take stock of the opposing carrier strengths, these holding the key to the outcome.

New carriers

Under construction for the Japanese Navy was the 34,200-ton (full load) *Taiho*, looking very much like the British carriers that influenced her and complete with a flightdeck almost four inches in thickness. A third great ship of the Musashi Class, the *Shinano*, was being completed as a 71,900-tonner, but in spite of her size she could carry only 47 aircraft. Five enlarged Shokakus never proceeded beyond the planning stage but a series of 15 improved Hiryus, named the Unryu Class, was started but only three were destined to be completed.

The remainder were passenger liner conversions, except for the reconstruction of the former seaplane carriers *Chiyoda* and *Chitose* together with the *Ryuho* from a slower auxiliary. Seaplanes were used extensively by the Japanese for fleet reconnaissance and, after Midway, they converted the 29,900-ton battleships *Hyuga* and *Ise* into hybrid carriers, retaining four twin 14-inch turrets forward and amidships but having the after end rebuilt to provide stowage for over 20 aircraft.

All this was small beer compared with the American programme, which was at last bearing fruit. The *Essex* (CV17) commissioned in May, *Intrepid* (CV11) in August and another *Hornet* (CV12) and *Wasp* (CV18) within days of each other in November. All were big ships able to stow around 100 aircraft, but Nimitz himself was yet to wait awhile. During 1943 US strength was augmented by the complete nine-ship Independence Class of CVLs built, it may be recalled, on 33-knot cruiser hulls and carrying up to 45 aircraft. Not only were they and the constant streams of CVEs by then coming forward but also the aircraft and aircrew to man them. In contrast with the almost carefree profligacy with which the Japanese expended their trained fliers, the American system was to pull them out after a given number of missions and use them to form the nuclei of fresh wings for the new carriers.

New aircraft

The material quantity was matched by its quality. Out went the well-trusted F4F fighter in favour of the new F6F Hellcat and, later, the distinctive gull-winged F4U Corsair. With the .50-calibre machine gun

Facing page: Loading a 21-inch torpedo on to a Grumman Avenger preparing for a strike early in 1944.

Below: A squadron of Chance Vought F4U-2 Corsair night fighters being prepared for take-off on the flightdeck of CV11 USS 'Intrepid'.

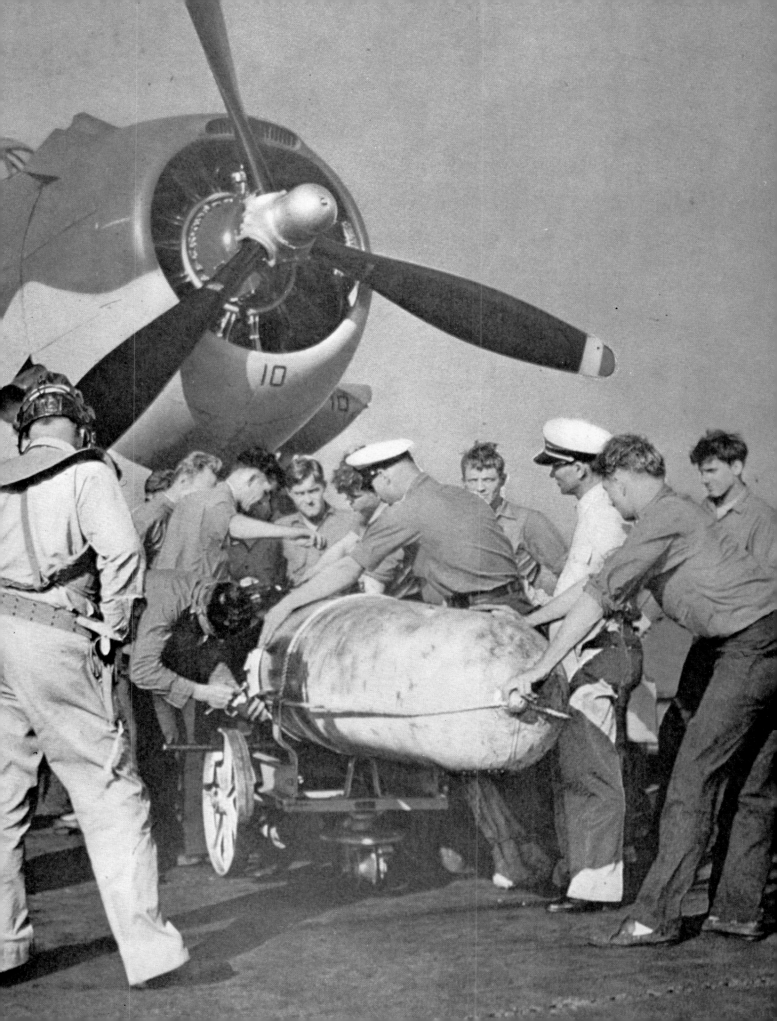

The F4U Corsair came into operational use in the Pacific during 1943 in time to play a vital part in turning the tide against the Japanese. A total of more than 12,000 Corsairs was built, the Brewster and Goodyear companies adding to the parent Chance Vought production. This picture shows a Goodyear-built preserved F4U-1 flying during a Confederate Air Force air show in Texas.

being partnered by 20mm cannon, the Zeros were to be matched in manoeuvrability and outgunned. The Avenger TBF, after its disastrous Midway debut, was being accepted as an excellent replacement for the prewar Devastator and the Dauntless was about to leave front-line service as the Helldiver went into quantity production.

Late August 1943 saw the American Pacific Fleet complete its preliminary exercising and it then formed a series of task forces to strike at various 'soft' targets to blood the new aircrews and F6Fs. The new CVs and CVLs hit Marcus and Baker Islands on 31 August-1 September and Tarawa on 19 September. On 5-6 October no fewer than seven new carriers, organized as TF14, flew about 750 sorties against Wake. These annoyances were on a far-flung scale and the enemy began to react, moving his main fleet strength from its established base at Truk in the Carolines (well positioned for the Solomons campaign) to an advanced anchorage at Eniwetok, at the northern end of the Marshalls. This was exploited by *Saratoga* and *Princeton* in early November by a strike against Rabaul which seriously damaged five heavy cruisers.

In November the Japanese were caught flat-footed by an unprecedentedly powerful three-pronged American assault on the Gilberts. Reduced temporarily to only one carrier, *Zuikaku*, the powerful Imperial Fleet was powerless to intervene in the face of Spruance's force, which included six CVs, five CVLs and eight CVEs carrying a total force of nearly 900 aircraft. The larger carriers were organized as TF50 in four task groups to ensure total air superiority, with the CVEs rendering local cover to order over the landing zone.

Two carriers torpedoed

The enemy commander, Koga, sagely refused to be drawn into a surface action and used his land-based aircraft to the full. A low-level raid by 16 'Betty' bombers out of a setting sun succeeded in torpedoing the CVL *Independence* which, though severely damaged, was saved by her regular navy subdivision and withdrew under her own steam. It has already been mentioned that the CVE lacked these essentials, a fact brutally underlined only three days later, on 23 November, when I-175, one of 18 Japanese submarines in the area, put a salvo of three torpedoes into the little *Liscombe Bay* just off Makin Island. She sank with heavy loss of life after about 20 minutes of explosions so violent that falling debris hit a destroyer three miles away.

Losses were accepted as inevitable in this, a dress rehearsal for greater things. Ashore, the enemy disputed every inch of territory, particularly on Tarawa, but he was doomed from the outset as he could not be reinforced as long as TF50 held the ring. Within a week it was all over and the Japanese braced themselves against the next obvious step, the invasion of the Marshalls. Their forward base at Kwajalein was hard hit by six carriers in early December with the infliction of what had become an aircraft loss rate of anything between five and ten times that of the Americans.

Six CVs and six CVLs, reorganized as TF58, spearheaded the Marshalls operation with eight CVEs again mounting shore support and AS cover. After a week the objectives were achieved, after resistance that reached new heights of fanaticism with Japanese fatalities reaching 98 per cent of

110

the defenders of Eniwetok. Within days, on 17 February 1944, nine carriers of TF58 under Mitscher, escorted by Spruance with a heavy surface group, mounted a 1250-sortie strike on the long-inviolate enemy fleet base at Truk. Swamping the defences, the marauders sank about 45 ships and destroyed 200 aircraft.

On to the Marianas

Like a biblical scourge, the force then turned northwest to the Marianas, a sensitive link in the enemy's inner defence ring. He lost a further 170 aircraft in probing raids by the Americans on Guam, Tinian and Saipan, and the Japanese Navy could no longer ignore these pointers to the next amphibious assaults. The Japanese ships had been reorganized into three balanced groups, each built around a trio of carriers. Unable to use devastated Truk, they were to be based on the Palaus, a fact well appreciated by Mitscher, who hit the area with ten carriers at the end of March in an operation aptly named Desecrate. Koga received brief warning and saved the bulk of his fleet by scattering it at sea, but losing over 30 vessels that were caught still in harbour. The first attack, on the 30th, almost totally destroyed the air forces; that night they were reinforced only to be shot out of the sky again on the following day. Nearly 250 aircraft were lost in a seven-to-one ratio, with the Americans following the simple minimum requirement adumbrated by Nelson — annihilation.

April and May 1944 saw TF58 elements switch flexibly to facilitating the advance along the New Guinea coast, at the northern end of which lies the island of Biak upon which the enemy had built a number of airfields to control the southern approaches to the Philippines. Its invasion on 27 May looked like producing the desired reaction from the Imperial Fleet, then at Tawi Tawi in the Sulu Archipelago, but, in the very act of preparing its strike against the American amphibious forces, it was diverted by grave news from the north; the Marianas, too, were being invaded.

Every Japanese airfield in the group was devastated by TF58, (by then 15 carriers strong) between 11 and 13 June and over 280 aircraft were destroyed, mostly on the ground. Ozawa finally sailed with the main body of the fleet on the 13th, joining up on the 16th with the second force under Ugaki east of the Philippines. He was counting on a total of nearly 1000 aircraft to give him parity with the Americans, not only those aboard his nine carriers and seaplane carriers but about 500 more in airfields ashore. They were on islands ringing the zone and the plan was to use them as staging posts for the refuelling and rearming of aircraft, enabling them to. attack the Americans on either leg.

On course for battle

A couple of years earlier, Ozawa would have been unstoppable, but things had changed. After one of his reconnaissance aircraft reported TF58 on the afternoon of the 18th, Ozawa made his dispositions, with a van force of three light carriers each with a powerful escort (including the giant 18-inch gunned battleships *Yamato* and *Musashi*) spaced well apart in separate groups and in

A Nakajima B5N 'Kate' torpedo bomber, hit by AA fire from the carrier it was attacking during the Marshall Islands actions in December 1943, disintegrates as its torpedo falls harmlessly away.

Left: Many hands make
light work of manoeuvring a
Grumman F6F Hellcat into
position for warming-up
before take-off.

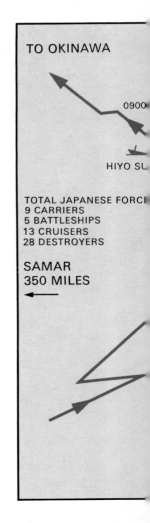

TO OKINAWA

0900

HIYO SU

TOTAL JAPANESE FORCE
9 CARRIERS
5 BATTLESHIPS
13 CRUISERS
28 DESTROYERS

SAMAR
350 MILES

line abreast. About 100 miles astern followed the Main Force of the other two large groups, each built around three larger carriers and with Ozawa wearing his flag in the new *Taiho*.

Sighting reports by American submarines gave Spruance adequate warning of his enemy's approach but he based his plans on the protection of the Saipan landings, grouping his fleet into five separate bodies, four built around three or four carriers apiece and the fifth a surface strike force formed around no fewer than seven battleships.

Ozawa's exact position was not determined until the evening of the 18th, when he transmitted a long radio message exhorting his shore-based aircraft to a maximum effort on the morrow and seemingly unaware that these same forces had already been drastically culled by American air strikes. Spruance reacted calmly enough, not turning on to an attacking course until first light on the 19th.

Turkey shoot

By 07.30 the first strike of 73 aircraft had left

Ozawa's leading carriers, timed to arrive as the Americans were recovering from a heavy attack by land-based aircraft — which never materialized. At 08.00 the first division put up a second force of 130 aircraft, followed at 08.30 by a third of 49 from the second division, and then a fourth, to bring the number of Japanese aircraft airborne to 370. But hardly were they away when *Taiho* was hit by a single submarine torpedo and was rapidly engulfed by fire. The aviation spirit that fed the flames also drained below into badly ventilated spaces, generating fumes that finally detonated at about 11.00, destroying the ship; Ozawa had already transferred to a cruiser. Within 20 minutes the veteran *Shokaku* was smitten by a salvo of three torpedoes and at 14.00 she, too, blew up and the Flying Crane flew no more, taking with her a large part of Ozawa's second-wave aircraft.

At about 10.00, American surveillance radar displays came alive with the echoes of the first Japanese aircraft at about 150 miles range. Spruance coolly waited a further 20 minutes before reversing course and putting up a maximum number of fighters with freshly filled tanks. All flightdecks were cleared of strike aircraft, which were sent to attack the island airstrips, whose potential was well appreciated. For four hours the Japanese aircraft flung themselves against a barrier of over 400 Hellcats working in shifts. Between 300 and 350 were destroyed by the Americans for the loss of 29; minimal damage was inflicted on TF58 and the day has gone down in history as the great 'Marianas Turkey Shoot'.

As the longer-legged Japanese planes were working out to their maximum range the Americans still had not pinpointed Ozawa's position. The latter, in turn, did not believe his losses and, assuming the aircraft to be safely ashore, turned northwest to meet his tankers and top-up bunkers to renew the fight the following day. Spruance spent the night steaming for the spot where the enemy was thought to be.

Strike at last light

Ozawa occupied the following forenoon refuelling and coming to terms with the fact that only about 100 aircraft remained to him. Throughout a frustrating day the Americans sought him until finally, at about 16.00, he was pinpointed at a range of 275 miles, a near maximum for that late

hour. Within an incredible ten minutes over 200 American aircraft took the air, 85 Hellcats covering Avengers and Helldivers.

Out of a dusk pocked with flak the strike bored through the enemy CAP, fatally damaging the second division's *Hiyo* with two torpedoes and severely damaging *Zuikaku*, *Chiyoda* and *Ryujo*. They returned with dry tanks after darkness and Mitscher eased their problems — and earned near-immortality — by ordering the fleet carriers to 'light up'. Starshells, signal lamps and decklights blazed in a glorious madness that invited submarine attack but brought his fliers home. Eighty or so aircraft were lost in landing or ditching or simply being jettisoned from flightdecks to make room for more. Pilots put down on any ship that could accept them and all but 50 survived the day.

Action could not be resumed on the 21st as the chastened Ozawa retreated towards Okinawa and the Americans were frustrated at having had only one swipe, even though the enemy was three carriers the poorer.

Japanese War Cabinet resigns

Spruance's main preoccupation, had, nevertheless, to be in his major responsibility for covering the amphibious landings and his

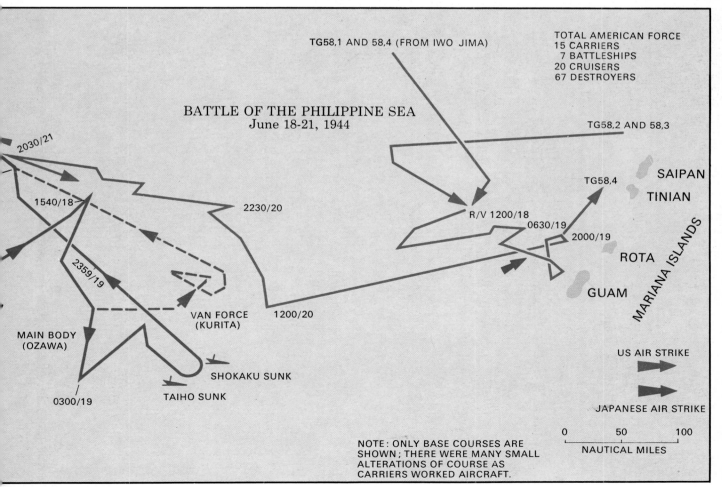

BATTLE OF THE PHILIPPINE SEA
June 18-21, 1944

TG58,1 AND 58,4 (FROM IWO JIMA)

TOTAL AMERICAN FORCE
15 CARRIERS
 7 BATTLESHIPS
20 CRUISERS
67 DESTROYERS

TG58,2 AND 58,3

2030/21

1540/18

2230/20

R/V 1200/18

0630/19

TG58,4

SAIPAN

TINIAN

2000/19

2359/19

ROTA

MARIANA ISLANDS

VAN FORCE
(KURITA)

1200/20

GUAM

MAIN BODY
(OZAWA)

SHOKAKU SUNK

TAIHO SUNK

0300/19

US AIR STRIKE

JAPANESE AIR STRIKE

0   50   100
NAUTICAL MILES

NOTE: ONLY BASE COURSES ARE
SHOWN; THERE WERE MANY SMALL
ALTERATIONS OF COURSE AS
CARRIERS WORKED AIRCRAFT.

113

participation in what came to be known as the Battle of the Philippine Sea was inevitably coloured by it. Even so, it was the greatest of the large-scale carrier battles and had far-reaching effects, notably in the destruction of the greater part of the enemy's airpower; the loss was shortly to be visited upon him in a terrible nemesis. A further bonus was the total despondency suffered by the Japanese upper echelons. Ozawa wanted to resign, and shortly after the fall of Saipan the War Cabinet did resign and Nagumo, that most doughty of opponents, committed suicide because of what had befallen them.

During the next few months the American Fleet acted in support of operations to take and consolidate key points in the Western Carolines and the Palaus and the island of Morotai. The two axes of the US advance were obviously converging upon the Philippines and the enemy would surely contest them bitterly as their loss would open the way to an assault on the homeland itself. During August 1944 the controversial Spruance was relieved by Halsey and some fleet redispositions were made, although Mitscher retained immediate command of the fast carrier groups.

Shortage of pilots

From early October 17 carriers of TF38, as the fleet was now known, organized in four groups, operated against Luzon, Formosa and Okinawa to draw the enemy's attention from the chosen assault area in the Leyte Gulf. The planned attrition of these strikes was even more effective than could have been hoped for the Japanese threw in — and lost — the greater part of the newly trained pilots intended for their carriers, by then repaired and increased by the freshly commissioned *Amagi* and *Katsuragi*. So few pilots remained that naval plans for the defence of the Philippines had to be recast around defeating the Americans by surface units only, a forlorn hope against a fleet so well endowed with flightdecks that it could afford to devote 11 CVEs to ferrying duties, topping up the 1100-odd aircraft in the attack carriers and a further 18 CVEs for close support of the actual landings.

Only four Japanese carriers could be even partly equipped with aircraft and on the principle that a carrier — like a gun without ammunition — looks effective until proven otherwise, Ozawa was given the desperate

Below: Even more hands are needed for this chore of clearing a crashed Hellcat from the deck of a British escort carrier operating with the East Indies Fleet in March 1945.

mission of acting as a sacrificial decoy. TF38's carriers were to be irresistibly lured away so that the Japanese surface ships, covered by land-based aircraft, could penetrate to the landing area.

A powerful force, built around seven battleships, was based on Lingga, near Singapore, and sailed on 18 October for Brunei in northern Borneo, a move stimulated by obvious American preparations. They arrived in time to hear the news of the landings at Leyte on the 20th and left again on the 22nd in two groups. The main strength, under Kurita, was given the task of forcing a passage to the Leyte Gulf via the Sibuyan Sea and the San Bernardino Strait. The remainder, under Nishimura, was to attack simultaneously after transitting the Mindanao Sea and the Surigao Strait, having been reinforced en route by Shima's cruiser force, which had left the Pescadores on the 21st.

Coat trailing

Meanwhile Ozawa's four allocated carriers, whose escort included the two hybrid Ise-class battleships (each without aircraft), left Japan on 20 October to trail their coats northeast of Luzon. Toyoda, the Japanese C-in-C, reasoned, correctly, that a man of 'Bull' Halsey's temperament could not fail to take the bait. For that to happen, however, the force had first to be seen but, with a contrariness so much a feature of war, it completely eluded the American patrol submarines. On the other hand, Kurita, who wished to remain undetected, ran into two

Above: A Japanese 'Jill' torpedo bomber so far surviving an intense hail of AA fire during the American carrier attack on Truk in the Carolines in February 1944.

submarines west of Palawan early on the 23rd, losing two heavy cruisers (including the flagship) and having a third disabled. Shima, too, was reported as he raced southward to join the yet-undetected Nishimura.

Frustrated after a day of inactivity Ozawa had his flagship, *Zuikaku*, advertise his presence with a long radio transmission on the evening of the 23rd. In spite of over 100 US fleet units in the area, that also seemed to be undetected as TF38's attention was concentrated to the south and west; Nishimura, too, had been located by the forenoon of the 24th.

First blood to the Japanese

First blood of the day went to the Japanese when a raid by shore-based aircraft put a bomb through the flightdeck of the CVL *Princeton*, a unit of TF38's most northerly group. Exploding below, the projectile started uncontrollable fires but, with an overdone 'don't give up the ship' gesture, other ships lay close aboard to play hoses on the flames and were severely damaged when the carrier was racked by a devastating and fatal series of explosions. This aerial effort on the part of the enemy left Kurita uncovered and, in what became known as the Battle of the Sibuyan Sea, he was assailed by wave after wave of American aircraft from all three available task groups.

Although other ships were damaged, the 'Aunt Sally' was the super-battleship *Musashi*, which was eventually put down by an almost-unbelievable 18 to 20 torpedo and twice as many bomb hits. Under these blows, Kurita was forced temporarily to reverse course and his despairing transmissions were received by Ozawa who, still undetected, promptly mounted a strike by his tyro-pilots on the US carriers. But as a ploy to get himself noticed, this, too, was doomed to failure as the Americans were already too hotly engaged with land-based aircraft and preoccupied with attempts to save the *Princeton* to conjecture on the origin of the latest pestilence.

Ironically, Halsey had by then become concerned that no Japanese carriers had been observed and fell prey to the theory that his enemy was occupying his attention with his surface forces while preparing a massive carrier strike in another quarter. The situation was, of course, precisely the reverse but it did stimulate the American commander to reconnoitre the hitherto unsearched northern sector.

The bait taken

At long last, by mid-afternoon, Ozawa was on the map but at too great a range to be attacked before dark. Even so, his efforts were about to be rewarded as Halsey,

116

obviously reacting to a possible solution to his concern, swallowed the bait and turned northward with his fast battleship force and all four of the Third Fleet carrier groups to be in a position to attack at first light on 25 October. In truth, the Japanese carriers had between them only 24 fighters, four torpedo aircraft and one dive-bomber, but if fully complemented they would have been more than matched by two of TF38's groups. Halsey's decision to withdraw virtually everything while three separate Japanese surface groups were known to be abroad is inexplicable, yet so accurately foreseen by Toyoda.

Meanwhile Kurita, far from beaten, had turned back on course at about 17.00 on the 24th, towards a now unguarded San Bernardino Strait. His appearance promised to be the more effective because Admiral Kinkaid at Leyte Gulf did not appreciate that Halsey had withdrawn completely; indeed he (Kinkaid) was concentrated with his own surface forces under Oldendorf to cover the Surigao Strait to the south, through which he had correctly anticipated that Shima and Nishimura would attack that night. Consequently, at 23.00 on the 24th Kinkaid, content that he was about to inflict a bloody nose on the force from the south, was oblivious of his mortal danger from the north, where Kurita was threading the strait with darkened ships.

Toyoda's plan had called for a synchronized dawn attack on the gulf from both north and south. Had that happened it could hardly have failed but Nishimura, bent on glory, tore into the Surigao Strait, leaving Shima well astern. Oldendorf's ambush was expertly prepared; first the enemy was harried by torpedo-armed PT boats, then by destroyers attacking in the classic manner so well practised by the Japanese themselves and then, as they emerged in line ahead from the narrow waterway, had their T crossed in textbook fashion by six waiting battleships.

Battleships obliterated

Nishimura's two battleships were obliterated and so were three destroyers; only a cruiser and a destroyer lived to fall back on to Shima's force, 30 miles astern. Uncharacteristically for a Japanese commander, he reversed course and pulled out, harried all the way into the Mindanao Sea, only to suffer yet another loss the following day from aircraft. In absolute contrast to this debacle, Kurita was into open sea and running down the east coast of Samar. If there was joy in the American camp, it was about to be quenched.

Kinkaid's close air support at Leyte was supplied by 16 CVEs organized into three groups. On 25 October the CAP was airborne by 05.00, which was fortunate as, in the pre-

Smoking AA guns as a Japanese dive bomber attack on a US carrier is driven off, with Avengers and crews on the flightdeck, during an action near Leyte in December 1944.

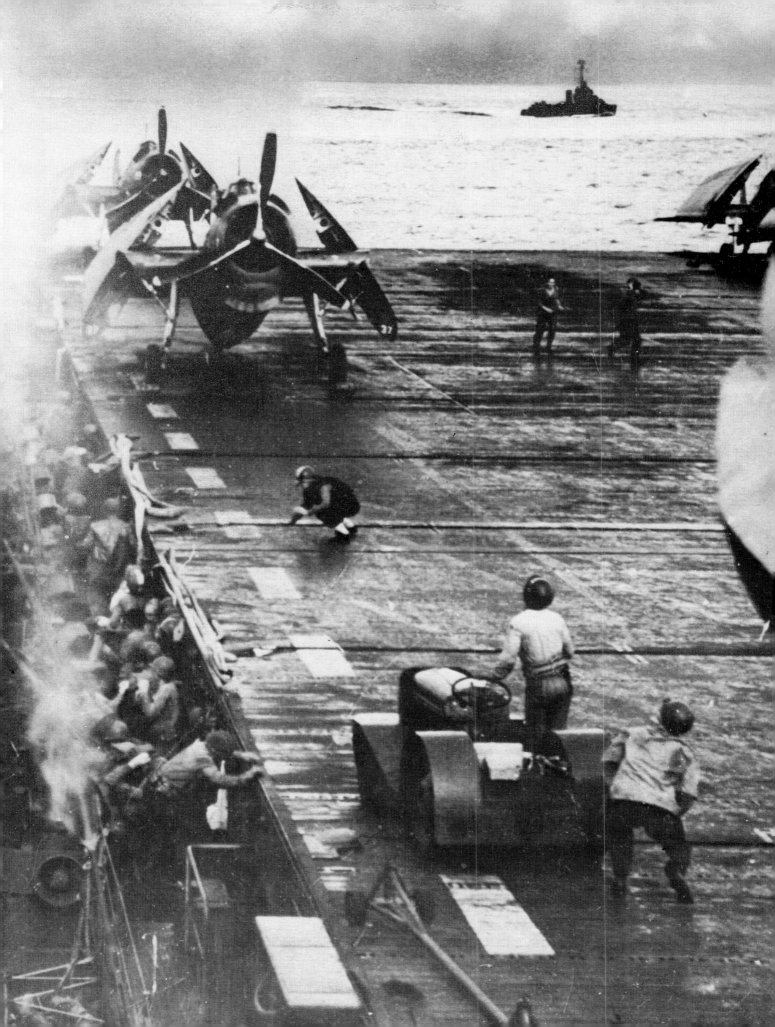

Dramatic picture of a Japanese Kamikaze manoeuvring his Zero to crash into the deck of an American ship towards the end of the Pacific battles. During the Samar action five US carriers suffered hits from suicide pilots.

dawn gloom, it sighted Kurita's force immediately to the north. Understandably, the nearest group, TF77.4.3 (or Taffy 3), requested verification of the sighting report, which proved unnecessary as the massive tophamper of the Japanese loomed through the uncertain visibility. For a brief uncomprehending spell the Americans gazed on the spectacle of four enemy battleships, eight cruisers and 11 destroyers. Kurita, on his part, could not believe his luck, having apparently caught a main carrier group totally unprepared. If it was true, everything depended upon hitting hard before it could get its aircraft aloft and, in his anxiety, he ordered 'General Chase' and his attack lost all cohesion.

Between them, the three CVE groups, given warning, could have mustered enough striking power to destroy Kurita in detail, but this was surprise, only one group was present, and aircraft were away already on a dozen distant missions. Taffy 3's commander, Admiral C. A. F. Sprague, did what he could, radioed for assistance, made smoke, and scattered into a dozen convenient rain squalls. Aircraft, armed or not, were all sent up to make feint attacks and the small destroyer and DE escort made heroic efforts at torpedo attacks. Kurita's resolution, fortunately, had been already dented by his battering in the Sibuyan Sea and he was content to lie back as the little CVEs steered desperately from the last salvo in a forest of white columns thrown up by the *Yamato's* huge 18-inch projectiles, 16-inch from the *Nagato* and 14-inch from *Kongo* and *Haruna*, laced liberally with 8- and 6-inch from the cruisers.

Carriers saved

Desperate though the situation was, Sprague was falling back gradually southwards on the battleships of Oldendorf, heading up fast from Surigao. Kurita was well aware of that advance and also of the rapidly increasing American aerial activity as Taffy 1 and 2 came into the fight. He was under severe pressure from what was really only a small destroyer force prepared to sell itself dearly in the best traditions of the service and he was taking damage. Meanwhile, the CVEs were saved mainly by the fact that the great enemy armour-piercing projectiles passed through their thin skins without exploding; even so, *Gambier Bay* foundered after being riddled. So close was the range that the carriers' 5-inch guns could be brought into action and, as Sprague manoeuvred frantically, he was exhorted by his gunnery officer to 'hold on and we'll get 'em with the 40-mils'.

At 09.25, suddenly, incredibly, Kurita's nerve broke at the thought of the retribution which had to come. Sprague's men leaned wearily on their hot guns and watched the enemy melt away into the haze. 'Dammit, they're getting away', Sprague heard one of his signalmen say, but the relief was absolute at five carriers still afloat. Had the Japanese held on it would have been doubtful whether Oldendorf's elderly ships, short of ammunition from the previous night's action, could have effectively prevented them from creating mayhem in the massed amphibious ships and transports in the gulf.

Enter the Kamikaze

But the battle off Samar was not yet done; five carriers of various groups had Japanese aircraft deliberately crashed into them — the sinister Kamikaze had arrived — but only one ship, the *St Lo*, was fatally damaged. The carriers were not the first to suffer from suicide dives; that dubious distinction had gone to an Australian cruiser smitten four days previously.

After a few indecisive manoeuvres meanwhile, Kurita hot-footed it back for the San Bernardino Strait like a boy discovered in an orchard. Neither Oldendorf nor the reluctant Halsey could hinder him, although aircraft of the nearest carrier strike group did make ineffective contact. As the

Curtiss SB2C Helldivers running-up engines on the flightdeck of an American Casablanca-class escort carrier prior to take-off during the 1943-44 Pacific battles. Note the F (flying-off) flag is still at the dip position.

Japanese entered the sanctuary of the strait at 21.30 one of the strangest actions of the war drew to its close. It should never have happened. For the relatively trifling cost of two CVEs, two destroyers and a DE, the Americans were allowed to recover the situation and stave off what could have been a great disaster.

Meanwhile, what of Ozawa? At 02.00 on 25 October (as Kurita was sweeping down the Samar coast and Nishimura was being dismembered) radar-fitted aircraft from the CVL *Independence* detected his force east of Cape Engaño, the most northerly point of Luzon. Intent upon his vision of destroying the Japanese main carrier force, Halsey was boring through the night with the fast battleships of TF34, trailed by the three available carrier groups of TF38.

Forced into action

Ozawa was pinpointed at first light and 150 aircraft were away in short order. The Americans were there in only an hour and, although met by heavy flak, were surprised to see only a dozen Zeros. It was all that the Japanese had but, true to his mission, the enemy admiral turned north to lure Halsey

ever farther away from his post. The *Chitose* was so severely mauled that she sank within an hour, leaving her compatriots damaged in varying degrees. By that time the American commander was receiving frantic transmissions from Taffy 3 and his growing suspicions that all was not well were resolved into reluctant action by a radio message from Nimitz, CINCPAC himself, at Hawaii, peremptorily requesting clarification as to what *was* going on off the eastern Philippine coast.

TF38's second strike at about 10.00 had left the *Chiyoda* sinking and, as the aircraft returned, Halsey reluctantly reversed TF34's course, having to leave Mitscher to finish the job, but he was too late either to aid Sprague or to prevent the withdrawal of Kurita's force to safety for a while.

Mitscher, adequately enough, went on to destroy both the *Zuiho* and, most satisfyingly, the *Zuikaku*, the last of the quartet that had violated Pearl Harbor. Ozawa, surprisingly, salvaged most of the remainder of his force, including the two hybrid battleships, and the complex series of actions known collectively as the Battle of Leyte Gulf were ended.

Getting ready for the final stages of the Pacific war, an American carrier unloading Corsair fighters on to lighters for delivery ashore at Guian in the Philippines.

The Japanese carrier 'Zuiho', under heavy US attack during the closing stages of the Battle of Leyte Gulf. The 'Zuiho' was one of four carriers destroyed during the action, which effectively heralded the end of the Imperial Japanese Fleet.

Air power decisive

The enemy had fought courageously and his plans had worked well but, except for the old-style gunfight in the Surigao Strait, the result hinged on his lack of air power, both land- and carrier-based. On 24 October the Imperial Japanese Navy was a potent force; by 26 October it was a collection of survivors that was never again a fleet. Leyte Gulf had cost it four carriers, three battleships, ten cruisers, nine destroyers — and the last of its morale.

Even so, the enemy was not finished and then began the hour of the Kamikaze, one of the war's most cost-effective weapons. Its pilots needed fanaticism and only a modicum of training; if an aircraft could fly, it was suitable and, in addition, had twice its usual range because it needed no fuel for a return trip. Above all, it exerted a powerful psychological effect and this, together with damage to many of its ships, including seven carriers, caused TF38 to haul off temporarily from its primary mission of supporting the reconquest of the Philippines. It returned after a brief period with extra fighter and AA complements, and a burning desire to clean out every enemy island airfield, an ongoing task that occupied the group until the surrender.

Shipping squandered

One of Japan's great failings as an island power had been a failure to profit from Great Britain's experiences and to safeguard her merchant fleet. Although essential for her survival, she squandered it with a cheerful profligacy, having no more than a token convoy system, few escorts and no organized series replacement programme worthy of the name. American submarines particularly took a heavy toll and, by the later part of 1944, the enemy was in deep trouble. Crash construction produced some of the desperately required vessels but four of the first five escort carrier conversions fell victim to the very submarines that they were built to counter.

Indeed, a month after Leyte, they were accompanied to the bottom by the largest carrier yet, the *Shinano*, converted form the third Musashi-class battleship hull. This great ship, fresh from her builders, without aircraft (and, apparently, without damage control), ran into a 'rookie' American submarine on its first patrol. Six torpedoes, six hits, and a career was stifled at birth.

Fleet train formed

In November 1944, the British Pacific Fleet came into being, formed around a nucleus of four fleet carriers. With two battleships and half a dozen cruisers in attendance, it equated roughly to one of the Third Fleet's task groups. Without doubt, the Americans considered the Pacific 'their' war and a certain amount of political manoeuvring was required to gain acceptance of a British presence. Having arrived it found itself with the requirement for establishing the 'fleet train' so essential for supporting warships on extended operations, particularly as it would be 5000 miles from its main base in Sydney, Australia.

Reporting for duty in mid-March 1945, the BPF was given an apprenticeship task in the suppression of the Japanese aerial activity expected to be stimulated by the American assault on Okinawa. This small but strategically important island was barely 500 miles from the Japanese

---

THE BATTLE OF LEYTE GULF
October 24-25th 1944

OZAWA'S FORCE (FROM JAPAN)
4 AIRCRAFT CARRIERS
2 BATTLESHIPS
3 CRUISERS
8 DESTROYERS

ZUIHO
ZUIKAKU

2359/24

CHIYODA
CHITOSE

1900/25

SHIMA'S FORCE (FROM FORMOSA)
3 CRUISERS
7 DESTROYERS

1030/24

0630/25

LUZON

COMBINED FORCE

0820/25

TG38,3

2359/24

HALSEY'S FORCE

SAN BERNARDINO ST.

1800/25   2359/24

0800/25

KURITA'S FORCE
5 BATTLESHIPS
12 CRUISERS
15 DESTROYERS

0200/24

MUSASHI

PANAY

SAMAR

LEYTE

OLDENDORF'S FORCE

SUBMARINE ATTACK

NEGROS

SURIGAO ST.

YAMASHIRO AND FUSO

2230/24

0100/25

MOGAMI

PALAWAN

SULU SEA

MINDANAO

NISHIMURA'S FORCE
2 BATTLESHIPS
1 CRUISER
4 DESTROYERS

0   100

NAUTICAL MILES

BORNEO

● POSITION OF VARIOUS JAPANESE FORCES AT DAWN 24 x 44

While the USN was rolling back the Japanese in the Pacific the British were shattering such shipping as remained around German-held Northern Europe. Here Fairey Fireflies are landing on a British fleet carrier after attacking shipping off Norway in December 1944, with Barracudas spotted forward.

mainland and about halfway between it and Formosa. The previous month the equally small Iwo Jima had been taken after fanatical resistance, with the Third Fleet carrier group striking Japanese airfields and the CVEs hitting the island bases to keep the enemy's heads down.

Kamikazes had become a major nuisance and in that respect the 3-inch armoured flightdecks of the British carriers came into their own. All four were hit, *Formidable* actually having a hole punched in her deck and incurring a slightly twisted hull which she carried for the rest of her career, but none was out of action for more than a few hours while the mess was cleared up. Some of the unprotected American carriers, notably *Franklin* and Mitscher's flagship *Bunker Hill*, were fortunate to survive their damage. Many had to withdraw for major repairs but their thin skins were perhaps justified after plenty of carriers had become available in that they could stow nearly twice as many aircraft and this, together with their superb operating procedures, accounted for their complete ascendancy.

Huge losses

During the Okinawa operations, the Japanese lost about 4000 aircraft, almost half of them Kamikazes; the Americans lost 36 ships and about 5000 crewmen. Ashore, for the loss of 7600 men the Americans killed an almost unbelievable 172,000 of the enemy. Not until June 1945 was the island taken and the bone-weary carrier crews allowed to withdraw for a breathing spell after three months at sea.

The Japanese instinct for self-destruction was not confined to fliers alone. On 6 April 1945 the monster *Yamato*, with a cruiser and eight destroyers, left the Inland Sea with the very last available bunker fuel stocks aboard. There was sufficient to get them only as far as Okinawa, where they were to wreak the maximum havoc among the many ships anchored offshore before running themselves aground, whereupon the crews were to go ashore and fight to the end. The ships were spared this final indignity by being sighted soon after their departure and swamped the following day by almost 400 aircraft from 13 carriers. Only four destroyers survived the attack, which cost the Americans only ten aircraft.

From early July both US and British fleets worked over the nearly helpless Japanese mainland almost at will but the enemy's collapse in August made the final act of invasion unnecessary.

123

THE NUCLEAR ERA

Jet age giants

Previous page: The mighty 'Nimitz' (CVN68), name ship of a class of three nuclear-powered monsters of 82,000 tons displacement, over 1000ft long and capable of making 35 knots and operating 90 jet aircraft. 'Nimitz' is pictured here in the Mediterranean in 1978.

Suddenly, it was a world again at peace, a world without employment for either the men or machines that had won it. The former departed in their ill-fitting new suits for factory and office and the latter, for the most part, went 'into mothballs'. Every suitable creek had its trot of ships newly reduced to reserve, the sunlight glinting dully from the silver-grey cocooning spun over essential fittings.

Around the world the US Navy had deployed about 41,000 aircraft, dwarfing the Royal Navy's complement, not yet at its first one thousand. Both fleets had ambitious carrier-building programmes in hand and a surprisingly large number of hulls went on to completion.

US building continued

By VJ-Day, 15 August 1945, 16 of the Essex-class CVs had been completed and a further eight advanced to the point where it was economical to finish them, though more slowly. Six, CV50-55, had been cancelled at an early stage leaving two, *Reprisal* (CV35) and *Iwo Jima* (CV46) as incomplete hulls eventually sacrificed in tests to destruction. For the better part of two decades the Essex-class carriers were to form the backbone of the American CV force, supplemented at first only by the already briefly mentioned Midways, laid down late in 1943 and incorporating hard-won lessons of the early war years.

Requirements for space boosted the

Right: Nerve centre of HMS 'Ark Royal' (R09), one of only two of the planned British Audacious-class fleet carriers of contemporary design and intent with the Midways but of rather smaller parameters all round. 'Eagle' was the second Audacious-class carrier.

Below: USS 'Midway' (CV41), also one of a class of three (Coral Sea), was of late war years design to take the massive complement of up to 137 aircraft. She was completed shortly after the end of the war and was the first American carrier to adopt the British angled deck innovation, although the 'Antietam' was the first US angled-deck carrier at sea in 1953. 'Midway' is shown here at a much later date with a brace of LVT A7 Corsair IIs overflying.

dimensions and the displacement leapt from the 27,000 standard tons of the Essex-class to over 40,000, largely accounted for by a 3½-inch armoured flightdeck, worked in as a result of first-hand knowledge of repairing damaged British carriers that had been mauled by bombs to an extent that would have destroyed a lightly built American ship. To reduce their susceptibility to fire, the newcomers' single hangar could be subdivided by fireproof curtains and, with an elevator serving each section, flying operations could be continued from a flightdeck obstructed by an island of minimum cross-section.

As with the CV9 hulls, a fleet speed of 33 knots was required which, for the giant 968-footers, meant a 40 per cent increase in machinery power, from 150,000 to 212,000shp. Where British carriers accepted a small aircraft complement as a penalty for protection, the Midways were to compromise on neither number nor size of aeroplanes and, as these had rapidly increased in size with increases in power, range, armament and protection, it was small wonder that the planned 137 aircraft needed a carrier so large as to be rated CVB from the outset — battle carriers in every sense.

Rushed to completion, *Midway* (CVB41)

was just one month too late to see the war's end and was followed one month later by the second of the class, CVB42, named for the newly dead President, *Franklin D. Roosevelt*. The third, *Coral Sea* (CVB43), was completed in 1947 and a further trio, CVB44, 56 and 57 were cancelled.

British carriers exported

Britain's over-ambitious wartime programme has been dealt with briefly in Chapter Five. Only three of the 13,200-ton Glory-class light fleet carriers were ready in time to get to the Far East and they had no time to make an impact. A further three were completed early in 1946 and two more emerged as maintenance aircraft carriers complementing the earlier *Unicorn*, which had been obliged to serve in a conventional role. Of the first pair of the ten-ship Glory Class, *Venerable* became the *Karel Doorman*, the Royal Netherlands Navy's first carrier and the *Colossus* hoisted the French Tricolour as the *Arromanches*. The French already operated an ex-British CVE *Dixmude*, and it was a feature of the early

postwar period that several smaller fleets operated carriers for the first time.

Six Majestic-class ships (enlarged Glorys of 14,000 tons) were also under construction, but none was to see service under the White Ensign. Only three were completed, *Terrible* and *Majestic* becoming the Royal Australian Navy's *Sydney* and *Melbourne*, and the *Magnificent* serving the Canadians as the *Bonaventure*. Both these Commonwealth navies had grown to full stature during the war and it was fitting that they should acquire what had become the world's undisputed capital ship.

Yet another British small-carrier project was the eight-ship Hermes Class, which was designed to full warship standards, compared with the light fleet carriers' mercantile features and utility appointments. To raise the speed from 25 to 30 knots power was more than doubled, from 40,000 to 83,000shp. They were about 50 feet longer and their capacity was increased from 40 to about 50 aircraft. Only four were completed, namely *Albion*, *Bulwark* and *Centaur*, joined considerably later by the

Above: Pilot's view of the angled deck on the landing approach to 'Ark Royal'; the mirror landing sight with its vertical and flanking green horizontal lights is visible on the port hand.

much-modified nameship *Hermes*.

Finally, there were the fleet carriers, the 37,000-ton Audacious Class of four ships, to be followed by the 45,000-ton trio of Gibraltars which would have rivalled the Midways had they ever been built. Only two of the Audacious Class were completed, as *Eagle* and *Ark Royal*, something over 800 feet long, extremely well protected and capable of stowing nearly 100 of the then current aircraft. They were to be much modified during their long careers.

Carriers under the atom bomb

Much of this, however, was still in the future and the fleets immediately after the war found themselves in a new period of transition as they started to cope with the Nuclear Age. In July 1946 the United States staged a controlled nuclear explosion in the midst of a large fleet of surplus ships anchored in Bikini Lagoon. Expended there were the tired old *Saratoga* and the newer CVL *Independence*.

Another aspect of the transition was the arrival of jet-propelled aircraft. Much research during the war had produced the successful German Me262 which, properly used, might have paralysed the Allied daylight bombing effort, and the British Meteor, which entered service in time to hunt the V1 cruise missiles. The Americans, of course, were also deeply involved in similar development, and by the end of 1943 were flying the first jet aircraft designed for carrier use, which became the McDonnell FD Phantom (not to be confused with the F4 Phantom II).

First jet landings

Meanwhile, the Ryan Corporation tested the water with a strange composite aircraft, the FR Fireball, with a radial engine forward and a turbojet aft. Early trials with this hermaphrodite were being conducted at the close of hostilities and it first went to sea in November 1945. During that month the piston engine suffered an inflight failure and the aircraft, perforce, made the first-ever landing by jet on a flightdeck, and that aboard the little CVE *Wake Island*. The event pre-empted a series of trials planned by the Royal Navy for the following month by a modified Vampire on the light fleet carrier *Ocean*, which were completed without hitch. Only a few FD Phantoms were built and they were soon displaced by the more-powerful F2H Banshee, but to an FD fell the distinction of making the US Navy's first planned deck landing in July 1946, on the *Roosevelt*.

Increasing size and weight of aircraft had, of course, been causing headaches to carrier designers for some time; fewer could be stowed, decks needed to be both longer and stronger; each problem spawned another. Powerful jet engines provided much higher speed and permitted smaller wings which, in turn, reduced drag. But the low-speed characteristics of jet aircraft were inferior, requiring higher take-off and landing speeds and threatening another leap forward in flightdeck sizes. That that never occurred was due to an outburst of British innovations equal to those that had first produced the carrier itself.

The angled deck

First came the angled deck. All carriers up to that time had had an axial deck with the forward third the province of the catapult and aircraft ranged for taking-off. The after two-thirds were for landing-on and a pilot,

Left: First use of carrier-based jet aircraft in battle was in the Korean War but early jet range and load limitations meant that they could be used only in the fighter role. USS 'Essex' (CV9) mounted the first jet strike against Korean Communists in August 1951 using F2H Banshees. This picture shows an F9F Panther landing on the 'Bon Homme Richard' (CV31) when she was about to depart for Korean waters.

once committed, relied on picking up the arrester wires. If he did not, all that remained between him and the forward park were good brakes and the deck barrier; the former were of little use on a wet heaving deck and the latter was expensive of both aircraft and nerves.

Researchers at the Royal Aircraft Establishment at Farnborough reasoned that, if the landing path were to be angled slightly to port, aircraft would be able to touch down over the starboard quarter and, in the event of a misjudgment, hit the throttle and go round for another attempt, as their path would flank the forward take-off zone instead of being aligned with it.

As if reluctant to believe that any idea could be so simple and yet work, both the US Navy and Royal Navy began by remarking the flightdecks of one carrier apiece, *Midway* and *Triumph*. These simple simulations were successful and modifications were worked into the Albion-class carriers then fitting out. First at sea, however, was that on the Essex-class *Antietam* (CV36) which carried out 4000 landings without problem in the first half of 1953. The trials established also that fewer arrester wires (with their heavy gear) were necessary and that elevators could be utilized better. Other carriers received the new deck at their first major refits.

Another British carrier innovation, the steam catapult, here shown in action as HMS 'Ark Royal', flies off a Phantom all-weather ground-attack aircraft during an exercise, with guided-missile destroyer HMS 'Fife' beyond and Wessex helicopter on standby.

The steam catapult

The second great development was the steam catapult. Earlier catapults, whether using hydraulics, pneumatics or cordite charges, were viewed as an alternative to be used if sufficient wind-over-deck was lacking. Angled decks invited the greater flexibility and efficiency permitted by simultaneous launching and recovery of aircraft but, as noted, take-off weights had increased to the point where catapults were often of insufficient power. In the new design, the long cylinder laid below the flightdeck drew steam from the ship's boilers to accelerate the shuttle; the bridle arm connecting it to the aircraft passed through a slot with a double flexible sealing strip. (Railway engineers had used the arrangement in the 1840s on the atmospheric railway but had been defeated by, inter alia, rats, which found the tallow-soaked leather seals much to their taste.)

HMS *Perseus* tested the first sea-going installation in 1952 and the Americans again adopted the idea rapidly, putting a pair into the *Hancock* (CV19) in 1954. Over 250 launches were carried out with a wide variety of aircraft and high reliability and good launch rate were recorded. Engineer officers with doubts regarding the quantities of steam drawn off found that the ship's speed was not affected. The extra gear

forward required the plating-in of the open forecastle deck, a feature normal to British carriers but not seen in US naval practice since the Lexingtons; the new arrangement was termed the hurricane bow and improved seakeeping in addition.

And mirror landing sight

Finally came the mirror landing sight (MLS). It is evident that to land an aircraft on a limited length of flightdeck requires the pilot to approach at the correct attitude and height to touch down as far aft as possible. The deck landing control officer, or batsman, operating in an exposed position right aft indicated to a pilot his attitude and when to cut his engine, although the latter had his attention divided by having also to watch his instruments. With low landing speeds the system worked well enough but as aircraft landing speeds increased and the resultant nose-up approach tended to restrict the pilot's view, reflexes were stretched to the utmost and the need for a new system produced the MLS.

The new device, which replaced the batsman, is essentially a stabilized mounting carrying a large curved mirror into which can be projected a white light, reflected back along the flightpath at a vertical angle dependent upon the type of aircraft. By keeping the light central on the mirror's vertical axis, the pilot will maintain the correct height and, by keeping it centralized between two horizontal flanking green lights, he remains horizontal and centralized on the flightpath. A later refinement translated air speed to a tone heard by the pilot through his headset; if he maintained a known frequency he kept the correct speed without recourse to looking at his air speed indicator. The US Navy again adopted this British all-weather device and sea-tested it in the *Bennington* (CV20).

War again

Introduction of these new developments was given urgency by the fact that the major fleets again had a war on their hands. Both in Europe and the Far East, a legacy of the war had been to create political vacuums by the collapse of established governments, a situation all too easily exploited by any armed force, usually erstwhile guerilla or partisan, well-blooded and often Communist. Korea was one such area, divided by the 38th parallel into the South, administered by the Americans, and the North, a Soviet domain by virtue of Russia's entry into the war against Japan in its closing weeks; it was a move purely for political gain, reminiscent of Italy's declaration against Britain in June 1940.

The US had little interest in the area and having set up a government based on Seoul, departed. Russia had no such intent and, to achieve control of the whole, had trained a North Korean army which, backed by both Soviet and Chinese camps, invaded the South in June 1950. Condemnation by the UN Security Council was ignored and immediate action was thus taken with what was to hand.

The Royal Navy's Eastern Fleet was no more than a small squadron built around the light fleet carrier *Triumph*. It was placed under American control although their presence also had been run down to the extent that only one carrier, the *Valley Forge* (CV45) was available. Even so, the

The last piston-engined fighter for the British Fleet Air Arm was the Hawker Sea Fury FB11, a strong and nimble aircraft that fought very effectively at Korea from British and Australian carriers. The Sea Fury pictured is one preserved and maintained in flying condition and RN markings by a United States enthusiast.

Although the Korean War saw the debut of carrier-borne jet aircraft, most of the strike action there was left to piston-engined types. In this picture armourers are making a final check of the weapons carried by an F4U Corsair about to take off from CVE18 USS 'Sicily' on a Korean strike in November 1950.

two put together a strike against the North Korean capital Pyongyang, only eight days after the yellow flood swept inexorably southward.

The *Triumph* was still operating Seafires, whose frailties have already been noted, but she hung on until relieved by her sister *Theseus* with a more balanced striking force. Another Essex, the *Philippine Sea* (CV47), joined also and a pattern emerged which was maintained for the next three thankless years, of a British or Commonwealth 'Light Fleet' covering the west, or Yellow Sea, coast and the US Navy, based on nearby Japan, cruising the east coast.

Harsh conditions

Sharing a latitude common with San Francisco and the Mediterranean, Korean waters could be assumed agreeable. They are not. Summers are unpredictable but the winters are bleak to the point of generating

unwelcome memories for old Arctic Convoy hands, bitterly cold, visibility poor enough 'to make the seagulls walk' and ice — ice in sheets and ice in packs, solid enough to hazard a destroyer's thin skin. In addition, whereas even the most junior hand knew why he was fighting WW2, Korea was an alien place containing someone else's war, a place with little more substance than an outline seen faintly through a passing snow squall. What enthusiasm there was was given by the knowledge that the mixed UN battalions ashore had it far worse, shivering in their foxholes with their backs to the sea along the tiny remaining perimeter around Pusan, outnumbered and totally dependent upon carrier-borne air support.

Though jet-propelled attack aircraft were coming into service, the Royal Navy used only the tougher piston-engined aircraft with their greater payloads. Sea Furies and Fireflies constituted the main force, surviv-

ing innumerable heavy deck landings and action damage. The Firefly was a general purpose strike and reconnaissance aircraft and the Sea Fury was a fighter from the same stable as the Hurricane, strong but nimble enough occasionally even to get the better of the MiG15 jets which later made their appearance.

Carrier jets and helicopters

In contrast, the Americans used the full orchestra. The little CVEs returned with their bent-wing F4U Corsairs, which operated virtually at zero feet only yards in front of friendly positions, blasting any visible target with napalm, 5-inch rockets, bombs up to 1000 pounds and 20mm cannon fire; all that from a single-seat fighter.

The attack carriers deployed piston-engined Skyraiders and jet-engined Banshees and FD Phantoms. The jets still lacked load-carrying potential, though they were useful as pure fighter aircraft, but the AD1 Skyraider was designed as a strike aircraft and used as a low-level workhorse from which up to 8000 pounds of external stores could be hung. It was a superb aircraft that thrived on hard work and survived well into the jet age, even converted into air ambulance or cargo carrier.

A notable newcomer to the Korean War was the helicopter. To be sure, early versions had flown during WW2; the British experimented with a Sikorsky machine for spotting U-boats in the vicinity of convoys and the submarines, in turn, towed ingenious wind-powered helicopters which could bear a man aloft to spot the convoys —

shades of kite-towing British destroyers of 40 years earlier! Neither had any carrying capacity beyond an observer, but by the late 1940s the Sikorsky S-51 had advanced the genre sufficiently to be flown from carriers and relieve the usual destroyer 'riding herd' or station keeping to fish out any flier who ditched on take-off or landing. A variant of the successful Sikorsky design was built by Westland in UK as the Dragonfly. The year 1954 saw the introduction of the S-58 as a serious challenge to conventional aircraft in certain duties; it also was built by Westland under licence as the Wessex and is flying still in 1978.

Helicopters, or 'helos' or 'choppers' as they came to be called, were familiar first in Korea in communications, transport and ambulance roles. They were later used by the Americans in the assault mode ('vertical envelopment') successfully enough to inspire them to convert the CVE *Thetis Bay* in July 1955 into the first true assault ship; CVHA1 was the forerunner of many such. Once arrived, its potential seemed endless.

The British for instance, ever alive to the submarine menace, formed the first AS squadron in 1954 to exploit its ability to listen-in to a passive sonar, 'dunked' on a cable, while hovering and undetectable by a submarine.

Carrier nuclear capability

The great use of CVEs made by the Americans off Korea was in part because of the reconstruction programme in hand on their still new attack carriers. At that time the ultimate deterrent was still embodied greatly in the strike capabilities of the large carrier and the object was to operate large nuclear-capable bombers from flightdecks. Aircraft as large as the P2V Neptune had been successfully launched with jet-assisted take-off (JATO) and other requirements followed rapidly; more-powerful catapults, strengthened and angled flightdecks, 'special' weapons stowage and larger elevators all made for lengthy periods in dockyards.

A new breed of giants incorporating these

Below: As the role of the fleet aircraft carrier has widened, so has the variety of types in a carrier's complement. Here a twin-turboprop Grumman E2 Hawkeye airborne early warning and fighter control aircraft with its distinctive radome, which entered service in 1966, is taking off from USS 'Nimitz' in the Mediterranean in 1978.

Right: The Fairey (Westland) Gannet AEW3 is a British airborne early warning aircraft powered by a double turboprop engine driving contrarotating propellers. Its radar antennas are housed rather less conspicuously in an underslung pod. This picture shows a Gannet about to land on HMS 'Eagle' in 1970.

improvements was, in fact, in hand. The super-carrier idea went back to 1945 when a committee was formed to explore the merits of size and, as the 6A Project, produced a bewildering series of designs culminating in a 65,000-tonner, not far short of the monstrous *Shinano* in displacement but considerably longer at 1030 feet. No permanent island would obstruct its flightdeck, which would accommodate four catapults and three deck-edge and one stern elevators. Box construction would permit launching of aircraft up to 50 tons, aircraft which would provide the bulk of the ship's complement.

First super-carrier scrapped

The design was finally approved in 1948; she was named *United States* (CVB58) and laid down the following spring. But never had a ship so many vociferous critics, on cost and justification, and they won a major victory in having her scrapped almost as soon as construction started. It took the Korean War to convince Congress that it had acted over-hastily and, after two wasted years, another 60,000-tonner, *Forrestal* (CVA59) was approved. It would deploy the Douglas A3C Skywarrior which, with an all-up launch weight of 82,000 pounds (including a 12,000-pound nuclear payload) was the largest ever developed solely for carrier operation. The Skywarrior first flew in October 1952 but was not ready until March 1956, by which

time its deterrent strike role had been taken over by the Strategic Air Command.

US naval policy was still firmly wedded to the large-carrier concept, not for the defeat of an enemy fleet, for there existed no likely candidate at that time, but for the projection of power ashore under the shield of a local superiority so massive as to guarantee the realization of political aims. USS *Forrestal*, named for the Secretary of Defense who championed the carrier's cause, was completed in 1955 as leadship of a series of seven. Her great asymmetric flightdeck was 1039 feet in length and 252 feet wide at its maximum point, embracing 4½ acres. Her fleet speed of 33 knots demanded 250,000shp. More was to come.

Nuclear propulsion

USS *Nautilus* had commissioned in 1954 as the world's first nuclear-powered submarine and it was widely forecast that all warships would soon follow suit to enjoy the benefits of virtually unlimited range at high speeds. To gain experience the Americans built the nuclear cruiser *Long Beach*, the frigate *Bainbridge* and, to complete a homogeneous squadron, Congress decreed that the fifth Forrestal-class carrier should also have nuclear propulsion.

Thus came the *Enterprise* (CVAN65), the 'Big E', powered by eight pressurized water-cooled reactors capable of generating officially 200,000shp, but probably considerably more. A very small island was possible due to the absence of uptakes but her 'unlimited' range was slightly circumscribed by the fact that her escorts would usually require fuel and her own stores were consumable. Her clean appearance topsides was enhanced by the adoption of fixed 'billboard' radar arrays in place of the usual crop of rotating antennas. As the arrays were abandoned in subsequent ships, their effectiveness is perhaps questionable.

Suez — a model operation

No great naval power other than those already fully dealt with had built an operational aircraft carrier until, in 1955, the French laid down the *Clemenceau* (followed soon afterwards by her sister *Foch*) to join the four ex-American and ex-British carriers that they already operated. Before the new pair could be anything like ready, France found herself allied to her old rival, Britain, in what was to be the last echo of gunboat diplomacy — Suez. Both France and Britain regarded the Suez Canal as a vital imperial artery and when, late in 1956, Egypt's President Nasser declared it nationalized, its loss was unthinkable. A joint amphibious attack by both powers, synchronized with a land offensive by the Israeli army, was designed to reoccupy the zone and bring about Nasser's downfall.

Preliminary 'softening up' could be achieved by RAF bombers out of Cyprus but the destruction of the Egyptian Air Force required a powerful fighter force which could only be deployed by carriers. The British *Albion*, *Bulwark* and *Eagle* combined with the French *Arromanches* and *Lafayette* in a model operation; while the Israelis attacked the Egyptian Army from the east, two further British carriers, *Ocean* and *Theseus*, using helicopters in the first such military operation, spearheaded the attack from the west with commandos, who secured the dropping zone for a large-scale Anglo-French parachute landing, itself followed by an amphibious landing to put infantry and armour ashore. It was a textbook example of how to conduct a limited war and the carriers emerged with great credit. That the powers concerned bowed in the face of world displeasure and withdrew without being able to achieve their objectives is another story.

Carrier aircraft role widened

As well as the growing bulk of individual aircraft, the sheer number of machines necessary to undertake the widening range of duties and activities expected of carriers called for increased size. To the torpedo, strike and reconnaissance tasks of WW2 carriers were added anti-submarine (AS) and airborne early warning (AEW) duties. Only the US Navy had sufficient carriers to dedicate specific units to the new tasks; the Royal Navy had passed the zenith of its involvement with seaborne air power, retaining only the *Eagle* and *Ark Royal* of fleet stature, and a period was set even to their continuation in service.

New airborne radars and other electronic devices gave new meaning to 'the eye in the sky', in particular in their ability to detect potential threats both under the surface of the sea and beyond the horizon of ship-mounted equipment. As far back as 1944-5 the Grumman Avenger had been able to carry a search radar in a ventral fairing but, because of the then limited capacity of carrier-borne aircraft, it needed to operate with others to provide effective attack capability. The bulk of electronic equipment was progressively reduced as its range of capability was widened and that, added to the increasing ability of carrier aircraft, led during the 1950s and 1960s to a succession of machines adapted or developed specifically for AS and AEW duties. Among them were the electronic countermeasures (ECM) versions of the ubiquitous Douglas Skyraider; the Grumman twin-piston-engined Tracker and Tracer, twin-turboprop Hawkeye and twin-turbojet Prowler; and the Fairey (Westland) twin-turboprop Gannet.

The Tracer was notable for introducing the large dish-like radome fitted above the fuselage to house the massive radar antenna and a similar radome was fitted to the Hawkeye, but several later aircraft have managed to house equipment and antennas in less-conspicuous radomes or bulges. A spate of new and developed electronics, apart from specialized radars, was introduced progressively with these aircraft. It included the magnetic anomaly detector (MAD), designed to detect any metallic object on or under the water, and, with the Hawkeye, a collection of devices that formed Airborne Tactical Data System (ATDS), which processes the information it gathers before passing it to a Naval Tactical Data System (NTDS). All inputs to the NTDS from aircraft and other sources disposed in and around a naval task group are automatically assessed so that the group's resources can be optimally allocated to meet any threat.

During the period here under review the fleet carrier was becoming more and more concerned with AS warfare in the face of rapid Russian submarine construction. No longer burdened with responsibility for maintaining the West's deterrent, it was free to get on with the job that suited it best — that of sea control. But at sea the threat never remains static and the carrier had to make still further changes to meet it.

Another picture of a Gannet, wings folded, being hauled by tractor to one of the launching catapults on the 'Ark Royal', while a McDonnell Douglas F4K Phantom fighter is on the elevator about to be brought up to the flightdeck.

Goliath displaced

Facing page: USS 'Enterprise' ('Big E') with over half of her varied aircraft complement spotted on the flightdeck. 'Enterprise', first of the US Navy's nuclear-powered carriers, was completed in 1961 and formed part of a small nuclear-powered surface group, including a cruiser and a frigate, which set up prodigious cruising endurance records. In theory a nuclear-powered force could stay at sea for several years independent of propulsion and ship's fuel supplies.

Below: An LTV Aerospace F8E Crusader day fighter unwittingly demonstrates the effectiveness of the flightdeck barrier on USS 'Enterprise' (CVN65) when its arrester hook fails to engage a wire.

The Second World War put the West in rather the same position as Faust; having enlisted the help of a Communist Mephistopheles it discovered that the true reckoning came later. A Russia newly armed and restored in morale embarked on a quest for political gain before the ink on the peace treaties was dry and a world that should have been united by a hard-won peace was instead divided by the Cold War. Paradoxically, the Western fleets, swollen to their greatest-ever potential by a need to defeat sea powers, were now largely redundant as their new potential foe was a land animal, largely self-sufficient and with naval and mercantile fleets of small stature and expendable.

By the beginning of the grey 1950s, the main nuclear threat to Russian territory was vested firmly with the Strategic Air Command rather than with the great strike carriers but the latter's potential for the creation of a *cordon sanitaire* for the support of amphibious landings could not be ignored, and a new seapower was born. Stalin's 'big fleet' mentality reportedly included plans for four carriers but the technology required for forging such a weapon was too advanced and the Soviets went instead for a more feasible expansion of their submarine fleet and the production of long-range bombers armed with stand-off bombs.

Double-edged strategy

This combination of arms was canny because it not only promised a means of defeating a carrier task force without direct combat but also provided the weapons ideally suited to destroying the British merchant marine, as ever Britain's Achilles heel. To assist in this function the Russians built also the Sverdlov-class cruisers, anachronistic 16,000-ton monsters that could not have existed within a large carrier's working radius but which would have made formidable raiders.

With Stalin, the 'balanced fleet' idea passed also, for the time. Khrushchev knew nothing of sea power and concentrated afresh on the submarine production line. Though its product was very orthodox and heavily reliant upon captured German technology, its rapidly increasing numbers forced the West to create a new large anti-submarine force.

During the grimy Suez adventure of 1956, the Russians observed not only another instance of the naval arm's power to intervene politically but also their own inability to intervene materially at the correct level of aggression that would not trigger an armed reply — they lacked what is now termed flexible response. As it happened, the unimaginative head of the Soviet fleet, Kuznetsov, had been relieved in January 1956 by Admiral Gorshkov who rapidly demonstrated, not least through his prolific writings, a burning vision of a new navy, a navy cast in an almost imperialistic mould and powerful enough not only for defence and offence but also for influencing by its very presence. Gorshkov's target of a blue-water fleet was made the more attractive by the rapid withdrawal of the Royal Navy from its traditional spheres of interest.

Enter guided missiles

At the dawn of the 1960s the Russian Fleet was still deficient in all but submarines, of

which it by then had about 500. But they alone were not sufficient, for it had become an age of technology for which the Americans were infinitely better equipped. To retain a credible stance the Soviets had to match them and the key to superiority lay in the guided missile.

As already noted, the Germans had led the field with the radio-controlled glider bomb, an air-to-ground missile of unpleasant accuracy that was taken a stage farther by the Japanese, who used a human guidance system. Again the Germans were first with practical cruise and ballistic missiles in the V1 and V2 and, at the war's end, the brains behind them joined the camps of both East and West. To enable their ships to have any chance of engaging a large carrier, the Russians saw the advantages of the long-range surface-to-surface missile (SSM). By 1958 they had developed the SS-N-1, known to NATO as Scrubber, a three-ton turbojet monster capable of carrying conventional or nuclear warheads a distance of 100 miles, although the guidance methods of the time restricted it effectively to horizon range. It was deployed by the Kildin Class, the world's first true guided-missile destroyers.

The Russians then set about creating a successor, the 250-mile SS-N-3, or Shaddock, for use by both surface ships and submarines. As radar guidance cannot 'see' over the horizon, the realization of the full range can only be through a mid-course correction by a suitably placed aircraft or ship that can 'fix' the target directly and it is this tenuous link that is the vulnerable part of the system, a single eye that can be put out by the target itself. Strangely, the Krupnyi-class cruisers that took the Shaddock to sea in 1961 carried no aircraft.

West's response

The West's missile priorities were different; with adequate striking power in its carriers, the urgency was to produce a system to deal with the threat of the long-range bomber and its stand-off missiles. Specifically, in 1962 the threat was the Tu-16 (Badger) with a 3500-mile range and carrying the AS-2 (Kipper), a 3½-ton missile of 100-mile range. This combination paled before the imminence of the 9000-mile-range Tu-20 (Bear) capable of carrying the AS-3 (Kangaroo), a 300-mile weapon as big as a fighter and with a speed of Mach 2. Neither aircraft could better 600mph but each could launch its weapon from the very limits of a carrier's interception range.

The answer lay in an effective surface-to-air missile (SAM) linked to suitable surveillance and three-dimensional radars deployed by escorts in a distant defensive ring about the carrier. Two SAMs were quickly introduced by the Americans, the 70-mile Talos, which they tried, unsuccessfully, to deploy in rebuilt WW2 cruisers, and the 20-mile Terrier which, in spite of its comparatively small size, needed the new 4700-ton Coontz-class guided missile frigate to accommodate it. Another, smaller, SAM, the Tartar, was also under development.

Nuclear-powered Enterprise

All four Forrestal-class carriers (CV59-62) were completed by 1959 and then the nuclear-powered *Enterprise* (CVAN65) was followed by a quartet of improved conventional design, as the Kitty Hawk Class. Three out of the four were completed with a Terrier missile system; but it was only a 'last-ditch' weapon and the carriers' defensive strength was still vested firmly in their 85 aircraft. The Terrier was in fact not the first guided missile to be put aboard American carriers as, at the end of the 1950s, some units of the Essex and Midway classes deployed the ungainly Regulus I SSM on mobile ramps. It was not a success, probably because its reputed 500-mile range outstripped the available guidance systems.

Britain, meanwhile, at last had carrier aircraft worthy of the name in the Scimitar and Sea Vixen; they were shortly joined by the Buccaneer, a robust aeroplane designed to deliver a nuclear payload from below its enemy's radar coverage. In 1958, the *Victorious* had emerged virtually a new ship from an incredible eight-year refit, an exercise so obviously uneconomic that all five of her sisters were scrapped within its timespan. The *Victorious* was dominated by an immense rotating 3-D array that offered surveillance and direction up to great ranges and, for group protection, the 25-mile Seaslug SAM was available, its unlovely launcher marring the otherwise handsome County-class ships, then completing.

France commissioned the carriers *Clemenceau* and *Foch* in 1961 and 1963 respectively, but a planned 30,000-ton follow-on fell victim to economics. Both carriers were equipped with the indigenous Etendard IV fighter/bomber and Breguet Alise AS and reconnaissance aircraft, bolstered by the acquisition of a few F8U Crusaders purchased from the Americans.

Missile goes underwater

In the late 1950s there occurred another technological milestone that was eventually to influence the aircraft carrier's development, when the Russians converted seven Zulu-class submarines each to carry a pair of ballastic missiles. They were SS-N-4s (Sark) which could carry a nuclear warhead up to 350 miles, thus posing a threat that could not be ignored, particularly as the Zulus were followed by the Golf I and Hotel I

A Grumman E1B Tracker, a variant of the twin-piston-engined S2 Tracker anti-submarine strike aircraft, being manoeuvred by tractor on the flightdeck of the Australian carrier HMAS 'Melbourne'. The Tracer's top hatch is open. No. 3 crew members.

A Marine (M) version of the Jaguar light tactical support aircraft taking off from the French Navy's carrier 'Clemenceau'. The Jaguar is a product of the Anglo-French company SEPECAT (British Aerospace/Dassault-Breguet) and is operated from both the 'Clemenceau' and 'Foch'.

submarine classes, the latter nuclear powered. A stealthy and highly potent weapon system had arrived and Russia and the United States were soon locked in technological combat to guarantee that neither achieved a decisive lead.

In July 1960 America's first purpose-built nuclear-powered ballistic-missile submarine (SSBN), *George Washington*, fired the first A1 Polaris. With 15 more missiles aboard, each capable of a 1200-mile trajectory, she could threaten a very large Soviet littoral and AS warfare on both sides began to develop in earnest, each realizing that, in the event of war, every such craft would need to be destroyed, and immediately. There would be no room for half-measures.

By 1962 the US Navy had nine SSBNs at sea, each carrying 16 Polaris missiles and the later boats having the improved A2 version. Russia was now lagging badly but still held a lead in medium-range land-based ballistic missiles, giving Khrushchev the foolhardy idea of basing some of them in Castro's Cuba. How the upper echelons of the Supreme Soviet could ever have countenanced such a hairbrained scheme must remain for ever a mystery, for a moment's thought must have revealed that the world's greatest seapower could throttle the island's communications with no difficulty.

Having issued an ultimatum to the effect of 'get out or risk war', the Americans rapidly blockaded Cuba's approaches. Aircraft from

The first true aircraft carrier (though able to operate only V/STOL aircraft) built by Soviet Russia, the 54,000-ton 'Kiev', with Ka25 'Hormone' helicopters and Yak-36 'Forger' V/STOL aircraft ranged on the flightdeck, photographed from a RAF Nimrod aircraft north of the Hebrides in December 1977.

the *Enterprise* and *Independence* (CV62) dogged every one of the many Soviet freighters and warships in the area; escorts treated several submarines similarly and the world waited breathlessly for one of the giants to retreat from this eyeball-to-eyeball confrontation. Eventually Khrushchev faced the inevitable and his intense chagrin was epitomized by the returning trail of freighters with their shrouded deck cargoes. The total inability of his fleet to project power and sustain it could not have been more tellingly highlighted and, as the

tension eased, he made a solemn resolve to rectify this shortcoming. From the shame of 1962 arose the Soviet Navy that we see today.

Both East and West now had good cause to fear the other's submarines and the serious view taken by the US Navy was mirrored in its conversion of the greater number of the Essex-class carriers to AS duties. They were redesignated CVS and formed the nucleus of hunter-killer, or HUK, groups operating the S2 Tracker and the EA1 Skyraider (nicknamed Guppy for its prominent radome). Also carried was the Sikorsky Seabat helicopter, capable of obtaining cross-bearings on a 'sinker' by dunking sonar and disposable sonar buoys and homing-in on aircraft or ships for a kill. In 1961 the more-powerful Sea King helicopter was introduced.

Later Essex-class conversions acquired also a new sonar which could work both actively and passively. Distant back-up was provided by long-range shore-based patrol aircraft such as the Lockheed Neptune and Orion (as well as by the British Nimrod and French Atlantique) carrying search radar and a good weapon payload, and also MAD

A derivative of the F8 Crusader is the LVT Aerospace A7 Corsair II light attack single-seater, later versions of which are fitted with Allison (Rolls-Royce Spey) turbofan engines; the A7D carries a multi-barrel 20mm cannon in the fuselage and has points for carrying a 15,000lb load of varied ammunition or extra fuel. This one landing has neatly caught an arrester wire.

gear capable of detecting the presence of submerged submarines.

Escorts strengthened

The carrier's escorts received a boost in 1963 in the *Bronstein* (FF1037), the prototype of a new breed designed to carry its own helicopter pad and the Asroc, a rocket projectile with a range of six miles, fired from an eight-cell launcher to put a nuclear depth-charge or AS torpedo close aboard a submerged target.

Even with hardware such as this, the CVS could still spend much fruitless time in combing the ocean and it was to reduce this non-productive effort that the SOSUS project was undertaken, whereby a net of sensitive listening devices was permanently established on the seabed in selected areas, transmitting every waterborne noise to monitoring stations. There the noise patterns could be automatically analysed and compared with a library of sound signatures of all known vessels, enabling the type and position of each 'spook' to be established and, if necessary, intercepted.

With the carrier becoming such a real enemy to their SSBNs, the Russians had also to face the facts that, even equipped with their large SSMs, their surface ships stood little chance of destroying a carrier with a single strike, and that the launching ship itself would face almost certain destruction in the inevitable aerial riposte.

In 1962, therefore, there appeared the Kanin Class with the first Soviet SAM, the SA-N-1 (Goa) to cover the SSM ships. A promised improvement on the Goa, with its 16-mile range, lay in the 27-mile SA-N-2 (Guideline) but it proved a failure. After a few Kotlin-class destroyers were expensively converted for the Goa system the idea was abandoned in favour of the new 5000-ton Kashins, purpose-built 'double-enders' and the world's first major warships with gas turbine propulsion.

The dual-function 5700-ton Kynda Class arrived between 1962 and 1965 carrying two quadruple SS-N-3 (Shaddock) launchers, together with an SA-N-1 system to give them a better chance of surviving an attack. Still no helicopter was shipped and there was only a nominal AS armament. In a rapidly changing situation, their armament balance was wrong and they were superseded by the Kresta Is with only four Shaddocks and two SAM systems. The addition of a helicopter conferred a greater measure of operational independence and some AS potential.

Countering Polaris and Poseidon

With the Lafayette-class SSBNs of 1964, the Americans introduced the A3 Polaris, whose 2500-mile range enabled the submarines to operate far out and increased their practical launch area to an extent where the already

Above: One of the Royal Navy's versions of the McDonnell Douglas F4, a R-R Spey-engined FG1 Phantom fighter/bomber, afterburners accentuated in a dawn take-off from HMS 'Ark Royal' in 1970.

Left: Batsman on the brink as he flags in SH3D Sea King (Sikorsky S61B) anti-submarine and transport helicopter over the port catapult of a US carrier. The American national flag was painted on the side for safety identification while on operations in Mauritius.

Above left: A new shape and a new potential at sea, as on land, as a Hawker Siddeley Harrier 'jump jet' comes up on the elevator to the flightdeck of HMS 'Eagle', thence to take off and land without the trappings of catapult or arrester gear essential to the Buccaneers already there assembled and others.

rather weak Russian AS weaponry could not possibly cope. The design of the Kresta IIs dates from this period, the first unit appearing about 1968 and carrying two improved SAM systems in the new SA-N-3 (Goblet) and a pair of quadruple launchers whose bulk convinced observers that they contained a successor to the Shaddock SSM. They did not; they did introduce the SS-N-14, an AS rocket vehicle capable of putting a nuclear depth charge or torpedo on to a submerged target 25 miles distant, assisted by a hull-mounted sonar and the newly introduced Ka25 (Hormone) helicopter.

Having done their best to provide an antidote to the Western carriers that so threatened their own SSBNs, the Soviets then urgently sought a surface ship to complement their fleet submarines in neutralizing the American Polaris boats, which, they knew all too well, were about to be joined by the C3 Poseidon of double the payload and carrying independently targeted MIRV heads.

To that end, the Russian *Moskva* appeared in 1968, a radical rethink in being cruiser forward and carrier aft, a hybrid already foreshadowed by the Japanese post-Midway Ise conversions and the more recent French *Jeanne d'Arc* of 1963. At 18,000 tons, the two Moskva-class ships are of 50 per cent greater displacement, little

longer but immensely beamy aft where their flightdeck covers a hangar for about 18 AS helicopters. Hull-mounted and variable-depth sonars are carried, together with a twin-arm Asroc-type missile launcher forward and two quintuple AS torpedo tubes. No SSMs are shipped but there are two Goblet systems to deter aircraft from interfering with her tasks. With these ships the Russians demonstrated clearly that they considered the Western carrier threat subordinate to that of the SSBN.

British and American rundown

Great Britain, meanwhile, wrestling as unsuccessfully as Laocoon with the increasingly constricting coils of a wasted economy, had decided in 1966 to abandon the projected 53,000-ton replacement for *Victorious*. Known as CVA-01, it would have operated the newly acquired McDonnell Douglas F4 Phantom. With the political decision to withdraw almost entirely from East of Suez came the argument that the Royal Navy's attack carriers were now no more than expensive luxuries, and the battle-worn *Victorious* paid off for scrap in 1967. Only *Ark Royal, Eagle* and *Hermes* remained as front-line units, and *Albion* and *Bulwark* in the assault role with no fixed-wing capability. No replacements were planned and the course was all downhill.

By the end of the 1960s the US fleet, too,

was losing flightdecks at an alarming rate, with most of the smaller carriers and seven of the ageing Essex Class gone. The remainder of these versatile ships had been regarded as CVSs, humble AVTs (auxiliary aircraft transport) or LPHs (amphibious assault ship); the last-named lacked the angled flightdeck and operated only helicopters in support of the seven purpose-built 18,000-ton Iwo Jima-class carriers. Only 12 attack carriers remained — three Midways, four Forrestals, the *Enterprise* and four Kitty Hawks — all splendid ships, but even the best cannot be in more than one place at once. The days of the massed carriers of the middle 1940s were already history.

Too costly

It was not that the attack carrier was obsolete, merely beyond even the American budget. The first of a new class of nuclear carriers, *Nimitz* (CVN68), was under construction. At 91,400 full-load tons and 1092 feet long overall she was to be only marginally larger than *Enterprise* but would cost twice as much, that is, one billion dollars. She was commissioned in 1975 and the final cost was, in fact, 1.88 billion, and her two funded sisters, *Dwight D Eisenhower* (CVN69) and *Carl Vinson* (CVN70), exceeded two billion dollars apiece.

By comparison, the unit cost of the Kitty Hawks had been 250-280 million dollars and the Forrestals 175-225 million, yet they offered the same size of deck. Significantly, too, the first two of the Nimitz Class had originally been designated CVAN or nuclear

attack carriers. With the diminishing number available, however, they were commissioned as CVN, or multi-mission carriers, sacrificing some of their strike potential to operate AS aircraft, notably the Lockheed S3 Viking and Sikorsky SH3 Sea King. Other conventional ships were modified from CVA to CV.

Design circumscribed

Carrier design was being forced into a funnel. Fewer could be afforded, but each had to be of a size capable of operating the aircraft necessary for guaranteeing air superiority. Simultaneously, a portion of that superiority was sacrificed to deploy AS aircraft. Heated debate was generated within the US as it alone, apparently, pursued the carrier's development; the debate has continued since.

One thing was certain, particularly to those navies that were even more financially restricted; it was time for a change of direction in seaborne air power rather than abandoning it altogether. The helicopter provided one ingredient, being deployed now from many types of surface warship; another, more important, was to be provided by they who had contributed most to the evolution of the carrier, the British.

As far back as June 1966, HMS *Bulwark* carried out trials with a small aircraft then known as the Hawker P1127, or Kestrel. Though attracting little attention at the time, it introduced the principle of vertical/short take-off and landing (V/STOL) at sea. The aircraft was to return later as the Hawker Siddeley Harrier.

Facing page: One of the US Marine Corps' versions of the V/STOL Harrier, an AV8A strike/reconnaissance aircraft pictured on the amphibious assault ship USS 'Guam' (LPH9) during exercises to test and develop the sea control ship principle.

Below: Crewmen crouch well clear as the signal is made for the catapult launch of a Lockheed S3A Viking on USS 'John F. Kennedy' in the Mediterranean. The Viking is a twin-turbofan anti-submarine aircraft with improved and more-varied electronics that started to replace the Tracker on American carriers in the mid-1970s.

The end and a new beginning

After its active service debuts in Korea and at Suez, the helicopter began to evolve as a weapon system in its own right. By the late 1950s the US Navy had its Essex-class conversions and 20 escort carriers (regraded CVHE) operating the Seabat for AS use. Other CVEs, following the pioneering *Thetis Bay*, carried heavy helicopters for assault purposes; these conversions were not very cost-effective but provided useful experience for the Iwo Jima-class LPH amphibious assault ships then under construction. The latter looked like carriers but had no catapults, angled deck or arrester gear, being designed solely for vertical aerial operations and, in conjunction with the new dock landing ships and amphibious transports, underlined a growing shift of thought towards a modified form of force projection, with the various types of ship complementary in function and, between them, capable of transporting, landing and sustaining a military force and its heavy equipment.

Ever short of funds, the Royal Navy had converted a brace of Albions to assault landing ships, including the slinging of small landing-craft under davits. The two Fearless-class LSDs acted as back-up for the transport and landing of heavy vehicles and equipment.

New American class

To marry the functions of these various classes of ship, the Americans built the new Tarawa-class LHA amphibious assault ships, of which the first commissioned in 1976. With 820-foot flightdecks, they are little shorter than an Essex but cost nearly as much as a Kitty Hawk, which makes them very expensive 39,000-tonners. They have an axial flightdeck and cannot operate conventional fixed-wing aircraft, but they can stow up to 49 large helicopters and 2000 troops with their equipment, armour and wheeled transport. Four LCUs (landing craft utility) operate from a floodable dock aft and smaller landing craft are carried on deck. The Tarawas would appear to be the ultimate in assault ships, but, like the true aircraft carrier, they have suffered from their cost; four of the planned nine were

axed and much hard thinking would be likely to precede hazarding in a high-risk zone any of the five that were built. By operating heavy helicopters, this type of ship has also an enhanced strike capability in their ability to launch certain modified SSMs, for instance the French Super Frelon and the Exocet AM39.

But it is in the anti-submarine mode that the helicopter has made the greatest impact and any escort ship worthy of the name now carries at least one. First-generation frigates employed a small type such as the Westland Wasp or Agusta-Bell 204AS but limited payload usually produced an 'either/or' situation, either sensors or weapons, needing a third party for a successful attack. One solution was the helicopter cruiser, of which the Italians led the way with the *Andrea Doria* of 1964 carrying four small helicopters on a 6500-ton displacement, followed by the larger *Vittorio Veneto*, stowing nine. Each has Terrier SAM launchers which have the parallel function of firing Asroc projectiles.

HMS 'Bulwark', pictured here in her final role as a helicopter carrier, started life during WW2 as one of the planned Hermes-class 'stretched' light fleet carriers, but was not completed until 1954. She was converted to assault ship, or commando carrier, in 1959-60, with accommodation for about 750 troops and their transport and weapons.

Above: A Hawker Harrier
hovering before landing on the
small helicopter deck of HMS
'Blake', one of a pair of elderly
Tiger-class cruisers
reconstructed during the
1960s for operation of four
Westland Sea King heavy AS
helicopters. The Harrier has
successfully completed trials
on virtually every type of ship
that can operate aircraft of
any type.

Left: The first warship
specifically designed to deploy
its own helicopters to extend
its search and strike
capabilities was the Italian
Navy's 6500-ton cruiser
'Andrea Doria', which was
completed in 1964 with a
hangar and small flightdeck
aft for operation of four
Agusta-Bell AS helicopters. A
sister is the 'Caio Duilio'.

Both will probably acquire the larger and more versatile AB212 helicopter.

From 1965 the Royal Navy rebuilt the two Tiger-class cruisers to operate four Sea Kings from a large hangar-flightdeck structure aft, whose ungainly appearance has brought much criticism of the ships. Expensive though the conversions were, they were steps in the right direction, with the helicopters each carrying radar, sensors and weapons. The Russian Moskvas of 1968-9 project the same line of thought, since continued in the Japanese Harunas of 1973-4, each with three Sea Kings.

Limited offensive capacity

Even the best of helicopters can provide only limited offensive capacity to their carrier and it is in that ability that V/STOL shows promise. The Kestrel trials had shown to advantage the aircraft's fast response time, taking off without regard to ship's heading or wind-over-deck conditions and requiring neither catapult nor arrester gear. Its small payload was also apparent, as was the possibility of improving it greatly by allowing space for a short running take-off, reserving vertical take-off for necessity only.

Although the Navy appreciated what the aircraft could offer, it was far from obtaining it. As the Harrier, the unique new aircraft entered RAF squadron service as early as 1967, but the marinized version would

probably have sunk forever in a slough of political despond had not the US Marine Corps evaluated it at sea in the *Guam* (LPH9) and ordered sufficient for three full squadrons, so convinced were they of its potential.

America had got itself deeply embroiled in Vietnam, a war it could not win. With an increasing dearth of flightdecks, the free-wheeling air support of Korean days was difficult to provide even in an unopposed sea scenario. The farsighted Chief of Naval Operations, Admiral Elmo Zumwalt, a veritable latter-day Fisher in his fertile flow of ideas, proposed a sea control ship (SCS) to fill the gap. A simple 12,000-15,000-tonner, she would operate a range of helicopters and, as part of a group, service those of other ships. Limited strike capability was to be provided by a flight of Harriers, to be built in America under British licence, which would rapidly lay sonobuoys around a suspect (for the slower helicopters to follow up), deal with an enemy snooper or a mid-course-correction aircraft or strike directly at an SSM launcher.

Paralleling the earlier CVEs, the SCS would have virtually no protection outside her aircraft and would exist to establish temporary air superiority over a task group or in a low-risk landing zone. By keeping to a basic specification, the US Navy hoped to

commission eight SCSs by 1981 at a total cost of less than one Nimitz-class carrier but, although the SCS philosphy was well proven by the *Guam* in an interim capacity, funds were not voted and another interesting carrier project foundered before its launch.

The Invincible Class

More happily, the Royal Navy had argued successfully that, to remain a reckonable force after the amputation of its carrier arm, it still needed to deploy air power at sea. So, in 1973, was ordered HMS *Invincible*, the first anti-submarine or through-deck cruiser (CAH), euphemisms acceptable to the vociferous anti-carrier lobby. Of a size with Zumwalt's still-born baby, the British ship is far removed in concept, being able to operate with the fastest fleet group and sacrificing capacity for a fine hull, yet still able to stow ten Sea King equivalents and five V/STOL aircraft of a size, if necessary, greater than that of the Sea Harrier. Forward, she will have the first example of another British idea, the 'Ski Jump', an inclined ramp designed to accelerate the aircraft into the air after a short take-off run, and so providing greater payload or range than would be possible with vertical take-off. Propelled by four Olympus gas turbines of 112,000shp, with full carrier electronics and a Sea Dart SAM system (but

Two further pictures of US Marine Corps Harriers during sea control ship trials in the Atlantic with USS 'Guam'. Also featured in the big picture is a Boeing Vertol CH46 Sea Knight transport/utility helicopter which can carry 25 equipped troops or about 3 tons of stores.

no guns), the design is expensive at £150 million and in no way to be regarded as a cheap substitute for the conventional carrier but as a versatile warship in its own right. Two further units are on order.

In the same size bracket should be mentioned the much-deferred French PA75 project for an 18,500-ton (full load) carrier with a 662-foot flightdeck and capable of operating either helicopters or V/STOL aircraft. The bold difference is that it is planned to instal nuclear propulsion.

Russian competition

That the West should not neglect the continued development of the carrier was dramatically underscored in 1976 when the Russian *Kiev* passed through the Bosphorus

for the first time. In layout not far removed from a CAH, she had a size closely akin to that of an American Midway. However, whereas it had taken the US Navy a quarter of a century of continuous development to reach that stage, the Russians arrived after a couple of years of experience with the Moskvas!

In the *Moskva* the Russians appear to have seriously underestimated the potential of V/STOL aircraft. Although they had the Yakovlev STOL Freehand flying while the *Moskva* was under design, they completed the ship, and her sister *Leningrad*, with the forward end of a short flightdeck blocked off completely by a veritable cliff-face of superstructure, acceptable for helicopters but denying the V/STOL even the shortest

Upper: While numerous experiments and developments were in train to find new ways of providing seaborne airpower back-up, carriers of the old conventional kind were in action again when America became embroiled in the Vietnam war. Here a flight of McDonnell F4 Phantoms is being refuelled by a Grumman KA6D Intruder shipboard tanker on the way to a strike over North Vietnam in 1972.

Lower: Construction proceeding early in 1978 on HMS 'Invincible', Britain's first of a class of three anti-submarine (through-deck) cruisers, designed specifically to operate the V/STOL Harrier and heavy AS helicopters.

rolling take-offs, and subjecting all aircraft to a massive degree of turbulence. Carrying the names of the two greatest Russian cities, they would seem to have been regarded initially as the ultimate, but trials with the Yak in the Mediterranean exposed their limitations and only the two were built.

Bristling with weapons

The Kievs, of which at least three will be constructed, carry their superstructure offset to starboard and flanked by an angled flightdeck of two-thirds the ship's length. For the rest, the ships bristle with every weapon and device to prevent interference with their primary mission, that of destroying submarines at any distance from Russian soil. Their first line of attack is with at least 20 Ka-25 (Hormone) helicopters carrying sensors and weapons, backed up by the ship herself, whose wake formation betrays a bow sonar dome of homeric proportions and a variable-depth unit aft. Once within range, she can put a nuclear depth charge or homing torpedo close aboard a submerged target with the SUW-N-1 launcher forward and dispatch any still surviving with ten torpedo tubes or two 12-barrelled rocket launchers.

Between five and ten of the later V/STOL Yak-36 (Forger) are carried to protect the ship from attack and to offer a measure of strike capacity. Eight SS-N-12 launchers forward are believed to be capable of smiting an enemy ship with a nuclear payload up to 250 miles distant, with no shortage of air support for mid-course correction, and thus offering a threat even to an opposing strike carrier, should one venture too close. Any aircraft that succeeded in penetrating the *Kiev's* screen would be confronted with two 20-mile SA-N-3 (Goblet) and two 10-mile SA-N-4 systems and four 76mm guns. Incoming SSMs that cannot be fooled by her extensive ECM can be shot out of the sky by either the SA-N-4s or four six-barrelled Gatling-type guns, automatically laid and designed to shred a missile by a cloud of fragments. As if all this was not enough, it is suspected also that the *Kiev* has a measure of amphibious capability.

Strike carrier still master

Even so, no Kiev or equivalent, whatever its mix of aircraft, could hope to match a large American strike carrier, which still remains unchallenged. Capable of a response flexible enough for all situations, from evacuating civilians to a full-scale nuclear strike, it can deploy up to 85 front-line aircraft such as the Grumman A6 Intruder and LTV Vought A7 Corsair II, covered by the Mach 2.3 Grumman F14 Tomcat, all with a performance that no vectored-thrust aircraft could hope to match. Even with the growing

size of aircraft, the carrier has always proved elastic enough to accommodate their needs, resulting in life-spans long by normal warship standards. The first postwar American attack carrier, USS *Forrestal*, was commissioned as far back as 1955 and a Service Life Extension Program (SLEP) due to commence shortly will modernize each of the large units in turn to extend their useful life to 35, or even 40, years.

The three Midways are too small and aged to be SLEP candidates and the first, *Franklin D. Roosevelt*, paid off in 1977.

Another view of the Soviet carrier 'Kiev' photographed from a RAF Nimrod over the Mediterranean, and a close-up of one of the 'Kiev's' V/STOL Yakolev 'Forger' aircraft hovering over the flightdeck taken from the frigate HMS 'Torquay' in the Atlantic.

With all the changes taking place and still to come, it will take many smaller ships to provide anything like the strength and flexibility of the force carried by the modern American giant carriers. Here a strike/reconnaissance Grumman A6 Intruder lands on USS 'Nimitz' to join a variety of other aircraft, including the very potent Grumman F14 Tomcat swing-wing fighter.

'Rosie's' final deployment was to demonstrate that the Harrier could integrate perfectly with conventional aircraft operations, particularly in providing cover during the vulnerable times of launch and recovery of strikes, periods at which, it may be recalled, both sides had been badly caught out during WW2. An experimental additional flightpath was marked out for the Harriers, angled from the port overhang to the starboard bow. When circumstances permitted, rolling take-offs were made; when not, they launched and recovered vertically from any suitable position. It will be apparent that they could do so equally well from badly damaged flightdecks, with the added advantage of having self-starting engines that need no external power units. Their performance might not be top-rate but in desperate times any air power is better than none.

End of the super-carrier?

With *Coral Sea* due to be phased out in 1981 and *Midway* by 1985, only 12 large (and ageing) flightdecks will be left to the US Navy. A planned fourth Nimitz, (CVN71) has been axed and it would seem that the only way that carriers of such a size are built again would be if the Russians take the initiative and produce an enlarged follow-on to the Kievs, capable of operating normal fixed-wing aircraft. Memories of the total dominance of the large carriers are still fresh and, if the Soviets build, so will the Americans. Otherwise, natural evolutionary forces will demand that the super-carrier gives way to smaller variants and it is to them that designers are now devoting their attention.

The proposed American 22,000-ton 'V/STOL support ship' is likely to be quashed on the same grounds as the sea control ship, having a similar aircraft/helicopter complement and 'lacking in versatility'. Its category is as much a euphemism as the British 'through-deck cruiser; it cannot be labelled aircraft carrier, because Congress's so-called Title VIII legislation demands that all such ships be nuclear powered. The navy prefers gas turbines.

A more likely runner is the CVV, a 58,000-ton conventional carrier stowing a flexible mix of aircraft 50 to 55 in number. Its 900-odd-foot flightdeck would give statistics close enough to those of the *Kiev* to make justification the easier.

Candidate for special attention

There is, moreover, one more argument against the task group built on a super-carrier. So valuable is it and of such great threat that it makes good sense to allocate long-range ballistic missiles exclusively to

Above: The Anglo/French Westland/Aérospatiale Lynx AS helicopter has been ordered in quantity by the navies of France and Britain, and by several other navies. It can carry a very wide variety of weapons, including 20mm cannon, homing torpedoes and a range of missiles, and is capable of operating from small ships in rough seas. Here a Lynx is seen undergoing trials on the French frigate 'Tourville'.

Facing page: Another fine picture of USS 'Nimitz' taken in the Mediterranean in 1978, showing the launching of one of her Tomcats.

its destruction. Satellite observation now enables new co-ordinates to be fed into its control at almost hourly intervals. Fired from deep inside enemy territory and plunging with its thermonuclear head from the stratosphere at an unstoppable speed, this weapon is virtually impossible to counter and needs only to fall within a reasonable radius to be total in its effect.

The US Navy is, therefore, considering another alternative known as the 'air-capable Spruance'. It is a 30-knot ship of 7800 tons with an extremely capacious hull, normally fitted out for AS warfare but capable of being built with a 300-foot flightdeck forward, separated from a 100-foot deck aft by a large boxy hangar/superstructure. From eight to 14 aircraft, depending upon the V/STOL to helicopter mix, could be stowed without need of elevators, and have adequate space forward for a rolling take-off and the pad aft for vertical recovery. Little rearrangement of the existing hull and machinery would be necessary, keeping development costs to a minimum, and the ship would be able to mount a multi-purpose air cover for any group of ships.

Other designs

Other fleets move in more orthodox directions. The Italians have under construction the 13.250-ton *Giuseppe Garibaldi*, of a size with the American sea control ship but closer to the British through-deck cruiser philosophy in both speed and armament. Her capacity will be 18 large helicopters or 16 Harrier-sized V/STOL aircraft. The Spanish Navy has acquired Harriers for use on its ex-CVL *Dedalo* and might build an SCS for themselves, while the Indians are also purchasing the aircraft to extend the active life of the ageing ex-British light fleet carrier *Vikrant*.

The British company Vosper Thornycroft has produced an extremely interesting design for a 6000-ton 450-foot 'Harrier Carrier' to carry eight aircraft. The proposal is for gas turbine propulsion, but with simpler diesel drive the ship would be a possible successor to the CVE. The design is aimed at smaller navies but none has yet been ordered and interest from the larger navies would depend upon a convincing argument that any future shooting war would last long enough for convoys and their

escorts to be needed. Even so, with V/STOL established, it could appeal for its cost-effective provision of more than just a token seaborne air force.

Experience has shown that however long a war, it is never of sufficient duration to permit detailed planning and construction once the shooting starts. As peacetime defence budgets will never permit an adequate number of carriers to be commissioned 'on spec', contingency plans need to be laid for rapid conversion of existing and suitable mercantile hulls. With that in mind the US Navy has commenced the Arapahoe project, to check the feasibility of a completely modular facility for the operation of about ten Sea King helicopters, designed around the 8-foot-square by 40-foot-long container so that it could be instantly put aboard a high-speed container ship.

A short step from this would be to try V/STOL aircraft in a similar mode. The modern supertanker (VLCC) offers an unencumbered deck often in excess of 1000 feet by 200 feet; though powered for only about 17 knots, it is very difficult to sink and could offer a convoy air cover with a minimum of conversion. Fast medium-sized roll-on/roll-off ferries are virtually purpose-built for operating V/STOL aircraft or helicopters, given a flat upper deck above vehicle decks with generous headroom and interconnected by ramps and elevators. No shortage of potential exists and it would seem that the merchant navy would, yet again, have a vital part to play in any real conflict.

Nothing can be certain but what cannot be gainsaid is the continuing requirement for air power at sea. With the technology available, a spate of very original designs can be expected as V/STOL really makes its mark. Without the need for vast flightdecks, even the smaller fleets are likely to possess ships which might or might not be termed aircraft carriers yet will be dedicated to the operation of air power in one form or another.

Postscript

On 4 December 1978 HMS *Ark Royal* slipped into Devonport at the end of the last commission of a British strike carrier. Laid down in the distant war-torn days of March 1943, she had reached the end of the road and, not for the first time, the Royal Navy was among the first to abolish a class of ship that it had been instrumental in developing. It was no coincidence, however, that at the same time it was announced that the third through-deck cruiser was to be named, not *Indomitable* as expected, but *Ark Royal*, symbolic of the continuation of air power at sea with the Royal Navy.

A sight no more to be seen — a busy deck scene on the last of the British Navy's fleet aircraft carriers, HMS 'Ark Royal', in the Mediterranean a few months before she finally paid off at the end of 1978. It shows Buccaneer low-level strike aircraft being serviced. The honoured name Ark Royal dates back to the first Elizabethan era; a galley built at Deptford, on the Thames, in 1587 as the 'Ark Raleigh' was bought for the Queen's Navy and renamed 'Ark Royal'. The name lives on in the third of the Invincible-class anti-submarine cruisers now building.

APPENDIX 1 - Some notable Aircraft Carriers

name	nationality	year completed	displacement tons	length overall feet	shaft hp	speed knots	approx no of aircraft	remarks
Furious	Br	1917	22,450	786.5	94,000	31½	35	final version battlecruiser conversion
Argus	Br	1918	14,550	565	21,500	20	20	ex-Italian liner *Conte Rosso*
Eagle	Br	1920	22,500	667.5	50,000	24	21	ex-Chilean battleship *Almirante Cochrane*
Hosho	Ja	1922	7500	552.5	30,000	25	21	
Langley	US	1922	12,700	542	7150	15	30	ex-collier *Jupiter*
Hermes	Br	1923	10,900	600	40,000	25	12	
Béarn	Fr	1927	21,150	597	35,000	21½	42	battleship conversion
Lexington	US	1927	33,000	901	180,000	33¼	90	Sister to *Saratoga* battlecruiser conversion
Glorious	Br	1928	22,500	786.5	90,000	30	48	battlecruiser conversion sister to *Courageous*
Akagi	Ja	1928	30,000	782.5	91,000	31	60	*Kaga* (1929) a slower (27kt) half-sister. Later both 28 knots, battle-cruiser & battleship conversions
Ryujo	Ja	1933	10,600	591	65,000	29	42	
Ranger	US	1934	14,500	769	53,000	29	80	
Yorktown	US	1937	19,800	827	120,000	33½		sister to *Enterprise* (1938) and *Hornet* (1941)
Graf Zeppelin	Ge		23,000	863	180,000	33½	42	launched 1939 never completed
Soryu	Ja	1938	16,000	746	15,300	34½	63	sister *Hiryu* 18,500 tons
Ark Royal	Br	1938	22,000	800	102,000	31	72	
Wasp	US	1940	14,700	741	75,000	29	84	
Illustrious	Br	1940	23,000	753	111,000	30½	36	class of six some single hangar deck, some two
Zuiho	Ja	1940	11,500	712	52,000	28	30	sisters *Shoho* (1942) *Ryuho*
Shokaku	Ja	1941	25,700	845	160,000	34	84	sister to *Zuikaku*
Essex	US	1942	27,100	872/888	150,000	33	80	24 of class completed
Bogue	US	1942	7800	496	8500	18	28	escort carrier (CVE) typical figures
Taiho	Ja	1944	29,300	855	160,000	33	53	
Unryu	Ja	1944	17,200	742	152,000	34	57	three of planned 15 completed
Shinano	Ja	1944	64,800	873	148,000	27	47	ex-Musashi-class battleship
Glory	Br	1945	13,200	694	40,000	25	42	light fleet carrier class of six
Coral Sea	US	1947	45,000	968	210,000	33	135	class of three
Eagle	Br	1952	44,000	811	152,000	31	55	sister to third *Ark Royal*
Albion	Br	1954	22,000	737	80,000	28	32	class of three, third *Hermes* similar
Forrestal	US	1955	59,000	1086	260,000	33	70	class of four
Enterprise	US	1961	76,000	1102	280,000	35	84	first nuclear propelled carrier
Moskva	USSR	1967	15,000	645	100,000	30+	18 helicopters	cannot operate fixed-wing aircraft, class of two
Nimitz	US	1975	82,000	1092	280,000	35	90	nuclear-propelled, class of three
Kiev	USSR	1976	40,000	934	—	30+	24 helicopters	can operate V/STOL aircraft, class of three

APPENDIX 2-Pennant numbers of American Aircraft Carriers

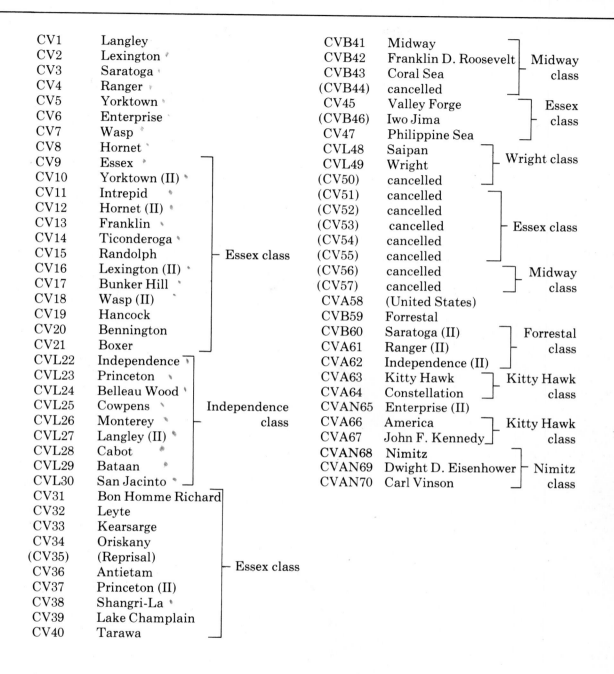

CV1	Langley	
CV2	Lexington	
CV3	Saratoga	
CV4	Ranger	
CV5	Yorktown	
CV6	Enterprise	
CV7	Wasp	
CV8	Hornet	
CV9	Essex	
CV10	Yorktown (II)	
CV11	Intrepid	
CV12	Hornet (II)	
CV13	Franklin	
CV14	Ticonderoga	
CV15	Randolph	Essex class
CV16	Lexington (II)	
CV17	Bunker Hill	
CV18	Wasp (II)	
CV19	Hancock	
CV20	Bennington	
CV21	Boxer	
CVL22	Independence	
CVL23	Princeton	
CVL24	Belleau Wood	
CVL25	Cowpens	
CVL26	Monterey	Independence class
CVL27	Langley (II)	
CVL28	Cabot	
CVL29	Bataan	
CVL30	San Jacinto	
CV31	Bon Homme Richard	
CV32	Leyte	
CV33	Kearsarge	
CV34	Oriskany	
(CV35)	(Reprisal)	
CV36	Antietam	Essex class
CV37	Princeton (II)	
CV38	Shangri-La	
CV39	Lake Champlain	
CV40	Tarawa	

CVB41	Midway	
CVB42	Franklin D. Roosevelt	Midway class
CVB43	Coral Sea	
(CVB44)	cancelled	
CV45	Valley Forge	Essex class
(CVB46)	Iwo Jima	
CV47	Philippine Sea	
CVL48	Saipan	Wright class
CVL49	Wright	
(CV50)	cancelled	
(CV51)	cancelled	
(CV52)	cancelled	
(CV53)	cancelled	Essex class
(CV54)	cancelled	
(CV55)	cancelled	
(CV56)	cancelled	Midway class
(CV57)	cancelled	
CVA58	(United States)	
CVB59	Forrestal	
CVB60	Saratoga (II)	Forrestal class
CVA61	Ranger (II)	
CVA62	Independence (II)	
CVA63	Kitty Hawk	Kitty Hawk class
CVA64	Constellation	
CVAN65	Enterprise (II)	
CVA66	America	Kitty Hawk class
CVA67	John F. Kennedy	
CVAN68	Nimitz	
CVAN69	Dwight D. Eisenhower	Nimitz class
CVAN70	Carl Vinson	

APPENDIX 3 - Some notable Aircraft used at sea

	Nat	Type	in service	power hp or st	max speed mph
Short 184	Br	torpedo bomber/reconnaissance	1915-19	260	90
Sopwith Baby	Br	bomber/reconnaissance	1915-17	130	100
Sopwith 1½-Strutter	Br	fighter bomber/reconnaissance	1916-18	130	105
Sopwith Pup	Br	fighter/reconnaissance	1916-18	80	110
Sopwith Camel	Br	fighter/reconnaissance	1917-20	150	125
Sopwith Cuckoo	Br	torpedo bomber	1918-23	200	105
Blackburn Dart	Br	torpedo bomber	1921-33	450	110
Fairey Flycatcher	Br	fighter bomber	1923-34	400	133
Martin T4M	US	torpedo bomber/scout	1927-37	525	114
Boeing F2B	US	fighter	1928-32	425	160
Fairey IIIF	Br	spotter/reconnaissance	1928-36	570	120
Boeing F4B	US	fighter	1929-37	500	180
Vought Corsair	US	fighter	1930-41	550	165
Mitsubishi A5M	Ja	fighter	1940-42	785	250
Nakajima Type 90	Ja	fighter	1931-37	450	200
Hawker Osprey	Br	fighter/reconnaissance	1932-39	645	176
Fairey Swordfish	Br	torpedo/spotter/reconnaissance	1936-45	750	140
Consolidated PBY Catalina	US	patrol bomber	1936-45	2×1200	185
Supermarine Walrus	Br	spotter/reconnaissance	1936-45	775	135
Douglas TBD Devastator	US	torpedo bomber	1937-42	900	205
Nakajima B5N,	Ja	torpedo bomber	1937-45	1000	240
Grumman F3F	US	fighter	1938-41	950	265
Blackburn Skua	Br	fighter/dive bomber	1938-41	890	225
Fairey Albacore	Br	torpedo bomber	1940-43	1130	161
Fairey Fulmar	Br	fighter	1940-45	1100	280
Vought OS2U Kingfisher	US	reconnaissance	1940-49	450	170
Aichi D3A	Ja	dive bomber	1940-44	1300	265
Grumman F4F Wildcat	US	fighter	1941-45	1200	310
Hawker Sea Hurricane	Br	fighter	1941-45	1450	342
Vought SB2U Vindicator	US	dive bomber	1941-45	750	260
Douglas SBD Dauntless	US	dive bomber	1941-43	1200	255
Mitsubishi A6M	Ja	fighter	1941-45	1150	350
Curtiss SB2C Helldiver	US	dive bomber	1942-47	1900	285
Chance Vought F4U Corsair	US	fighter/bomber	1943-52	2250	415
Fairey Barracuda	Br	torpedo/dive bomber	1943-46	1650	240
Fairey Firefly	Br	AS strike/reconnaissance	1943-56	2250	385
Grumman TBF Avenger	US	torpedo bomber	1943-55	1750	260
Grumman F6F Hellcat	US	fighter	1943-46	2000	371
Supermarine Seafire	Br	fighter/bomber	1945-54	2350	450
Douglas A1 Skyraider	US	fighter	1945-62	2700	320
Hawker Sea Fury	Br	fighter/bomber	1947-54	2500	460
Fairey Gannet	Br	AS/strike/reconnaissance	1953-78	3050	300
Hawker Sea Hawk	Br	low-level fighter	1953-60	5200lb	560
de Havilland Sea Venom	Br	strike fighter	1954-60	5300lb	575
Douglas A4 Skyhawk	US	strike fighter/bomber	1953-76	11,000lb	685
Douglas A3 Skywarrior	US	strike bomber	1956-	21,000lb	610
LTV F8 Crusader	US	fighter	1956-	17,000lb	1100
Supermarine Scimitar	Br	fighter/reconnaissance	1958-63	22,500lb	710
Blackburn Buccaneer	Br	low-level strike	1961	22,000lb	M0.85
Sikorsky S58/Westland Wessex	US/Br	AS helicopter	1961-	1500	140
North American RA5C Vigilante	US	strike bomber	1962-	22,000lb	1600
Hawker Siddeley Sea Vixen	Br	strike fighter	1963-72	22,500lb	640
Hawker Siddeley Buccaneer	Br	low-level strike	1966-	22,000lb	M0.85
LTV A7 Corsair II	US	strike bomber	1967-	11,400lb	
McDonnell Douglas F4 Phantom	US	fighter	1969-	24,500lb	M2.1
Sikorsky S61/Westland Sea King	US/Br	AS helicopter	1970-	3200	160
Hawker Siddeley Harrier	Br	strike	1971-	21,500lb	740

ceiling ft	span ft	armament	crew	remarks
9000	63.5	1 MG, 1 14in torpedo	2	biplane/seaplane
10,000	25.7	1 MG, 2 small bombs	1	biplane/seaplane
13,000	33.5	2 MGs, 2 small bombs	1-2	biplane/seaplane
17,000	26.5	1 MG	1	biplane
17,000	27.0	2 MGs, 2 small bombs	1	biplane Type 2F.1
12,000	46.8	1 18in torpedo	1	biplane
13,000	45.5	1 18in torpedo or bombs	1	biplane
19,000	29	2 MGs, 4 small bombs	1	biplane
10,000	53	1 MG, torpedo	3	biplane
21,000	30	2 MGs	1	biplane
20,000	45.8	1 MG, 1 Lewis gun, 500lb bombs	3	biplane
27,000	30	2 MGs, 2 small bombs	1	biplane
18,000	36	3 MGs	2	American O3U biplane
32,000	36	2 MGs	1	'Claude'
32,000	31	2 MGs	1	biplane
25,000	37	2 MGs	2	biplane
10,500	45.5	1 MG, 1 Lewis gun, 1 18in torpedo or bombs	2-3	biplane
13-21,000	104	4 MGs, 4000lb bombs	7	monoplane amphibian
18,000	45.9	2-3 MGs, small bombs	3	biplane amphibian
19,500	50	2 MGs, 1 21in torpedo	3	
25,000	51	1 MG, 1 21in torpedo or bombs	3	'Kate'
33,000	32	2 MGs	1	biplane
19,000	46.2	4 .303 MGs, 1 Lewis gun, 1 500lb bomb	2	
20,500	50	3 MGs, 1 18in torpedo or bombs	3	biplane
26,000	46.4	8 .303 MGs	2	
18,000	35.9	2 MGs, small bombs	2	seaplane
35,000	47	2 MGs, 800lb bombs	2	'Val'
28,000	38	4-6 0.5 MGs	1	Martlet in RN
36,000	40	4 20mm cannon	1	
28,000	42	5 MGs, 1500lb bombs	2	Chesapeake in RN
25,000	41.5	4 MGs, 1 1000lb bomb	2	
35,000	36	2 cannon, 2 MGs, 700lb bombs	1	Zero-Sen/'Zeke'
29,000	49.8	2 20mm cannon, 1000lb bombs	2	
34,000	39.7	4 0.5 MGs, 2 1000lb bombs	1	
20,000	49.2	2 MGs, 1 18in torpedo or 1500lb stores	3	
28,500	41.2	4 20mm cannon, 2000lb stores	2	
24,000	54.2	4 MGs, 1 torpedo or 2000lb stores	3	Tarpon (some) in RN
37,000	42.8	6 0.5 MGs, 2 1000lb bombs	1	
43,000	36.9	4 20mm cannon, 3 500lb bombs	1	
33,000	50	4 cannon, 8000lb bombs	3	
36,000	38.4	4 20mm cannon, 2 1000lb bombs	1	
25,000	54.3	2 AS torpedoes, 1000lb stores	3	AEW version still in service
44,000	39	4 20mm cannon, 2 500lb bombs	1	
40,000	42.8	4 20mm cannon, 500lb stores	2	
—	27.5	2 cannon, 9000lb stores	1	
41,000	72.5	2 cannon, 12,000lb bombs	3	
58,000	35.3	4 cannon, 5000lb stores	1	
—	37.1	4 30mm cannon, 4 AA missiles or 4000lb bombs	1	
—	44	16,000lb stores	2	
—	56 rotor	2 AS torpedoes	4	
64,000	53	nuclear capability		
48,000	510	4 AA missiles, 4 500lb bombs	2	
—	44	16,000lb missiles, bombs or stores	2	
—	38.8	15,000lb stores	2	
70,000	38.4	8 AA missiles or 10,000lb stores	2	
10,000	62 rotor	AS torpedoes	4	
50,000+	25.3	cannon, bombs, missiles	1	AV-8A US Marines

INDEX

PICTURE CREDITS

Aéronautique (*via P. J. R. Moyes*) 24
British Aerospace 151; (*via M. J. Hooks*)
141b, 144t, 158
Charles E. Brown 28-9, 35b
Emy Conrad (*via Peter Kilduff*) 147
Fleet Air Arm Museum 57t
Ambrose Greenway 145, 150
Imperial War Museum 11, 13, 15, 16, 19, 21,
26, 32, 33b, 35t, 39, 40, 40-1, 57b, 64, 68-
9, 74-5, 76-7, 78-9, 89b, 90-1, 97, 100-1,
106t, 107 (*via MacClancy Press*) 71, 73;
(*via J. M. Maber*) 62
Inter-Air Press 124-5, 134, 141t, 156-7, 159,
160-1
Derek James front endpaper, facing title
page 17, 23, 25, 37
Michael Jerram 110, 131
Keystone Press (*via P. J. R. Moyes*) 49, 59,
98-9, 111, 115, 117
Peter Kilduff 126-7, 139, 143t, 144b, 154t
John M. Maber 8-9
MacClancy Press 54, 66-7, 92-3, 109, 112,
113

Marshall Cavendish Ltd 10, 27, 36, 42, 44,
44-5, 82
Clifford & Wendy Meadway 56, 89t, 103t,
104, 106t
Ministry of Defence contents page 135, 142-
3, 155t and b
Ministry of Information 105
Philip J. R. Moyes 48, 114-5, 123
Pilot Press 65, 83t
Planet News (*via P. J. R. Moyes*) 70-1
Royal Navy 130, 148-9
Michael Turner 127, 128, 137
Twentieth Century Fox 47
United States Navy title verso, back
endpaper 51, 120-1; (*via Peter Kilduff*)
12, 22t and b, 30-1, 33t, 52-3, 83b, 84-
5, 86, 93, 129, 132-3, 138, 146, 152,
153; (*via P. J. R. Moyes*) 43, 55, 58, 61,
81, 94-5, 96, 102-3; (*via M. F. Jerram*)
127t
Vickers Ltd 154b
Vought Corporation 108